Of Cradles and Careers

A Guide to Reshaping Your Job to Include a Baby in Your Life

Also by Kaye Lowman
The LLLove Story
Especially for You

Of Cradles and Careers

A Guide to Reshaping Your Job to Include a Baby in Your Life

KAYE LOWMAN

LA LECHE LEAGUE INTERNATIONAL
Franklin Park, Illinois

March 1984

Printed in the United States of America
84 85 86 87 9 8 7 6 5 4 3 2 1
Book and cover design by Lucy Lesiak
Photo credits are given in the Appendix
Library of Congress Catalog Card Number 84-080085
ISBN 0-912500-14-X

To Cecil and Lucille,
who provided the foundation,
and
Laurie, Andy, Amy, and Carrie,
who provided the reason.

Contents

Foreword

■ Every expectant mother is faced with the question, "Should I breastfeed my baby?" But when you're a working mother, the question becomes more complicated; you're also faced with the dilemma of how to make that work.

The first question, whether or not to breastfeed, was an easy one for me to answer. My position on "Good Morning America" exposed me to the latest findings; I had the experts at my fingertips (doctors, psychologists, nutritionists, and other health specialists). They all told me the same thing—breastfeeding would be one of the best gifts I could ever give my child—a gift of good health, along with all those necessary antibodies, and just as important—a gift of love, warmth, and security.

"But how to do it?!" Like many other working mothers, I was faced with a real problem: How could I provide this nurturing for my child and yet continue my career?

I found out that I was pregnant with my first child the week I began working for "Good Morning America" as a field reporter. It was a few days after delivery, while I was away enjoying my newborn, that the decision was made to make me the co-host. Now the pressure was really on! ABC needed me to come back to work as soon as possible. It was really a problem for me because all I really wanted to do at that point was to stay home and play with my baby's toes. But how could anyone pass up such a wonderful job opportunity? It also meant a workday that began at 4 A.M., and a fast-paced, demanding schedule which would include a lot of travel. However, it was an offer I just couldn't refuse.

I had not planned to take Jamie to work with me, but as the time drew near, it seemed to be the only answer. Breastfeeding was that important to me.

ABC also had not planned on my coming back to work with my baby, but to get me into the anchor seat faster, they agreed to let me bring Jamie and to provide a nursery on the set.

It was a new and unprecedented move for ABC, but the only way for them to get me back. In fact, it actually changed policy in many companies, as I later found with the many wonderful letters I received from women around the country.

I can't honestly tell you that it was easy. Bundling a sleeping baby to take her out into the cold morning air, feeding her between tapings, and trying to maintain some decorum in my office—which now included baby swings, cribs, and changing tables—it was a difficult juggling act. But boy, was it all worth it!

I also breastfed my second daughter, Lindsay, by adjusting my work schedule and spending more time at home with her. It is my belief that the care I took of myself while pregnant along with the breastfeeding experience had a tremendous impact on how healthy, loving, and secure my children are today.

I can't possibly imagine not having had that unbelievable bond that breastfeeding developed between myself and my daughters. In those early months there was that first communication with my baby, her gorgeous, dark eyes looking up into mine silently saying, "I need you!" Those eyes were my constant reminders that what I was doing was the right thing.

Joan Lunden Krauss
ABC Television Network
"Good Morning America" co-host

Introduction

■ This is a book about women. Women with careers; women who become mothers. Women who are deeply committed, both at home and at work.

This is not a book about whether to work or whether to stay at home. Nor is it a book questioning the value of full-time mothering or comparing one style of mothering to another. Nor is it about quality time versus quantity time.

This is a book about an emerging lifestyle and the women who are creating it. A lifestyle that does not pit one part of a woman's life against another, but embraces both her need to work and her desire to be a mother.

This is a book about women who cope with enormous demands, yet never lose sight of what is most important in life; who understand the intense needs of young children, yet insist on the right to raise a family while pursuing professional goals. This book is about women who are willing to make the personal sacrifices necessary to achieve their goals.

This is the story of women who are revolutionizing the workplace.

And giving it a heart.

Part 1

Baby and Briefcase: A new perspective

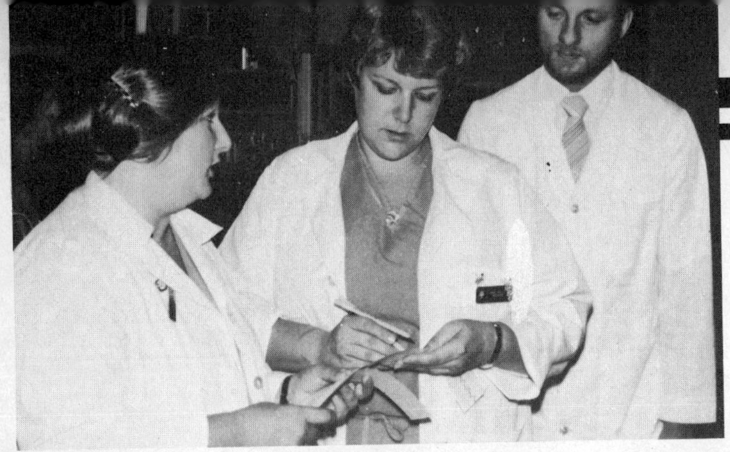

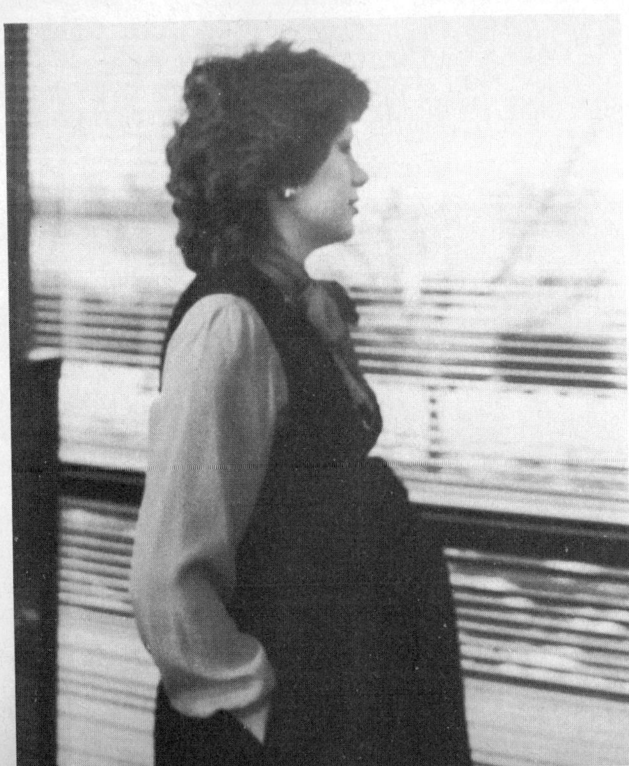

Chapter 1

Birth of a Baby
Change of priorities

"While I was pregnant, there was no question in my mind that I would return to work full time. I would just find someone to care for my baby while I was at work. Simple, right? I thought so until Jonathan was born. Then all of my simple plans vanished. After he was born, going back to work was no longer important. In fact, I did not want to return at all. Jonathan depended on me so much. How could I possibly leave him with some stranger?

"But as my six-month leave drew closer to an end, I realized that I had to return to work in some capacity. My husband was in the process of changing jobs and his new income would not be constant. I had to work, but I wanted to be with my baby.

"The solution? I compromised and went back to work twenty-five hours a week. By getting off at 2:00 P.M. every day, I would only miss one breastfeeding, and I would be away from my baby fewer hours per day than if I worked full time."

Chris Akin, Jonathan's mother, and thousands of career women-mothers like her, are at the root of a movement that is changing the landscape of the American workplace almost as profoundly as the Industrial Revolution changed it a century ago.

In ever increasing numbers, and with a zeal and determination born of the bitter realization that "having it all"—a full-time career, a fulfilling marriage, and an adorable baby—is nothing more than a sure fire formula for creating a never-ending cycle of guilt, frustration, and fatigue, women are throwing the nine-to-five work ethic overboard and replacing it with flexible work options that were largely undreamed of only a few years ago.

"Women are realizing that they have been sold a bill of goods," says Coralee Kern, a successful entrepreneur who is now one of the country's leading experts on alternative work pattern trends.*

"We have lost a generation of children in our country because women have been led to believe that they should seek their primary fulfillment outside of the home. Now women are saying, 'I won't take it anymore. I won't work eight days a week, twenty-six hours a day for the company. The company won't let me have relationships, a personal life, time for myself. My kids need me and I need them. I want to be able to parent my children.' Parenting is an important experience that a great number of people have missed out on."

Baby or Career?

While the 1960s movement to liberate women by providing them with increased educational opportunities, broader career options and advancement opportunities, and new choices in individual lifestyles did indeed throw open the doors to a more fulfilling life for millions of women, it also created a host of dilemmas and, for many, a no-win situation of eventually having to make an either/or choice between having a baby and continuing to pursue a career.

As their biological clocks wind down, often at almost precisely the time that their professional lives are in high gear, many women wait in vain for the right moment to set aside their careers in favor of starting a family—a time that for many women simply never comes.

Angry and frustrated at being forced to make this all-or-nothing choice, women have begun reshaping traditional male-oriented work schedules into manageable pieces that permit a balanced blend of family life and career opportunities.

Factors other than personal fulfillment are also propelling women with young children into the work force: an uncertain economy and high unemployment, divorce, the spiraling cost of living, and a lack of cultural support for the career of full-time mother.

Whatever the reason behind her decision to seek outside employment, the bottom line for the woman with an infant or preschooler is the same: how to work outside of the home and still do the best she can for her child.

*See chapter 17 for more information on Coralee Kern.

Effects of Separation

This boom in working mothers with babies and preschool children has spawned a whole new body of research studying the effect of regular, prolonged separation from mother on the infant and young child. Hardly a week goes by without yet another such study being reported in the media. One study directly contradicts another about the effect (positive or negative) of a day-care environment on the young child, the importance (or lack of it) of an at-home mother, the disastrous (or favorable) influence a mother's working has on the socialization skills and maturity level of her young offspring.

Parents of young children, tired of hearing all the contradictory advice, are turning a deaf ear to the experts and tuning into their own feelings, relying on their own instincts to guide them in making choices about how their children should be raised.

What many of these parents are deciding is that finding an alternative to leaving the baby forty or more hours a week is a top priority. The solutions to cutting down on the hours of separation are many and varied, but the reason for doing so is uniformly the same: the realization that babies need to be with their mothers, and mothers need to be with their babies.

■ Many women wait in vain for the right moment to set aside their careers in favor of starting a family.

"I was very aware of a strong desire to be with my baby, and felt grief at the thought of separation," states Dr. Carla Clark, a pediatrician from Tennessee. "I was reluctant to turn the responsibility for his development and teaching over to someone else.

"Bolstered by La Leche League and its philosophy, I became more and more convinced that babies need their own mothers. I made a commitment not to turn his care over to someone else."

Dr. Clark's solution to combining motherhood and her career was to stay at home for the first three and a half months of son Philip's life, and then to work three mornings a week, taking the baby and the sitter to the office with her. "This way I was able to be with the baby before starting to see patients, between patients, at lunch, and then we would all drive home together. This enabled me to nurse him and be with him during the workday."

Some mothers, like Susan Novara, a teacher from Michigan, are able to plan ahead and delay starting a family until they feel they can afford to live on one income for an extended period of time.

"My husband and I waited a long time to have a child," explains Susan. "I worked for six years before my daughter was born. I wanted to be the one to raise her. I didn't want a babysitter to have the fun of seeing her grow. We waited to have a child until I could leave my job and stay home with her. I was at home full time until Lindsay was sixteen months old, and then I went back to teaching just four hours a day."

The Mother-Infant Bond

Other mothers, like Carol Britton, find that they are somewhat surprised by the intensity of the mother-infant bond.

"After experiencing childbirth and the breastfeeding relationship, it became extremely important to me to modify my work schedule," says Carol. "I knew ahead of time that I wanted to reduce my hours at work, but until I actually had a nursing relationship with my baby, I didn't fully realize the importance of the responsibility for nurturing another human being. And to me, that means being there whenever that human being needs you."

Denise Peacock, a social worker from Georgia, explains that she and her husband were always clear about their priorities.

"Years prior to pregnancy, we always knew that I would either remain unemployed indefinitely, or work only as little as possible. Our son Reid came first. He is a choice we made, a responsibility we accepted."

■ "Why have children if you don't intend to raise them?"

"It has always been my belief that the responsibility of having children is not in birthing them, but in raising them," says Susan Hahn, who sidetracked her career as a teacher and began a new career as a fitness instructor in order to minimize the separation from her baby and still use her teaching skills. "I originally thought that I would stay home for five months, but after five months I realized that no amount of money was worth leaving my daughter to be raised by a sitter. I fell in love with motherhood! I will have my whole life to go back and teach other people's children. I will have only a few precious years of my own children's youth to try to teach them to be loving, responsible citizens."

"I knew that I could not possibly manage holding down a full-time job, mothering a new baby, guiding an adolescent, and still maintain some semblance of a healthy marital relationship. Who has that kind of emotional resources?" says Margaret Risk-Bryan. "I feel that my baby needs me all the time. I don't think anyone can care for him as well as I can, and he deserves the best I can give him. But it is also important to me as an adult who has put herself through seven years of college and graduate school to continue the career I began."

Margaret's solution to mixing a career and family responsibilities: working as a free-lance editor, accepting only as much work as she can comfortably handle. "By working as I do, I feel that my life has continuity."

"My career has a secondary place in my order of priorities," states Lisa Holden, mother of a two-year-old and a five-year-old, who now works three days a week as a dietician. "There is no question that the decision to have children and to spend time with them has slowed down my career advancement. That at times has been a bitter realization. But I'm growing in joy and peace in the decision I've made. When I meet women who have decided not to have children for career reasons, or who have always worked full time regardless of their children's ages, I feel that I have the richer portion.

"It never occurred to me to keep working full time after the children were born. Why have children if you don't intend to raise them?"

Breastfeeding: a Priority

Current medical research has firmly established the importance of breastfeeding, and in a large percentage of cases, a woman's determination to seek a modified work schedule is based on her desire to breastfeed her baby.

When Patricia Wendt, an RN who worked in the federally sponsored Women, Infants, and Children's (WIC) program, returned to work, she took her baby with her in order to continue breastfeeding her. "I didn't want to try to force her into a schedule or give her a bottle just because I wanted to work," Patricia explains. "Why should she have to get second best? I felt that I belonged with my baby, so I arranged to keep her near me."

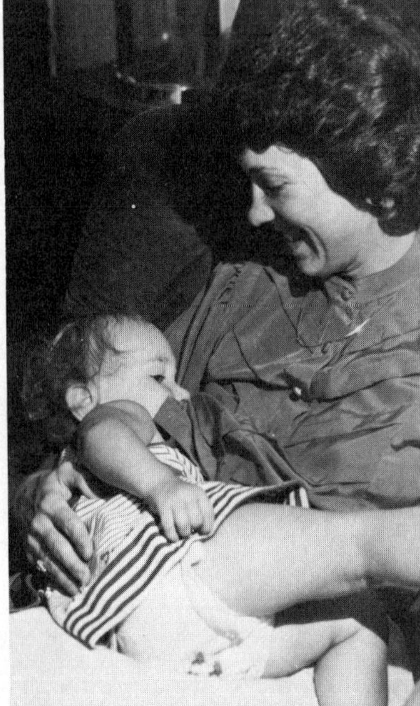

Psychologist Patricia Holliday takes time out to nurse her daughter Tiffany.

Sarah Forbush Jett, a dental hygienist who splits her job with another mother-hygienist, says, "I felt safer giving my son my own milk. I didn't want to subject him to a lot of chemicals (in commercial formula). It just did not seem natural to start his life off that way."

"My child benefited both physically and emotionally from the time we spent as a nursing couple," comments nurse Sheri Kelly. "Physically, because breast milk is filled with vitamins, minerals, natural immunities, and things we haven't even discovered yet; emotionally, because I was there to fill his needs in the way only I could fill them. It was important to me to make work fit my son's schedule so that I could nurse him."

Virginia McGowan, a teaching assistant at the University of Toronto and mother of an eleven-month-old daughter, speaks of her conviction that breastfeeding is doubly important in helping the working mother meet the needs of her baby.

> A baby is an awesome responsibility—a new life entirely dependent on his/her parents for physical and emotional requirements. Is there anything more important, or more satisfying, than meeting those needs? I think not. I firmly believe that breastfeeding is the best and easiest way to give the entire family a good start, both physically and emotionally.

Carla Bombere, graphic artist, does free-lance work so she can spend more time with her son Andrew.

Working has added a new stress, and breastfeeding has become doubly important now. The role of breastfeeding in meeting the nutritional and immunological needs of an infant has been well-documented. This information is relatively easy to obtain. Equally important, however, is the role of the nursing relationship in calming the baby, the mother, and thus the entire family! We have found that this pacifying aspect of breastfeeding has become increasingly important as our daughter's nutritional and immunological requirements decrease. Experience has shown us that stressful times can be short-circuited by a peaceful, soothing respite at the breast.

Making Choices

"I wanted to have it all," confesses Susan Miele, mother of twelve-year-old and fifteen-month-old daughters. "I wanted a great job, a loving spouse, and beautiful kids; I wanted to look great and keep everything running smoothly. I know the Superwoman myth is impossible to achieve, yet I kept yearning for it.

"But I think I've made the best possible compromise," says Susan, an attorney who now works part-time in state government instead of in a more lucrative, challenging position so that she can be more available to her toddler. "Every time I get fed up with my job, I remember that a certain amount of boredom is the price I pay for being able to get that big hug from those chubby little arms at 3:00 in the afternoon. It's worth it!"

Chapter 2

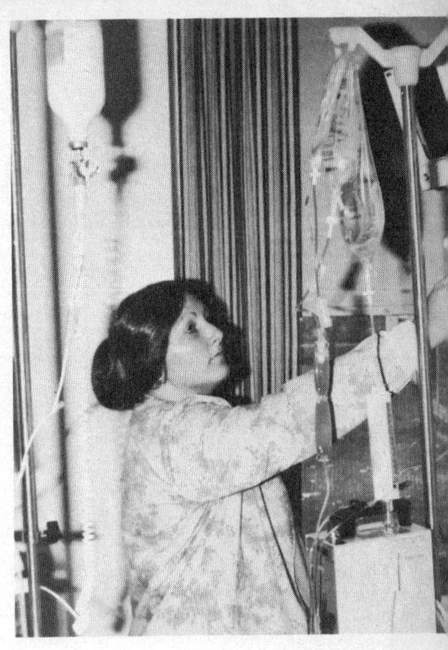

The Nine-to-Five Work Ethic

Bitter realizations, new directions

Much like the new kid on the block, the first wave of women who broke the dam and flooded the business world in the late 1960s found it imperative to follow every rule to the letter in order to play on the corporate team and win.

Once the major barriers to advancement into middle and upper management began to slowly fall away, women were determined to move ahead, regardless of the personal sacrifices involved. The first taste of victory had been too long in coming for these women not to do whatever they saw as necessary to prove themselves and take their hard-earned places in the corporate mainstream.

When affirmative action, women's rights organizations, class action lawsuits, and landmark U.S. Supreme Court decisions began to crack open the doors that had previously been closed, padlocked, and emblazoned with a sign reading "No Women Allowed," professional women knew that proving themselves every hour of every day, being a better "man" than every other man in the company, was their only chance for promotion and advancement. These women knew that they had to be twice as smart, put in four times as many hours, and, above all else, epitomize the perfect "corporate man" in order to be promoted ahead of their well entrenched male counterparts.

Like pioneers of every other age, these women endured hardships, harassment, humiliation, ridicule, and personal sacrifice in order to tame the frontier and open up the new land that held out the promise of equal employment opportunities, equal pay for equal work, and respect for a job well done—regardless of the sex of the person who did it.

Through the next decade, women gradually were able to simply take their place in the working world, without having to fight for, and then guard, that place. While discrimination in the areas of salary and promotional opportunities were hardly things of the past, women could be fairly confident that they would be accepted into the workplace and that pay increases and promotions, although still often coming more slowly than they should, would come.

Lois Jansen combines her career as a chemical engineer with being a mother to son Jacob.

By the mid to late 1970s, the influx of women into the labor force had given career women one of the things they needed most: strength in numbers. At last these women could relax enough to take a deep breath and stand back for a moment to look at what they had won, how far they had come, and what price they had paid to get there. Though hardly surprising, the answers to these questions were sobering. The battle, if not the war, had been won, but a personal life, home and family, and the ability to fill the role of wife and mother headed the list of war casualties. In the process of beating the men at their own game, these women had gained the world but had lost an important part of themselves.

For many women, the realization came too late. Some judge had long ago declared their marriage dead, and their relationship with their children was either mortally wounded or missing in action. The victory had been won, but the battlefield was strewn with broken marriages and shattered relationships.

What women were now able to see was that the workplace had been designed for men who had full-time wives at home, or for single people without family obligations. Nowhere was there any provision for accommodating the needs of a woman with family responsibilities. Working from nine to five, five days a week, meant that mothers had to leave home before their children left for school, that the children came home to an empty house every day, that dinner was soup and sandwiches or didn't get served until 8:00 P.M. (by a woman who was probably too tired to eat it), and that "free time" on the weekends had to be spent catching up on a week's worth of shopping, errands, and housework. If there was a baby involved, the stress load automatically doubled. With no one responsible for tending the home fire, it often smoldered and died. Hardly the stuff of which a happy home life is made.

Revolutionizing the Workplace

Enter a new generation, the second generation of working women. With the right to a good job more secure than it had been in the past, and with the educational and professional skills that give them real bargaining power, this second generation of career women is restructuring the American workplace—and giving it a heart.

Exhausted by trying to keep up with the myth of the 300% woman who can give 100% each to career, children, and marriage, women are revolutionizing the workplace by making it responsive to the needs of workers who are also mothers. They are refusing to accept that the price of a good job is the abandonment of home and family.

Tired of working hard at everything all the time, without ever having the satisfaction of feeling that they were doing their best for either family or career, women are humanizing the workplace by forcing it to become more responsive to the needs of the woman who wants to combine family and career, not sacrifice one for the other.

Eli Ginzburg, Chairman of the National Commission for Manpower Policy, has said that the demand by women for equal participation in the labor force "is the single most outstanding phenomenon of this century" and the most obvious force for change. As women break down occupational barriers, they are demanding new work schedules as well.

■ Women are refusing to accept that the price of a good job is the loss of home and family.

But in many ways, this revolution women are causing in the workplace has been a quiet revolution. They are not carrying banners or staging sit-ins. They are not taking corporate executives hostage or going on strike. Their demands are being made so quietly, most often on a case-by-case basis, that many other working women are still largely unaware of the revolution that is going on around them.

If you think you are alone in wanting to modify your full-time work schedule, take heart in these statistics:

- The proportion of women in the labor force will increase from 48.4% in 1977 to 57.1% in 1990. The total number of working women will jump from 40 million in 1976 to more than 54 million in 1990, according to the Bureau of Labor Statistics.
- As of February 1980, there were over 15 million Americans working fewer than thirty-five hours a week by choice.
- In the last decade, the part-time segment of the labor force has grown five times faster than full time.

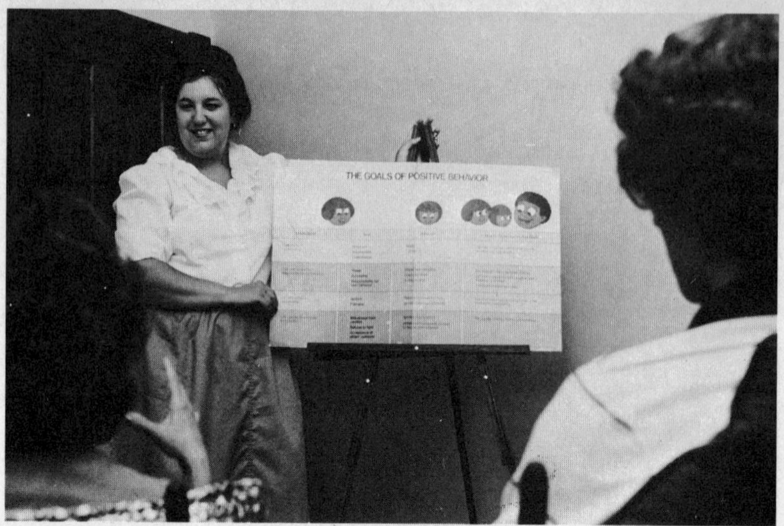

- In 1970, one out of every eight workers was part-time; in 1980 it jumped to one out of every 5.5 workers.
- The United States government now employs over 50,000 part-time workers.
- Between 1977 and 1980, over 20,000 new part-time positions were created in federal agencies.
- Over 2.1 million professional and technical people, managers and administrators, worked part-time regularly and by choice in 1980, an increase of 150,000 over the preceding year.
- 2.5 to 3.5 million workers, or about six percent of the labor force, were on flextime in 1977, and by the end of the next decade, 25 to 30% of all workers may have flexible schedules.
- By the mid 1990s, as many as 15 million workers could be earning their primary income by working for a company from their home.
- One out of every four at-home workers is a woman. There has been a 43% increase in the number of people working from home since 1972, according to the Bureau of Labor Statistics.
- About 3 million professionals have chosen to work less than thirty-five hours a week. Their number has grown 63% since 1976, and the rate of increase since then has been four times as great as other part-timers.
- Women occupy two-thirds of all part-time professional positions.

Sally Strosahl, clinical psychologist, conducts a parent education class, then takes time out to be with Kyle.

- 2.4 million people, or one out of every five employed Americans, work less than thirty-five hours a week. Most of them are women.
- As of 1982, twenty-five states and the federal government had officially encouraged the use of job sharing and other forms of permanent part-time employment by passing legislation that specifically increased the opportunities for such work arrangements by supporting pilot projects designed to test the feasibility of allowing employees to reduce the number of hours in their current jobs.
- By 1990, two-thirds of all mothers and more than half of all mothers with children under six years of age will be working outside of their homes. Today, the "typical" American family is one in which no adult member is home from nine to five.

Evidence, if employers need any other than what can already be seen in their own companies, that many women want to work less than full time, is everywhere.

A Need for Change

"Families at Work: Strengths and Strains," the 1981 study of American families sponsored by General Mills, revealed that most women would choose part-time employment if they could afford the correspondingly reduced pay. Some 41% of the women who work by choice rather than necessity said they would prefer part-time over full-time employment. Fifty-one percent of women who hold executive, managerial, or professional jobs would like to work part-time. Most of the working women surveyed said they would continue to work even in the absence of economic necessity, but the majority also said they would prefer to work only part-time.

This $300,000 survey, conducted by Louis Harris and Associates, concluded that women are in the work force to stay, not only to help support their families, but also to achieve personal satisfaction.

At the 1980 White House Conference on Families, the development of more family-oriented personnel policies, such as flexible working hours, personal leaves, shared and part-time jobs, and transfer policies that consider the needs of the family, was the number one recommendation.

The Conference Board, an international business research organization, reports that in response to the rising number of women in their work forces, American corporations will begin to offer modified working arrangements in order to help employees mesh career and family demands. These options will likely include flexible working hours as a means of eliminating tardiness, Friday afternoons off in the summer for employees who choose to work longer hours Monday through Thursday, and flexible benefit packages which will allow employees to choose from a wide range of benefits, which someday may include child-care services.

Chapter 3

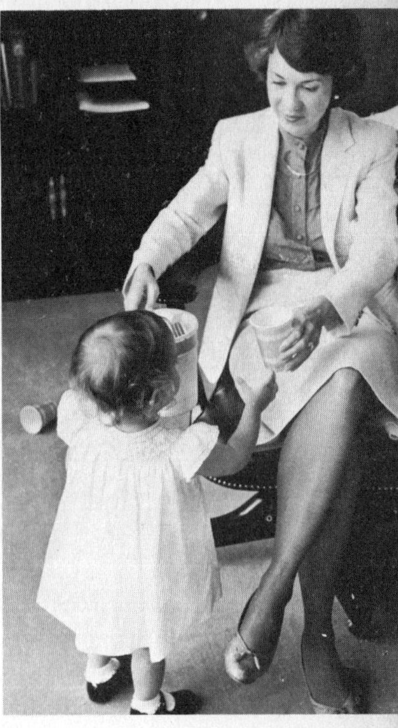

Flexible Work Options
How and where to find them

A funny thing happened on the way from the 1950s to the 1980s. The forty-hour workweek, which had been held sacred for decades, fell on hard times. A variety of flexible work patterns appeared on the scene. Part-time, flextime, and job sharing began to have an impact on the workplace.

People who wanted to work less than forty hours a week comprised the fastest growing segment of the labor force in the 1960s and 1970s. Why the sudden interest in modified work schedules?

"The great upsurge in the demand for part-time work came with the influx of women in the labor market," says Dr. Diane Rothberg, president of the Association of Part-Time Professionals.

Who Is Working Part-time?

Figures from the Bureau of Labor Statistics indicate that 14% of the country's professional and managerial workers are voluntarily choosing to work part-time. Seven percent of all male and 22% of all female employees are opting for less than full-time hours. Among professional women, there is a marked increase in the number seeking flexible work hours. Today, among women working part-time by choice, almost one-fifth are in professional and managerial occupations. "That's where you see the growth. That's where the trend is," Dr. Rothberg says. "Over the past decade the professional women's preference was translated into almost 700,000 new part-time professional positions.

"A sizable percentage of those working part-time are women with small children. Having family responsibilities is the leading reason that people choose to work part-time."

Other people with other reasons are also finding that a flexible work schedule suits their needs.

Barney Olmsted of New Ways to Work

"People in transition want to be able to work part-time," says Barney Olmsted, co-director of New Ways to Work, a San Francisco-based work research and resource organization founded in 1972. "Part-time allows those who are changing careers to keep their foot on one base while developing a foothold on another."

Different people want to work less than full-time for different reasons at different times in their lives. But one thing nearly all of them have in common is a long-term commitment to their jobs or professions.

"Historically, those working part-time were viewed as casual workers who were not committed to working and were less interested in their jobs than full-timers," Ms. Olmsted reports. "But we know this isn't the case. Most people who work part-time will want to go back to full-time once their reason for wanting a reduced schedule is over."

Women with young families who want to hold onto their jobs instead of dropping out for several years, people who are making a mid-life career change, and those who want to phase into retirement have been identified as the largest groups of people seeking part-time employment. Those who work in certain professions are also more likely than others to seek the part-time alternative at some time in their work lives.

"There is a lot of interest in part-time work among teachers and social workers and others who have people-oriented jobs," Ms. Olmsted points out. "These people used to take time out to relieve the pressure, but they can't do that now because there is no assurance they'll be able to get back in."

People with high pressure jobs—those that require a lot of client contact, a lot of creativity, or more than forty hours a week—are also good candidates for a reduced workweek at some time in their lives. Those at the other end of the scale who have very tedious, repetitive jobs are also more likely to want a break in the form of part-time work, according to Ms. Olmsted.

Who Is Hiring Part-Time?

Surprisingly enough, the federal government, with 2.8 million employees, turns out to be one of the most progressive employers in the United States. Several major pieces of legislation have been passed that have opened up job options in a whole gamut of occupational categories and levels.

- The Federal Employees Part-Time Career Employment Act passed in 1978 called for research and demonstration programs "determining the extent to which part-time career employment may be used in filling positions which have not traditionally been open for such employment on any extensive basis, such as supervisory, managerial, and professional positions," and for "determining the extent to which job-sharing arrangements may be established for various occupations and positions."
- A presidential directive issued in 1977, before the passage of the Part-Time Career Employment Act, required five federal agencies—the Veterans' Administration, the Federal Trade Commission, General Services Administration, the Environmental Protection Agency, and the Export-Import Bank—to begin experimental programs specifically aimed at giving older people, those with family obligations, the handicapped, and students greater opportunities for federal career employment.
- When the Comprehensive Employment and Training Act (CETA) was re-authorized in 1979, it advised: "In the designing and operating of programs, special consideration shall be given to provide for alternative working arrangements such as flexible hours of work, work sharing, and part-time jobs, particularly for older workers, and those with household obligations including parents of young children."
- The U.S. Postal Service employs a vast number of part-timers. Those who pass the Postal Service exam may be hired on a part-time flexible basis as letter carriers, mail sorters, baggage and parcel handlers, or customer service representatives. They accumulate sick and annual leave, and receive prorated health and retirement insurance.

Other Areas of Government

State governments are also doing a noteworthy job of creating flexible job opportunities. Some thirty-five states have supported policies or enacted legislation aimed at encouraging alternative employment options, and to provide benefits and promotional opportunities that had previously been available only to full-timers.

Wisconsin's experimental program, Project JOIN, opened certain middle and high level management positions to part-time workers. Three-fourths of those in shared positions are female, most of them married women with children under six.

Maryland passed the Permanent Part-Time Employment Act in 1975, setting a target of five percent as the proportion of all state jobs that should be open to part-timers. Pennsylvania, New York, and Massachusetts have all passed bills encouraging the hiring of more part-time workers at every level of state government.

California conducted an experimental program in its Department of Motor Vehicles that was so successful that the Reduced Worktime Act was passed in 1980, opening almost all state jobs to the option of part-time scheduling.

In the state of Oregon, two women share the job of administrative assistant to one of Oregon's highest elected officials, Secretary of State Norma Paulus.

Private Industry

More and more major companies in private industry are realizing that part-timers are just as dedicated and often more productive than their full-time co-workers, and are offering a variety of alternative work options.

- Aetna Life and Casualty Company and Investors Diversified Services, Inc., both plan to turn their pilot projects for at-home data processors and clerical workers into permanent programs.
- Blue Cross-Blue Shield of South Carolina is expanding its at-home work program.
- Xerox employs permanent part-timers in its branches throughout the country. Some are employed for less than twenty hours a week, others for twenty to forty hours a week. Those working more than twenty hours are entitled to full benefits, while those working less than twenty hours receive only certain fringes.
- Connecticut General Life Insurance Company employs 200 part-timers, most of them clerical. Connecticut General has found that there is as much productivity from part-timers as full-time employees, and that absenteeism and turnover have been kept to a minimum.
- Control Data Corporation's bindery in Selby, Minnesota employs *only* part-timers—249 of them, and almost all of them women with child-care responsibilities. Company-

wide, Control Data employs about 5,000 people under modified working arrangements.*

- The Equitable Life Assurance Society of the U.S. has endorsed part-time jobs at all levels. This policy, adopted in 1976, was seen as the solution to the problem of a chronic shortage of actuaries and computer programmers, but has now spread to a wide range of jobs.
- Honeywell, Inc.'s Micro Switch Division in Marlborough, Massachusetts was one of the first plants in the Boston area to adopt mothers' hours.
- Sears, Roebuck and Company has 107,000 permanent part-time employees who receive life and long term disability insurance, as well as pensions and profit sharing. Including its seasonal help, part-timers account for more than half of Sears' 400,000 employees.

Other large corporations offering alternative work options include: Eastman Kodak, Massachusetts Mutual Life Insurance Company, Campbell Soup Company, Trans World Airlines, Inc., United Air Lines, Maytag Company, and Lockheed Missiles and Space Company, Inc.

Where to Find Flexible Jobs

As a whole, public sector organizations, most notably education and government, offer the best prospects for landing a less-than-forty-hour-a-week job. The white collar worker often has a better chance of landing a part-time job than her blue collar counterpart.

Dr. Diane Rothberg quotes the Bureau of Labor Statistics as showing that at the professional level, teachers, librarians, and health care professionals have the greatest number of part-time positions. Writing and editing, computer programming, accounting, psychology, social work, and counseling are career fields that also have a high percentage of part-time jobs.

In *A Part-Time Career for a Full-Time You,* JoAnne Alter says that the service fields offer the best opportunities for part-time work, and lists these service areas that employ the greatest number of part-timers.

- **Health Care**—direct patient care, plus medical, dental, technical, and administrative support.
- **Education**—for adults as well as for children, and particularly for those with physical or learning disabilities or other special needs.
- **Day Care**—preschool and after-school programs for children of working parents.

Diane Rothberg, President of the Association of Part-time Professionals

*See chapter 16 for more information on Control Data Corporation.

- **Home Services**—household maintenance, home repair and improvement, painting, decorating, and lawn care.
- **Social Services**—counseling and therapy, public assistance, support services for the elderly and handicapped, and related services.
- **Business Support Services**—clerical, legal, advertising and public relations, information and financial services, equipment maintenance, and commercial cleaning.
- **Leisure Services**—travel, sports, recreation and entertainment, and vacations.
- **Personal Services**—beauty and grooming, repair of household appliances, automobile maintenance, care of clothing and personal belongings, and other services related to individual needs.

In *Job Sharing,* Gretl S. Meier lists the following occupational categories as good bets for a shared position: teacher, administrator, program developer, secretary, receptionist, clerical worker, counselor, social worker, psychologist, researcher, technician.

The top ten professions practiced from the home, according to *Women Working Home* by Marion Behr and Wendy Lazar are, in order of the number of women involved in each occupation: artist, craftperson, writer, consultant, teacher, advertising agent, attorney, salesperson, therapist, and secretary-typist.

Data Resources, Inc., reports that there are now 15 million information-manipulation jobs—such as computer programming, financial analyst, and writing—that could be done at home.

The part-time work that is the easiest to get, according to Stephanie Azzarone, author of "Shorter Hours, Fuller Lives," is "in the hard-to-find specialized skills. These include accounting, engineering, and, especially, data processing."

The Bureau of Labor Statistics reports that during the 1980s the major growth areas will be in white collar jobs in clerical and related fields, transportation, energy and the environment, computers, sales, health care, education, and office support systems.

The Legal Profession

A few professions have been particularly resistant to accepting anything less than forty, fifty, sixty, or more hours a week. Highly trained professionals in competitive, demanding fields have largely either had to accept the unrelenting hours expected of them or drop out completely.

But even in such hard driving professions as law, signs of change are apparent. Female lawyers, like females in every other profession, feel they should not be forced to choose between their careers and their desire to have a family. As more female attorneys begin to juggle the bar and the baby, options are slowly beginning to open up. A program titled "You, Your Child, Your Career" sponsored by the Barclay Group, a placement service for lawyers, focused on the conflict facing female lawyers who don't want to sacrifice job for children or children for job.

"Speakers at the meeting described a variety of ways to mesh the obligations of home and work: a part-time schedule, a change of specialty to one that permits flexibility, switching to the less competitive and time consuming public sector, working at home," reports a story published in the *New York Times*.

■ "Many of the new generation entering medicine are questioning the extraordinary demands in their training."

Even though new options requiring fewer hours at work are emerging for the lawyer-mother, those with their eye on a partnership still face formidable obstacles, according to the *Times* report. "One criterion determining who shall become a partner is the number of billable hours the lawyer has to his or her credit; the more hours the better."

Since sixty-hour workweeks are not uncommon for lawyers and those who are serious about getting ahead often put in eighty or more, a lawyer-mother who insists on time with her children will be at a serious disadvantage until enough female lawyers bring enough pressure to bear to modify these expectations for a woman with a young family. Odds are that once the stigma associated with fewer hours is broken, a good number of lawyer-fathers who want a chance to be more than spectators in their children's lives will heave a sigh of relief and head home to the kids.

The Medical Profession

There are even signs that the medical community, long known for its insistence on the total commitment of mind, body, and soul to the profession, is slowly beginning to realize that there may be a better way.

The Harvard Reduced Schedule Residency project provides for a shared schedule for those in its Graduate Medical Education (GME) program, allowing two physicians to share one house officer position, each working two-third to three-fourths time. This overlap in the sharers' schedules is designed to ensure continuity of patient care and time for participation in educational activities.

"A major premise underlying the work of the Harvard project," according to *Job Sharing* by Gretl S. Meier, "is that many of the new generation entering medicine are questioning the extraordinary demands in their training. Men as well as women want to combine training time with other commitments—research, family, personal avocations, or other medical interests. Moreover, because the training time is coming to be seen as a period when professional identity is formed, the need for 'maintaining one's humanness' is crucial both professionally and personally. Professional concerns center on the effect of long hours on the quality of care delivered, the sensitivity to patient needs under long periods of stress, and the educational saturation point for physicians who are being trained in a clinical setting."

Unions and Part-time

A few unions have become involved in the move toward increased part-time work options, but most have either opposed it or have been silent on the issue.

As the guardians of the worker's right to a full day's pay for a full day's work, unions have tended to view the trend toward part-time employment with distrust, fearing that employees at some time in the future may be forced to accept part-time status, even though they want to work full time. Unions are particularly wary out of concern that employers might want to switch their entire labor force to part-time in order to avoid costly fringe benefits.

"Unions have traditionally been opposed to part-time because they feel all workers want to work full time," explains Dr. Rothberg. "There aren't benefits with part-time work, and they're concerned about worker exploitation."

But here, too, the sheer number of people seeking part-time work is causing unions, like employers, to take a second look.

"We've seen a number of unions push for part-time work alternatives, but they do it only when their members express an interest," observes Barney Olmsted. Unions for service employees, parole officers, and social workers are among those that have become involved in part-time work issues. Not surprisingly, these are unions with a high percentage of female members. Unions with a large percentage of blue collar employees have shown less interest.

The National Education Association has come out in favor of voluntary job-sharing, making it the first national labor organization to adopt a formal resolution in support of this new work arrangement, according to the Association of Part-Time Professional's national newsletter.

"We're seeing some movement as more women come into unions," Dr. Rothberg says. "Instead of viewing part-timers as casual workers, unions should use this as an opportunity to build more membership and get more benefits for part-time workers."

"Unions will protect the interests of their members," New Ways to Work's Barney Olmsted states. "Those who want to be able to work part-time need to make their voices heard in the union. It's a way to upgrade part-time work."

Chapter 4

The Reduced Workweek
Trend of the 80s

There are all too few examples of situations in life where everyone comes out ahead, but providing flexible working arrangements is one of those rare instances that creates a win-win situation where both employee and employer have everything to gain, and little, if anything, to lose.

In an article titled, "Mutual Aid: Firms and Job Seekers Find Benefits in Part-Time Work," *Wall Street Journal* reporter Joann S. Lublin reports that: "A recent Labor Department study found that part-time employees generally provide higher productivity, greater loyalty, and less absenteeism than full-time employees—while putting less strain on company payrolls. The study, covering sixty-eight major corporations, concluded: 'Employers are going to be money ahead using part-timers.' "

The article goes on to quote William B. Werther, Jr., a management professor at Arizona State University and an authority on work patterns, as saying, "The trend for the next two decades will be toward more part-time work," with part-timers becoming "a much more significant part of the work force."

Employers consistently report that part-time employees are just as dedicated and productive as their full-time co-workers. They're grateful for the opportunity to work less than full time, and are willing to "go the extra mile" for their employer in return. Because they have time off during the week, they take care of personal chores and doctor's appointments on their days off rather than on company time. They take fewer sick days and waste less time socializing around the coffee machine.

Along with reducing salary and benefit costs, there are other pluses for the employer as well. Giant Food, Inc., a Washington-based retailer, found that the average full-timer's late arrivals cost the company 7.4 days of work in a year. This amounted to twice as much work lost due to tardiness by full-timers than by part-time employees.

Being able to reduce or eliminate overtime is another bonus many employers are discovering. By using part-timers during regular working hours along with full-time employees, or after hours in place of full-timers, many companies are finding they are able to make sizable reductions in the amount of overtime being paid out.

Offering the option of part-time work hours has also helped solve critical manpower shortages in some occupational fields, particularly nursing. The lure of shorter hours has brought many nurses back into the hospital in recent years.

Job sharing, flextime, and permanent part-time options are increasingly being seen as an effective recruitment tool in occupational fields where the competition for qualified personnel is particularly fierce.

Part-time work may also have a positive effect on current high unemployment rates by giving two willing participants the option of sharing one job. Part-time work gives workers more time to spend with their families, provides an easier means of making a mid-life career change, and allows more time to pursue educational and leisure activities.

One of the most positive signs of change in recent years is the more widespread recognition of part-timers as career-oriented employees. Employers are increasingly willing to invest in training and developing their part-time labor force.

Interest in various forms of permanent part-time employment originated in client-oriented public service agencies, according to New Ways to Work's *Job Sharing in the Public Sector*.

"Social workers, probation officers, teachers, librarians, mental health workers, and public assistance workers, all of whom are in high stress 'caring' professions, have most frequently expressed the need for alternatives to full-time employment," which often leads to burn-out, reduced productivity on the job, and disruption in employees' personal lives. "Job-sharing teachers, social workers, and probation officers consistently point to higher productivity, less stress, and greater job satisfaction as benefits valuable to both the individual and the organization."

Benefits of Part-time

The Part-Time Employment Program in the California State Department of Motor Vehicles allowed for eight to thirty-two hour workweeks in either shared, split, or part-time arrangements. Some 238 employees participated in this program, with 95% choosing half-time arrangements. The final report on this project noted that:

- productivity was as great as that of full-timers.
- there was a decrease in the use of sick leave.
- there was savings due to a reduction in the amount of overtime that had to be paid.
- the only increase in costs was for health care benefits, because regulations specified that those working over twenty hours per week had to be given full rather than partial benefits.

Of this program, Gretl S. Meier reports in *Job Sharing* that "Participants perceive the advantages in terms of their personal lives, job attitudes, and motivation to work. They list as a particular disadvantage the limited upward mobility because of slower promotion rates. Ninety-eight percent of the respondents indicated that they felt better about their jobs since they began to work fewer hours. Quality of life was improved because they had more time for families, school, leisure, and community activities. Tax advantages from reduced incomes, reduced strain from demanding jobs, and the ability to commute during 'off hours' were also cited. The work situation was improved because employees achieved a more satisfactory balance between their jobs and the rest of their lives. They reported less fatigue, increased work satisfaction, enjoying the job more, and needing to use less sick leave and vacation time for personal reasons."

Clinical psychologist Sally Strosahl gets home from work early so she can be with Kyle and Andrew.

A job-sharing program initiated in 1977 in Santa Cruz, California found that by using job-sharing as a recruitment tool, it was possible to attract highly qualified people who were more interested in flexibility at work than top salaries, and who viewed the opportunity to job share as a form of compensation.

After initiating job-sharing in one percent of its jobs in 1976, the city of Palo Alto, California found that "both job-sharers and supervisors agreed that job-sharing reduces fatigue and increases energy," according to *Job Sharing in the Public Sector*. Turnover was reduced because several employees were convinced to restructure their jobs rather than leave them. "Sharers were overwhelmingly positive about the effects of job-sharing both on their home life and their work life. Five out of six sharers reported higher morale because job-sharing allowed more time to pursue personal interests, go to school, or use their talents at work *and* raise a family."

Attitudes Change Slowly. Even though study after study confirms that part-timers perform as well or better than full-time employees, exhibit more job satisfaction, have less absenteeism and tardiness, and lower turnover, part-timers are still seen as "different" from the mainstream employee, which often translates into reduced promotional opportunities. As part-timers integrate themselves more and more fully into the work force, this will become less of a problem. For now, part-timers as a whole continue to suffer job discrimination on the basis of reduced advancement opportunities, fewer fringe benefits, and lower salaries.

Dr. Diane Rothberg of the Association of Part-Time Professionals believes that managers are not taking the issue of part-time work as seriously as they should because the information hasn't been pitched at the right target.

The media have been trying to introduce the idea of part-time work, but they are doing it in women's magazines. They are not talking to managers. Part-time hasn't really been played up in the business journals, so management is still not taking it terribly seriously.

The movement for permanent part-time work is one of the hardest issues, because it is done on an ad hoc basis. In the future, workers may unite to press for it.

Women Take the Lead

"I have a hunch that as there are more and more women who have invested ten years in their career and run up against their biological time clock, we will see even more of an increase in the forces for change in the traditional work patterns," says Nancy Inui of FOCUS, a private, nonprofit organization in Washington state that promotes the development of alternative work patterns.

"And as women increasingly move into management and are in a position to make these kinds of personnel decisions, there will be more understanding and support for alternative working situations. They'll be a whole lot more supportive of other women.

"Occasionally we run into women who are not supportive (of alternative working arrangements)," Ms. Inui continues. "They buy into the idea that the company should own your soul." But, overall, she feels that the climate for innovations in the workplace is extremely favorable, partially because "what happens to women is going to happen to men, too. The husbands of the women who want these changes and are working for them will be affected," and they in turn will support such options where they work.

Ms. Inui feels that managers are slowly beginning to change the way they view work, and that this change will make alternative work options easier to integrate into the workplace.

"As new types of managers come up through the ranks, there will be more enlightened supervisors who will view work not as a forty-hour chunk of time but as an end product. They will break away from the idea of work as a chunk of time at a place of business. They will see that workers can put in time at their own pace—days, nights, weekends—as long as they produce. They'll view the job not in terms of hours, but in terms of the job itself. Who cares where and when the news release was written as long as it was done on time? As this idea takes hold there will be a lot more flexibility for jobs that are not dependent on using certain equipment in a certain place. Both employees and employers need to think creatively about all of the possibilities that exist."

Since 1976, FOCUS, which Ms. Inui describes as a "high volume, low budget operation helping to implement alternative work patterns" has listed over 4,000 positions in the Seattle area for permanent part-time and job-sharing positions. With 3,800 drop-ins at their office in 1982 alone, FOCUS is seeing that people of every age group and occupational category are looking for alternative work situations. "This is a good sign," Ms. Inui explains, "because the broader the base for social change, the more likely it is to happen."

■ **"More enlightened supervisors will view work not as a forty-hour chunk of time but as an end product."**

Mothers are likely to be one up on other people when requesting non-traditional work options. "I think that people who want an alternative work arrangement so they can have more time with small children have an advantage," Ms. Inui says. "Even the most hard-bitten boss will be more sympathetic to motherhood than he would be to someone who wanted to write the great American novel or practice the cello."

The likelihood of being able to institute a change, mother or not, will be heavily dependent on the style of the particular company. Those with rigid personnel policies will be less likely to have corporate hearts that can be warmed, even by the needs of a tiny newborn.

"The best bet is going to be a company with a certain management style," Ms. Inui points out, "the kind that believes 'happy workers are better workers.' " On the other hand, "companies that are basically rigid are going to be a whole lot less receptive. Things like a strict dress code are usually dead giveaways."

Changes Are Near

The trend is clear: Companies are becoming more and more employee oriented, and mothers who want to negotiate a modified work schedule stand to benefit from this new direction in employee relations.

So says Mary Lou Maxie, a consultant with Buck Consulting of New York, a sixty-five-year-old employee benefits consulting firm that helps major companies design and audit their benefit programs. With a list of over 700 major corporate clients, including 400 Fortune 1000 companies, Ms. Maxie is in a good position to watch important trends develop, and she feels strongly that the time has never been better for mothers with infants and toddlers to succeed in negotiating an alternative work situation.

"Companies want to do what is best for the employee because it's good for the company, too," Ms. Maxie explains. "It really works to the employer's advantage (to agree to a modified work schedule). Women who are given this kind of arrangement feel obligated to the employer. They will try to do more work in the time they are in the office. We find that absenteeism is much less in these situations than in cases where the mother is working five days a week. If she's only working three days, she'll be sure she's there those three days.

"The employer really benefits. He has an employee who is producing as much, or almost as much, as a full-time employee, but he's only paying 60% of the salary and benefits."

A willingness on the part of employers to talk about a modified work schedule began showing up about 1979, but particularly in the last two years more and more companies are saying yes to these kinds of arrangements, Ms. Maxie observes. "Banks, consulting firms, the administrative end of large manufacturing companies, and oil companies are doing a lot in this area."

As more and more employees ask for this kind of arrangement, employers will realize that this is something employees want, and they will accommodate the need. It is important to remember, Ms. Maxie points out, that "employee benefits evolve because of employee interest. Employees get particular benefits because they go to the employer and say, 'We need this. This would make life easier for us.' Benefits are designed to make the employee happy and improve morale."

As Dr. Diane Rothberg comments, "Changes are coming because of the demands of the workers, particularly women."

Part 2

Creative Work Schedules: Making room for motherhood

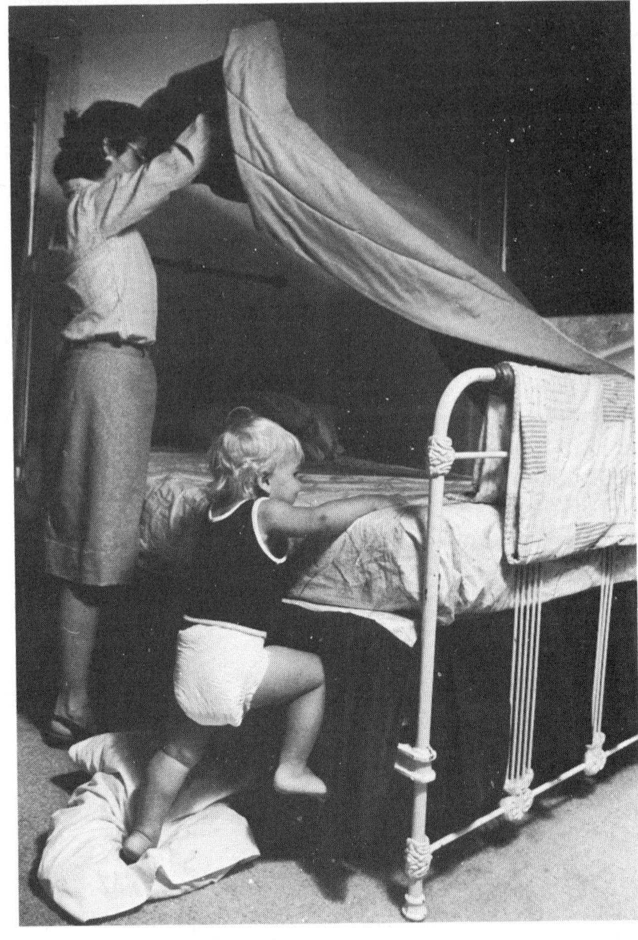

■ Chapter 5

Permanent Part-time
Popular alternative to the forty hour week

■ The key to successfully negotiating a modified working arrangement, as FOCUS President Nancy Inui says, is to make it easy for the employer to say yes.

In most cases, the employer will find it easiest to say yes if the modification you are after is the conversion of a full-time job into a part-time job. Why? Because almost all employers have had some experience with part-time employees, although perhaps not with an upper level professional or managerial position such as the one you have your eye on. The employer probably already has some sense of how to supervise a part-time employee, as well as some idea of what he or she can expect from a part-timer. Job-sharing, flextime, and work-at-home programs are more likely to be unknown quantities, but he or she will probably be able to relate to part-time work, at least conceptually.

So the odds are more likely to be in your favor if the alternative arrangement you are after is the conversion of a full-time job into a permanent part-time position. Permanent part-time is currently the most prevalent alternative to the forty-hour week.

Mother Hours

How does permanent part-time work fit in with the needs of a career woman who wants to modify her working hours in order to be more accessible to her baby?

Very well, according to those who have done it. A three, four, or five hour workday means a shortened period of separation and, depending on the age of the baby, only one or two missed nursings. Some clever mothers and cooperative babies even manage to synchronize mother's work hours with baby's naptime, further minimizing the sense of separation.

Although working shortened daily hours is the most common part-time arrangement, some mothers work two or two-and-a-half days a week instead. This has the advantage of giving mother and baby five uninterrupted days a week together, but for the breastfeeding mother it has the drawback of increasing the number of missed feedings to four or five in a single day. It will almost certainly be necessary for the mother to pump her breasts in order to remain comfortable, and even an "older" baby will be likely to need several bottles during her absence. Most important, longer periods of separation are also generally more difficult for the baby/toddler to accept.

Some mothers have little choice other than to work two long days instead of four or five short ones, while others deliberately choose this system feeling that five uninterrupted days with the baby is adequate compensation for two long days away from home.

Health Care Workers

If your professional skills lie in the health care field and, most particularly if you are a nurse, your chances of finding part-time work have recently increased dramatically.

The chronic and continuing shortage of nurses has forced hospitals to come up with attractive arrangements to lure women back to the patients' bedsides. Hospitals across the country are finding that the opportunity for part-time employment is an effective recruitment tool for nurses who otherwise would hang up their nursing caps for an extended period of time after their firstborn arrives.

One hospital in South Carolina even ran display ads in the local paper pitched at the nurse-mother. "Full-time mother, part-time nurse," the headline read. "Motherhood is a full-time job. Now North Trident Regional Hospital can offer you the opportunity to keep your hands in your other career—nursing. Individualized orientation and schedules to meet your needs. Innovative abbreviated shifts—when even part-time nursing is more than you can handle at this busy time in your life."

An added bonus in the trend toward increased numbers of part-time nurses is that administrators are recognizing that nursing's chief occupational hazard, burn-out, is far less of a problem among those who are working less than full time. The floor nurse's ability to be caring and compassionate probably rises in direct proportion to the reduction in stress she finds through her shortened work-week.

Mothers who are registered nurses are finding that hospitals are willing to accommodate their need for part-time work, and that there is often some element of flexibility in selecting a schedule that is satisfactory to all.

The current tight economy is throwing this situation somewhat out of balance, since there are more nurses than ever looking for work to help meet the family's financial needs, while at the same time the hospitals' patient loads are at a low ebb because federal funds have been cut and people are postponing elective procedures. None-the-less, in many parts of the country the outlook for finding good part-time nursing jobs is excellent.

Scheduling Options

Mary Doll works two to four days a week from 3:00 P.M. to 11:00 P.M. as a pediatric nurse, with her husband assuming responsibility for their year-old son while she is gone.

"The position I have now was created for me," Mary explains. "My employer seems to be glad to still have me here since I have acquired many skills and the ability to fill-in in a number of different areas. My co-workers seem to be glad that I can work and still spend a lot of time mothering my son. This flexible arrangement has enabled me to continue pediatric nursing, which I love."

Nurse Mary Doll works on a flexible schedule because of her son Evan.

Janis DePar works on an "optional" basis. "I let the staffing people know when I am willing to work. I usually work one 3:00 to 11:00 P.M. shift during the week, and one 3:00 to 11:00 P.M. shift during the weekend. My next door neighbor cares for the baby from 2:30 to 4:30 P.M. when my husband gets home. He brings the baby to the hospital and we all have supper together. When I get home at 11:30 P.M., I usually nurse Nicki. It is the most relaxing thing to do after a hard evening of work in the operating room. I can't imagine working and not nursing my baby."

Sharon O'Shaughnessy knew she wanted an extended maternity leave even though "Initially, upon requesting a six-month leave of absence, my employer tried to dissuade me, using the reasoning that my full-time position could not be held for me. She offered me the usual three months plus two weeks of holidays plus two weeks' leave of absence. I said no, that I would take my chances on finding work when my six months were up. Even at that time I had doubts about wanting a full-time job while mothering.

"When no part-time job was available at the end of the six months, this same person (herself a full-time working mother) encouraged me to remain on staff on a casual basis until a part-time job became available, which I did. My fellow nurses were delighted—and envious!"

■ "It was important to me to make my work fit my son's schedule so that I could nurse him for the first year of his life."

Sharon now works days every second weekend, and an occasional extra day or night. "As an outgoing individual who enjoys working with people in my field, I feel that I am happier and more contented because I work two days a week."

Cynthia Lee took an "on call" position "which requires me to work one day a week, if asked. It has no benefits, but it allows me to keep up my nursing skills, and doesn't require me to take Michael to a caretaker very often. My co-workers think it's ideal, if one can afford to do it."

Cheryl Kruwel works from 11:20 P.M. until 7:20 A.M. two nights a week and every other weekend.

"Initially, I found that if I worked more than two days in a row my milk supply decreased," Cheryl reports. "So we set up a permanent schedule that was agreeable to everyone in the department. My only request was that I not work more than two days in a row, so we settled on Monday, Tuesday, and Saturday the first week, and Sunday, Thursday, and Friday the second week. This schedule allows me to get the rest I need."

Nurses like Cheryl who work all night have to devise some system for child care while they sleep during the day. Cheryl's mother was the answer for her.

"Fortunately, my mother lives nearby. I arranged to pay her for babysitting. After working all night I go home, pick up the baby, and drive to her house where I can sleep. She takes care of my son while he is awake, and when he needs to nurse she brings him to me. Many times he cuddles in and we sleep together."

Shari Kelly, who is separated from her husband and must work to support herself and her baby, works the night shift four times a week. She receives full benefits for her thirty-two hour workweek.

"It was important to me to make my work fit my son's schedule so that I could nurse him for the first year of his life," Shari explains. "I tried a schedule of one day on, one day off so that I wouldn't be away from my child every night, but I wasn't able to get enough sleep and found this absolutely exhausting. Then I went to a schedule of four days on and three days off. This works much better for me."

Shari's son was used to a family bed and she says, "I miss it and I feel he does, too. He stays with his grandparents during the night while I work. During the day he is with me, but I am so tired from working all night that I am impatient for his naptime so that I can sleep. I come home exhausted just as he is perked up for the day, but I am forced to work at night until he is old enough for me to return to work full time."

On the plus side, Shari has found her co-workers to be very supportive of her desire to continue nursing while she works. "No one objects to covering for me while I am 'doing my thing' (pumping my milk). They've been good-natured and even tease me about still 'doing my thing' even though the baby is now a year old."

Claudia Lupia works on an "on call" basis. Working on call enables her to choose the days and shifts she wants to work each month, and also gives her the flexibility to work as much or as little as she likes, depending on eight-month-old Michael's needs.

"Initially I tried working twenty hours a week after Michael was born," Claudia reports. "But when he (and I) showed signs of separation anxiety, I began working only three or four nights a month. The hospital nursing office calls me every month listing the shifts that are open for the coming month, and I pick my hours."

In addition to the flexible schedule and reduced hours, there have been added bonuses in this arrangement for Claudia. "Working less frequently has made me enjoy being a nurse again," she says. "And by working on call, I have the chance to work all over the hospital and gain additional experience."

Some Drawbacks

Carolyn Ashcraft, an LPN, worked the 3:00 to 11:00 P.M. shift three days a week after her first baby was born, and found her co-workers reaction to her arrangement was "mostly favorable, but I was not allowed to bring her into the hospital to nurse. As a little baby she slept a lot in the evening, which is why I chose that shift. As she grew older (twelve to twenty-two months), it did not work out as well. She napped at the time I was leaving, and it was upsetting to her to have me gone when she awoke. Since I only worked part-time, sometimes I was there and sometimes I wasn't."

Cynthia Jones, also an LPN, had other problems. "My co-workers were not particularly supportive. After the first few weeks, they got tired of relieving me for ten minutes so I could go pump my breasts. But I said if they could have ten minutes for a cigarette break, I could have ten minutes to pump milk for my baby."

More Options for Nurses

When her baby turned six months old, Diane Lack began working on call for the same hospital where she had been employed for several years before the baby's birth. The termination of this arrangement after a year due to budgetary cutbacks at the hospital turned out to be a blessing in disguise for Diane, who then discovered med-pool.

"Med-pool is like a secretarial pool, only for nurses," she explains. "For the past seven months I have been working one or two days a week, depending on their needs. In a med-pool, there is no minimum or maximum amount of days to work. Sometimes I must travel to other hospitals, but I make up to six dollars an hour more than I did when I was on the hospital nursing staff."

Some nurse-mothers find that motherhood and a non-hospital setting work well together. Pat Lewis remarks, "As a public health nurse, I have a very flexible schedule. When the children were small, I'd work two to four hours, then go home to nurse them. Now that they are older, I can leave work when I need to carpool, attend soccer games, or whatever. I work with patients in their homes and in clinic settings, and have always been available when my children were home sick. Since I am a back-up nurse I work when asked, and can say no easily. I find it hard to say no to work demands when we are short-staffed, but my family comes first. The patients will be there later, but I have to be careful not to postpone the needs of my family."

Carol Smith accepted her position with a health care agency when her baby was a year and a half old. "I provide relief nursing care in patients' homes and in institutions on an on-call basis. I am under no obligation to accept any assignment. I only accept weekend work and short shift assignments when my husband can be home."

Carol says that at the place where she worked before her baby was born, her employer and co-workers "seemed to understand and approve of my reasons for resigning when my baby was born, but at the same time I sensed a feeling that I might later regret giving up such a super job—days, good pay, and job security. But I wanted an intimate hour-by-hour relationship with my baby in the early years of his life. I wanted to be his primary caregiver.

"My present employer deals with many people in my situation, and is very good about working out arrangements that consider everyone's needs."

There is usually a price to be paid for not working full time, as nurse Edith Infinito who works twenty-four hours a week, points out. "There are fewer benefits and no upward mobility."

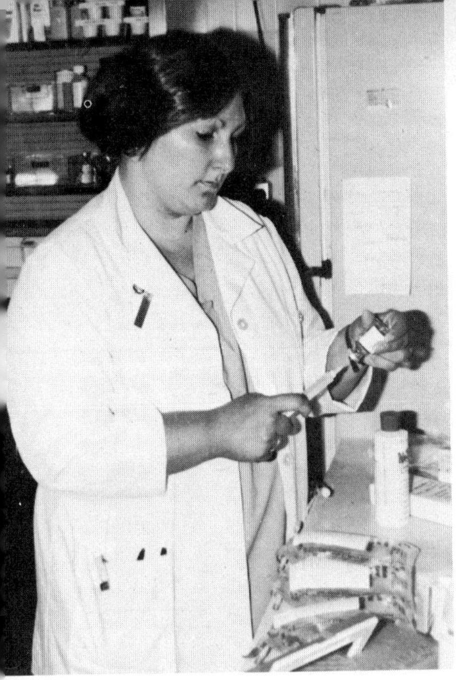

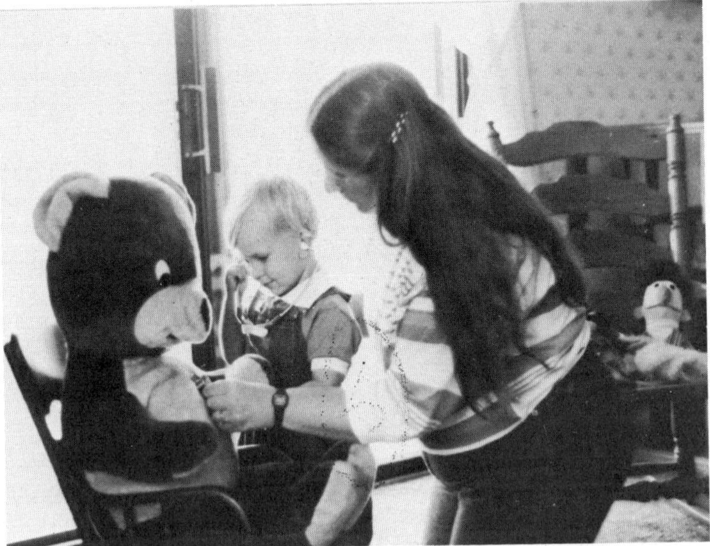

Diane Lack is continuing her nursing career on a flexible basis so she can spend more time at home with Ryan.

But, like many other mothers with young children, she feels that the trade-off of less money and status for more time at home with her one-year-old and three-year-old is a sacrifice worth making.

Other Medical Fields

Other areas of the medical spectrum are also accommodating to those who want to work part-time.

Dr. Yolanda Leparulo works twenty-five hours a week, without night call, on the faculty of a teaching hospital.

"Many women physicians do not consider half-time work," Yolanda comments, "but in a teaching job it is not hard to do. Working part of a day each day is easier for breastfeeding. I only miss one feeding per day. And I feel closer to my daughter because no day goes by without good times with her.

"Co-workers are generally helpful and tolerant. However, they tend to smile patronizingly when I leave work for the day at lunchtime. They seem to think the special things I do with her—like attending a toddler gym class—are a little far-fetched."

Dr. Leparulo feels she has achieved a good mix between mothering and medicine. "I am really glad to see my daughter when I get home, and I don't feel cheated at all. Serena usually naps two of the five hours I am away.

"I couldn't imagine giving up medicine; I would get so far behind. Housework accumulates faster than you can do it, and

■ Robin Peyson Nazimiez, Health Planner

I was not planning to return to work until baby Jason was at least a year old, but I found that we were not meeting our monthly bills, even though we were being frugal. When Jason was four months old, I got a call offering me an opportunity that was too good to be true. It was a small health care consulting firm not far from my home, and I could set my own hours. I found day-care arrangements for Jason and agreed to take the job on a one-month trial basis. I began working from 10:00 A.M. until 1:00 P.M. Monday through Friday.

As of today, I have been working approximately three and a half months. All, needless to say, has not been smooth. In August we all went on vacation to visit my husband's family for ten days. On our return, Jason was not happy to return to day care. I wanted to give it a little time to see if he would adjust, but he became more and more unhappy. He had begun to crawl while we were on vacation, and had begun to exhibit some signs of separation anxiety. As he became increasingly mobile, I think it was normal for this anxiety to increase. So in early September my husband and I sat down and arranged a new work schedule for both of us so that Michael, my husband, could take care of Jason for the three hours each day I would be at work. Jason is old enough now that he doesn't miss a feeding while I am gone, but I nurse him when I get home. On different days I work different hours—four to seven on Monday, Thursday, and Friday; two-thirty to five-thirty on Tuesday; eight to eleven on Wednesday. This is to accommodate my husband's job. He is a research biochemist and has a flexible schedule. We are still working things out, trying to find a schedule that is best for us all. Nothing ever stays the same, especially Jason! It is hard sometimes, as Michael is now often working nights and part of the weekend, but we are managing. La Leche League has been very helpful to me. ■

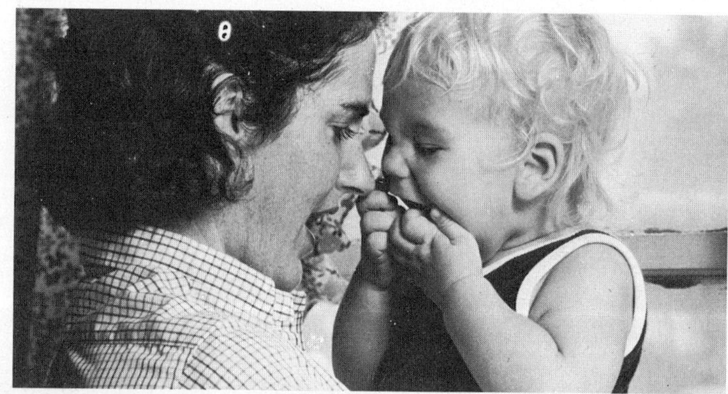

working gives me an excuse for having a messy house. But I can't imagine working full time, either. I would never see Serena."

Physical therapist Diane Corcoran worked half-time in a veterans' hospital when her firstborn was a baby, and now, since the birth of her second child, works part-time in a special education center.

Her new job permits her to work just a day and a half per week away from home. "I can do all of my paper work at home, bill my calls to the office, and schedule new referrals at my convenience, including evenings and weekends.

"In both cases, my employers wanted me to work full time," Diane admits. "But I live in an area where there aren't many other therapists to fill the job, so I can pretty much choose my hours and make the kind of schedule I want.

"I enjoy my work, and certainly enjoy being a mother. This arrangement gives me both."

Debbie Armstrong, also a physical therapist, works part-time on a contract basis for a hospital home health department. "I worked full time in the hospital as a physical therapist before the birth of my baby. I took a five-month leave of absence, and then switched over to the Home Health Department since there was a part-time opening when I was ready to return to work. I now do physical therapy on home visits. I am paid per visit and make up my own schedule, generally working about four hours per day. If the baby is sick, I can stay home or adjust my schedule as needed."

Pharmacist Jennifer Peddlesden went back to work part-time in a hospital pharmacy when her baby was nine months old. "The woman I worked for allowed me to stay home or come in late if there were any problems, such as my son being sick. My hours were flexible since I was not the only one on duty and my presence wasn't crucial."

But even with such accommodating arrangements, Jennifer quit her job after six months to return to being a full-time mother. "None of it worked well for my son. His reaction to separation always seemed to come after the fact. He would be clinging on my day off, get up to nurse at night, and demand much more attention than he did before I worked.

"My six months of working part-time convinced me how much a baby needs his mother full time. After nine months of not working, I found that I had not forgotten everything I ever learned, and that my brain did not go to mush after becoming a mother. I am confident that at some later date I will be able to pick up my career as a pharmacist again. Once convinced of this, I was very happy to quit and be a full-time mother until the kids are grown up."

Microbiologist Linda Caplan has found that "As a laboratory technologist, I am able to find work in a variety of schedules, and am especially sought after if I am willing to work weekends and holidays.

"When my first child was eighteen months old, I began working every other weekend. I then started picking up Fridays, and five months later picked up Thursdays, then every other Monday. I was averaging three and a half days a week until my second son was born. When he was ten months old I began working sporadically, filling in on weekends and occasionally holidays as well."

Linda finds that she has a lack of status on the job, with "no chance to become a supervisor, no chance for promotions, and little responsibility. However, psychologically, working this way feels good. I did not have to give up the career that I studied for years to achieve, and in which I have spent so much time working. I definitely feel a boost to my self-esteem, which has to be evident in my attitude toward my children."

People Who Help Others

Other "helping professions" are also showing increasing flexibility in willingness to modify work schedules to meet employees' personal needs.

Social worker Deborah Thorne found that her employer was "basically cooperative and understanding that being a parent is my priority." But she feels that she has "been given more work and a larger caseload in return for being able to work part-time."

Moira White, also a social worker who works half time, says that "my employer and co-workers have been extremely supportive. When we were having difficulty finding good child care, I was able to bring my daughter to work with me for meetings, and I could work at home."

Moira chose to work four hours, five mornings a week instead of three longer days. She explains her reason. "Emily has been able to continue nursing without any supplements. She adjusted readily to the fact that I was away each morning, but eagerly awaits my return. I tried to express my milk and leave some for her, but she would not take a bottle. She preferred to wait for me.

"We live in a moderately large city, and if I worked full time I would be away from 8:00 A.M. until 6:00 P.M. I could not stand to be away from the baby for that length of time. I feel fortunate to have been able to make such satisfactory arrangements. I have always wanted children and I love being a mother."

Family therapist Karen Combs who works twenty hours a week for the Iowa Department of Social Services feels that her "co-workers are very supportive. Some don't realize that I'm working part-time, although I talk about it as much as possible to encourage others to seek this alternative."

Karen says that there are no formal policies about part-time work. But she knew she did not want to work full time after her baby was born, so her immediate supervisor "was instrumental in securing this part-time position for me."

Canadian clinical psychologist Christine Sexton has a "boss who believes women should be able to have a career and a family," and so got the hospital to agree to having her work half time. She now works a maximum of three days a week "although while breastfeeding I worked shorter hours on four or five days in order to get home to the baby more quickly."

■ "My employer has been very supportive. . . . I was able to bring my daughter to work with me and I could work at home."

Like many professional women who at least temporarily trade their fast-track careers for part-time work in order to have more time at home with their babies, Christine found that her co-workers reacted with a mixture of feelings to her arrangement.

"There was a small amount of wonderment, and perhaps some thought of me as less than a true professional. Sometimes there is extra stress for my co-workers, since they have two half-time people to relate to instead of just one person."

Psychologist Kathy Moskowitz, who is employed by Kaiser-Permanente, also works twenty hours a week. "Mostly, people are supportive, although some have difficulty understanding that my child is my first priority. I do not presently take emergency calls, although I will have to do so soon."

Kathy says it is "difficult to 'shift sets' from home to work and vice versa. I am reluctant to leave the baby (nine months old) with a babysitter for recreation, since I am away from him while I work. My husband brings him to me to nurse at lunch two of the three days I work, but by the end of the day he really misses me.

"But I feel good that I can continue in my profession. For most of the time, Andy is with one or the other of his parents. My working gives him some special time alone with his father."

The Field of Education

Teachers, who often are required to be at school less than eight hours a day, are sometimes able to be more accessible to their children with the help of a willing principal.

As a teacher of multiply handicapped children, Monica Miele has only a twenty-seven hour workweek, and very flexible working conditions which enable her to juggle her job and her three preschoolers—three years, fifteen months, and four months of age.

"I am only required to be in school five and a half hours a day," she says. "I work five minutes from my home, so I often leave on my lunch hour to go home and spend the time with my children. Since I have a class of five- and six-year-olds, I bring my three-year-old to class on occasion to participate in parties and field trips. Once when

Teacher Bernita Frost often brings daughter Kristen along with her to school.

my son was fifteen months old, my mother-in-law could not babysit at the last minute, so I packed up my diaper bag and lunches and brought Andrew to school with me."

Monica has been fortunate to have a particularly understanding and supportive principal who "encourages me to go home on my lunch hour. He has never refused me time to leave school for a family problem. He enjoys seeing my son come to school with me and does not expect me to stay for after-school activities."

Bernita Frost, who teaches school in Zimbabwe, has the freedom to leave and go home to nurse the baby, or to have the baby brought to school for her to be nursed. "My working hours are short—7:45 A.M. until 12:45 P.M.," she says. "I am allowed to go home at intervals to feed the baby. The housemaid takes care of her during the mornings, and then I have the afternoons free to relax with her because the housework is all done for me.

"If I have to go somewhere with the pupils and can't get home to nurse the baby, the maid can bring her to school and I can feed her in the headmistress' office. I take the baby to school for afternoon and evening functions. The children love the baby and help to look after her at afternoon activities. All of the teachers and the headmistress are very cooperative and do not mind taking the class for a few minutes if I am delayed at home."

Biostatistician/epidemiologist Judith Simon worked six hours a day after her first baby was born, and half-time after the birth of her second baby. "Most of the time the hours are flexible and the atmosphere is casual. I can stay home when one of the children is sick, and often work at home in the evening after they are asleep. My employers and co-workers at SUNY (State University of New York) have been very supportive, and several co-workers have similar arrangements. My employers are happy to have classes well taught and studies well analyzed, and are not concerned about personal working arrangements."

Not Always Easy

Few working situations are perfect, and sometimes career women-mothers find themselves in the uncomfortable situation of feeling as though they are living in glass houses, with employers and/or co-workers watching every move.

"I feel that there is a lot of pressure on me," admits teacher Linda Erlebach. "I have to do things letter perfect, or the administration will take away my 'nursing privileges.' My employer feels I should be weaning my eight-month-old daughter—that nursing is something I'm 'hanging on to' to make me feel better. But my co-workers, who are mothers, are mostly supportive."

"At first it was very hard to work and be a mother," reveals Jacqueline Rojas, who teaches at a major university. "At work I thought about the baby, and when I was with the baby I thought about work. This still happens occasionally, but now I try to be more efficient while I'm on the job, and totally relaxed while I'm with the baby."

Kathy Arnold, who has a three-year-old and a sixteen-month-old, voiced the biggest hazard that faces every teacher-mother: "It is often difficult to have as much patience as I should with my own after I get home from wrestling with thirty-odd kids all day."

Hard to Replace

Those who have a sophisticated expertise in a hard-to-find skill can often write their own ticket when seeking modified working arrangements. Employers have too much invested in on-the-job training for these professionals to let them walk away from their jobs, and in some cases such an employee is not only expensive but difficult to replace.

Engineering and computer programming are two professions that currently enjoy such an enviable situation. The engineer or programmer who wants to reduce her workload in order to spend more time with her baby will likely find her request granted almost as a matter of course.

Other areas in private industry are beginning to pick up on the trend toward reduced hours for mothers who have small children. Some industries are more receptive to this idea than others, although not necessarily for purely altruistic reasons.

"I always tell women to get a job in a bank," says Pat Ibbs, associate editor of *Spencer Reports*, an employee benefits publication for Fortune 1000 companies. "AT&T is another good choice. They've both been hit with sex discrimination suits, and they must hire and promote a large percentage of women."

Because it now employs so many women, the banking industry as a whole is beginning to be more receptive to the needs of women in general, and career-women mothers in particular. The First National Bank of Boston is one such example. The bank has fifteen women who are working less than full time, all of them for family reasons.

"This has been going on for about three years," explains bank spokesperson Marion Gardner-Saxe, "although we have only had an official policy about part-time employment for about a year."

These are far from casual arrangements, and Ms. Gardner-Saxe says that part-time status is granted only in particular cases and for very specific reasons.

> Part-time status is granted only in the case of bank officers who represent a great deal of time and training that we don't want to lose. It is only available to those who are already employed by the bank full time, and who have proven their commitment to this bank and to their career. They must have a very good track record and strong support from their division that there is a clear need for them to remain with the bank.
>
> We will allow them to go part-time because of family responsibilities, their own health, or to ease into retirement. We are looking for people who can make a full-time commitment to their career, but we are willing to accommodate the need for less than full-time hours for specific worthwhile reasons for our better employees. We will limit these people to a certain maximum number of years that they can be employed only part-time.

The fifteen women working part-time at the First National Bank of Boston are all in high level positions such as loan officers, personnel officers, or vice presidents, with a full-time salary range of the mid 20s to the mid 40s.

"None of these women has taken a decrease in responsibility due to her part-time status," Ms. Gardner-Saxe continues, "and there have already been promotions. Promotions may take longer for those who are only working part-time, but so far there haven't been any complaints."

Responses Vary

Part-time arrangements can now be found in almost every sector of private industry, although some employers are markedly less receptive to the idea than others.

Chemical engineer Lois Jansen, mother of an eighteen-month-old son, found "there was considerable reluctance by my supervisors to having me work part-time. I have had to re-justify my special arrangements on many occasions. It took six months to convince them to approve a scheduled promotion and pay increase."

Lois, who works three days a week, says she continues to do essentially the same work she did before the baby was born, although "my assignments were modified to include projects with fewer time constraints and less need for daily contact with the production department. I spend a larger portion of my time assisting other engineers rather than working on projects I am completely responsible for. I have made myself available for consultation by phone when I am at home, and will change my working days if necessary to complete an assignment or attend a meeting."

Systems engineer Ruth Fleming, who has a seventeen-month-old daughter, found her supervisor to be very supportive of her twenty to thirty hour workweek. "His wife had educated him well about long term nursing and part-time employment," Ruth says. But even so, "Every once in a while my supervisor's boss asks me when I plan to return to work full time. Eventually I will have to give a date."

Beth Lindberg, a lead computer operator whose youngest child is sixteen months old, works three twelve-hour days and says, "This schedule has worked very well. I am able to nurse often on off-days. On workdays I nurse morning, evening, and at least twice during the night."

Beth and her co-workers devised their own schedule. "Six of us must cover the computer seven days a week, twenty-four hours a day. We all work three twelve-hour days a week. Our employer was enthusiastic when we proposed the new schedule, showing we could get all the work done. We gave up lunch breaks, and whenever possible we swap hours when someone is ill.

Computer operator Connie Seymour kept her old job after her daughter was born, but now works only from 2:00 P.M. to 6:00 P.M. "Since the workload decreased drastically after the sale of our company, I think it was a relief to have me volunteer to cut my hours. The work still gets done, and friendships are maintained on a daily basis. It is a very agreeable situation for a small office.

■ "Although being away from home is not always ideal, the coming home reunion is always great!"

"This short time away from the baby makes it easy to continue our nursing relationship. Although being away from home is not always ideal, the coming home reunion is always great!"

Ruth Titschinger works two eight-hour days a week as a word processor for Federated Department Stores.

"Federated maintains a staff of former full-time employees for on-call work," Ruth says. The system works very well and "my supervisor appreciates having an experienced, dependable person who does not require extensive monitoring. Because of my previous record with the company, I now earn top dollar for my part-time typing and general clerical duties."

Patricia Street works four days a week for the California State

Legislature from 6:00 P.M. until 11:00 P.M. which allows her husband to be with the baby while she is gone.

Patricia Street sometimes brings Connor and Cela to work with her.

"As soon as I had the baby, I knew that my plans for going back to work full time after my six month leave would not work. It was the reality of her vulnerability and helplessness, and the way she looked to me to protect her that changed my mind. I knew that I couldn't trust anyone else to give her what she needed on all levels—physical, emotional, and educational."

Patricia says that her career is "definitely in 'park,' but I have stumbled on a rare job opportunity, and my husband and I have been so grateful for the way it has worked out. There are too few of these situations available. The public needs to be more aware of these alternatives to the nine-to-five job since more families are finding it almost impossible to live on one modest income."

Real estate associate Michele Ruckgaber, whose daughter is now two and a half years old, has found that her particular line of work is quite flexible and accommodating to the needs of her baby.

"I suppose in some respects you could say I am still on an extended maternity leave," Michele says, "because the nature of my work is such that when I sell, I get paid. Right now I am just choosing to sell less."

Michele, who reduced her hours at work once the baby was born, says that, "Probably my co-workers didn't care one way or the other, but my brokers really resented my absence because they knew I wasn't selling as much as I had been selling before and consequently they weren't making as much money from me."

Michele says that her husband sometimes helps out by going on appointments for her, and that she has learned to do more of her work with her customers on the telephone.

"Knowing that the average appointment takes about two or three hours, I frequently took Heather with me so that I could nurse her on the way to or from the appointment, although we never nursed in front of customers.

"Very honestly, some business that I might have had has probably just passed me by. But I just took the attitude that my baby was more important than the money.

"Sure there were days when I did, and sometimes still do, miss the excitement of a full-time career, but when Heather and I are together I forget those feelings quickly. I really enjoy the chance to be myself with her; I don't have to get involved in the 'game playing' that goes on in the business world."

Denise Peacock took a part-time job as a secretary in the public relations department of a children's home when she was unable to find a part-time job in her field of social work. "My immediate supervisor is female and very supportive of my need to be primarily a mother. Interestingly, though, she is not as supportive of my continuing to nurse my sixteen-month-old son. The administration itself is tolerant but not supportive. I work six hours a day, three days a week. These hours are flexible—I can go in late or get off early as needed, and I am not far from my son."

Martha Katz-Hyman converted her full-time job as an archivist for the American Jewish Historical Society to a twenty-five hour a week job after her first baby was born. "The arrangement proved satisfactory to both my employer and my co-workers. There were other part-time employees, so the idea was not unusual."

Bookkeeper Julia Matusiewicz went back to work when her son was six months old for an employer who allowed her to take as much of the work home as possible. At times she also took her son into work with her.

But even such a flexible arrangement had problems. "I had trouble finding a sitter I could trust, and then after I did find one, she'd quit to go to work full time. After five months I decided it just wasn't working out and I quit."

Nancy Johnson, who works in the Civil Defense Department for the State of New York, returned to work in a different office but with the same job title on a half-time basis when her baby was ten months old.

"I worked mornings as a Senior Personnel Administrator," Nancy says. "After four months I was promoted to a higher level, Associate Personnel Administrator, in a different program but still half-time, working every morning. I shared a budgeted job item with another mother who also worked half-time. We did not share a work assignment, but instead had two separate and distinct roles in the office.

"Overall, the attitudes we encountered were very favorable. There was jealousy from the full-timers on sunny summer days when we left at noon and they continued to work, but other than that we all worked well together. When a position for assistant director of our program came up, it was offered to us half-timers first because according to the director he found us the most valuable staff members."

Mary Lou MacGregor found what she considers an ideal situation as a consultant for a cosmetics company.

"I work approximately fifty days of the year. The job begins at 11:00 A.M., giving me a chance to have a relaxed breakfast with the children, do a load of laundry, play a game, and get lunch together before going to work. I come home for lunch, my only break in the workday, and stay home for one full hour in the middle of the afternoon. This gives me a chance to nurse Christina, fifteen months, read four-year-old Owen a story, and then put them to bed for an afternoon nap so they can stay up a little later in the evening with my husband, Chris, and me.

"After I have been re-energized with lots of hugs and kisses, it's back to work until 6:00 or 7:00 P.M. The children sleep most of the late afternoon, then I am home for dinner and we have the evening together.

"Owen and Christina are with me almost constantly when I'm not working. We go together to the doctor, dentist, my hairdresser, exercise class, shopping, dinners, the movies, and almost anywhere else. It seems so natural, so wonderful, to be together. The joys of life happen when I am with my family. I am fortunate to be blessed with two wonderful children who have taught me new dimensions to the word love. I am a part-time working mother, but my thoughts, my love, my being, are for Owen and Christina all of the time."

Chapter 6

Job Sharing
Where one-half plus one-half equals more than one

Perhaps you've already heard the story of the remarkable Miss Neef. It's a classic among those who believe in flexible working arrangements.

Thomas Van Beek lives in Amsterdam. In 1961 Tom was a twenty-five-year-old executive in need of a private secretary. After a procession of unpromising applicants, a bright, charming young lady came to Tom's office. She was Miss Neef. Her references were impressive, her typing and shorthand more than adequate. Beyond her obvious secretarial talent, there was the aura of personal stability that Tom had been looking for. Miss Neef was hired on the spot.

She was an executive's dream. She was tireless. At the end of a long day, when even her young employer was exhausted, Miss Neef was as prepared to cope with her responsibilities as she had been before she went out for her brief lunch break.

The weeks became months, and the months, years. During the season of heavy business, Miss Neef did the work of two—a one woman miracle.

Then, in 1973, came the day Tom dreaded: Miss Neef wished to retire. As he thought about the splendid job she had done—really more than anyone could have asked of one person—Tom was determined that his remarkable Miss Neef should have the most lavish retirement party he could arrange.

It was at that celebration that the mystery of Miss Neef's boundless energy stopped being a mystery. For shortly after the guest of honor arrived, the guests of honor arrived. For twelve years, Tom had been convinced that his secretary had been doing the work of two. Instead, two secretaries had been doing the work of one. Two sisters, sharing the same job, worked half-time and split the paycheck.

They were identical twins.*

Tom, without even knowing it, got what an increasing number of enlightened employers are now actively recruiting—two for the price of one.

Job sharing—the sharing of one permanent, full-time job by two people who split the hours, responsibilities, and fringe benefits of the position—is perhaps the most talked about of the new flexible working arrangements.

Why all the excitement about job sharing? Because for the first time it has opened up jobs that must be filled on a full-time basis to those who only wish to work part-time. Job sharing has broken down the barriers to upper level professional positions that previously could not be obtained on a part-time, one-person basis.

Advantages to the Employee

Besides the obvious advantage of more personal time, there are a number of other pluses to the job sharing arrangement.

Depending on the particular job and the preferences of the employer, job sharers may work out a number of different arrangements, including working as a team on the same assignments, splitting tasks by interest or ability, or working different times of the day, different days of the week, or even different months of the year.

For mothers who are breastfeeding young babies, half-day arrangements are usually best so that mother and baby are not separated for more than a few hours at a time so that fewer feedings will be missed. Also, the shorter periods of separation are generally easier for the baby to handle. You may even be fortunate enough to be able to schedule your time away at work during baby's longest naptime, so that he'll only be awake for a short period during the time you are away from home.

While many part-time positions provide only greatly reduced fringe benefits—or no benefits at all—a shared position almost always includes 50% of all of the benefits to which full-time employees are entitled.

An added plus for the employee is the fact that half the salary for a shared position is usually higher than what the typical part-time job would pay.

On the job front itself, many job sharers report that the opportunity to share total responsibility, to be able to seek a partner's input on important decisions, is a real bonus. The loneliness at the top can become much less so when there is a thoroughly knowledgeable and equally committed partner to bounce ideas off of. There is strength in numbers, and job sharers sometimes find it easier to make innovative or complex decisions, knowing that each is there to back the other one up.

With jobs that can be split along the lines of areas of responsibility, each sharer has the option of selecting those parts of the job where her strengths or interests lie, and leaving the other parts to her partner who has the complementary skills needed to handle the position's other responsibilities. The most common and clear cut example of this kind of division of responsibility occurs among job-sharing teachers. One will teach math, English, and science, while the other teaches in her areas of greatest expertise—history, reading, and social studies.

Some partners have even reported being hired for a job that neither one of them alone was qualified for, but because of their combined abilities they were able to meet all of the requirements for the position.

To a man, or woman, job sharers report increased enthusiasm and energy for their jobs, increased job satisfaction, higher productivity, and freedom from "burn out."

Advantages for the Employer

For the employer, the advantages of job sharing are just as numerous, chief among them the ability to get the talents and energy of two people for the price of one. In the case of job sharing, one-half plus one-half equals more than one.

Higher productivity and lower turnover almost invariably seem to go hand in hand with job sharing. Increased productivity is particularly noticeable in jobs where the work tends to be boring and repetitious.

Job sharing is on the rise, and indications are that it will become an increasingly common option in the coming years. A study conducted in 1981 by Louis Harris and Associates for General Mills, Inc., revealed that twelve percent of the 104 companies surveyed already had some job sharing. Seventy percent said they expected to have it in the next five years.

Increasingly, employers are finding that they are money ahead when they restructure a job rather than lose a valued employee. Particularly among career women who have decided to start their families, modifying the job is often the key to retaining the employee. Rather than lose the employee altogether, employers are beginning to see the wisdom of pairing two people—not uncommonly both of them mothers with young babies—as a means of retaining professionals in whom the company has invested a great deal of time and training.

Social worker Cyndy Boesch found herself in just such a situation when she was expecting her second baby.

"I had intended to quit my job when the baby was born, but a co-worker who was also pregnant (with twins!) suggested we job share her position, each working four hours a day. This was as much time as I wanted to be away from my baby, yet it allowed me to stay current in my field and have some extra income. We share an office, and we also share the same sitter who goes to her house in the mornings, and to my house in the afternoons. It has worked out very well, both for us and for the state of North Dakota. Job sharing is an alternative that works both for the employer and employee."

Because of their reduced workweek, job sharers work all of the hours they are in the office, without any of the waste that is built into the typical eight-hour day.

■ "I think at first some people doubted our sincerity and assumed we'd call it quits, but they have been won over."

Dental hygienist Sarah Forbush Jett, who works two days a week and shares her job with another mother-hygienist who works three days, explains that, "I put in more energy and work harder the two days I am in the office than I would if I worked five days. I feel fresher in my job and enjoy it more. I have had several offers to work full time, but enjoy being with my two-year-old son too much to go back to full-time employment. I nursed for a little over a year, and being able to come home for lunch helped me feel that I was never away from him for too long. It was the perfect arrangement for me."

Job sharing is also coming to be viewed as an excellent vehicle for making use of the talents of the handicapped who are not able to work a full eight-hour day, students who are not free to work full time, and older workers who find job sharing an excellent way to phase into retirement. The pairing of an experienced and inexperienced worker provides a unique form of on-the-job training.

While increased productivity can often be objectively measured, a measure of the less tangible but no less important increase in employee loyalty is more difficult to come by. Yet employers quickly realize that it's there. Delighted at being given the opportunity to continue in their professional capacities even though they are not willing to work full time, job sharing employees willingly give the employer in excess of 50% of their professional time and ability in exchange for their 50% paycheck. Because of their circumstances, job sharers are *especially* committed to doing well on the job. They know they've been given a unique opportunity, and they're committed to seeing that it works. Everyone, it seems, comes out ahead.

The studies of job sharing employees all yield uniformly similar findings: Productivity and morale are high, absenteeism and turnover are low. In fact, absenteeism is often virtually eliminated because one partner is almost always able to cover for the other.

Job sharing also provides the employer with continuous coverage for the position. The ability of one partner to cover for the other means that a qualified, experienced person is always available to fill the position, even if one of the sharers is ill, has an accident, or decides to leave for whatever reason.

The company gets the talents of two people for the price of one, and the job sharers get exactly what they have been looking for—the opportunity to raise a family, continue their education, or pursue other interests while maintaining their professional status.

JoAnne Alter reports in *A Part-Time Career for a Full-Time You* that some banks in England have instituted a system of "twinning." "These arrangements, for clerical workers particularly, provide alternating weekly schedules for pairs of women, sometimes in the same job. 'Twins' care for each other's children as well as their own during periods when they are not on the job. Utilizing such auxiliary staff, the banks maintain, allows them to retain experienced personnel."

Selling the Idea

Even though the employer has as much to gain through the job sharing arrangement as you do, most sharers, like district court deputy Barbara Tickner, find that employers have to be sold, and sold hard, on the idea.

"I returned to work full time when my first child was eight months old," Barbara says. "It became apparent in the following months that I was not spending as much time with my son as I wanted to. I felt I was missing too many of the little things, the daily routines around the house. I was very pleased with my babysitting arrangement (my sister-in-law cared for Joshua in her home), but still I felt I needed more of a day-to-day role with Josh.

"I began a crusade along with my former co-worker to get permission for the two of us to share one full-time job. We really had to argue our case to convince them to try it on an experimental basis. Our boss finally agreed to it 'for a few months.' Well, that was three years (and one more baby) ago, and all is working perfectly. Now many mothers (and others) are following suit.

"I think the skeptics are no longer skeptical. We have not had any problems. I think at first some people doubted our sincerity and assumed we'd call it quits, but they have been won over."

Gene Turner, an administrator at Oklahoma State University, is one of those rare employers who initiated job sharing in his office. He explains his reasons:

"I created three job sharing positions in 1979 because it was nearly impossible for me to recruit good secretarial people. So I went to a non-traditional recruiting technique. I found there was a good pool of potential employees if I could be flexible."

Turner only gave his sharers one stipulation: "I told them that I want absolute coverage, and that I expect them to cover for each other when one is sick. It doesn't matter to me who works what hours. They cover for each other on a credit system, so I never have overtime. Each one gets half pay no matter how many hours they work in a given week."

How well has job sharing worked from his perspective as an employer? "I am getting 120% because each employee is giving me 60%, even though I'm only paying for 50%." Turner reports. "They arrive early, stay late, and call each other at night to be sure that nothing gets left undone."

Turner says he is quite alone in his innovative employment options, but very pleased with the arrangement.

"Other people at the university think I'm eccentric, particularly because universities are such bastions of the status quo. But when I retire or have my first coronary, maybe someone will say, 'Hey, maybe he was on the right track after all.'"

New York Life Insurance Company has a more sweeping job sharing program, which includes 160 positions and has been labeled "a great success." The shared jobs are staffed on a one-week-on, one-week-off basis, and have chiefly appealed to women who are re-entering the labor force.

Although theoretically almost any full-time job can be split, the fields that are currently offering the greatest opportunities for job sharing, according to *A Part-Time Career for a Full-Time You,* are medicine, education, administration, and personnel. By far, the greatest experimentation with this form of employment has taken place in the public sector.

Is Job Sharing for You?

Job sharing, although an ideal alternative for some, is not for everyone. An ability to communicate and a commitment to doing it on a regular, frequent basis, flexibility, a spirit of cooperation, and a willingness to talk over and share important decisions are crucial qualities for job sharers.

For those who need to "own" their work, who find it important to get credit for the job they do, who find it difficult to share either praise or responsibility, job sharing will become a problem instead of a solution.

Because the vast majority of job sharing situations are created as a result of an employee's request rather than the employer's initiative, and because the conversion of a full-time position into a job sharing arrangement is a slow, demanding process, a careful self assessment, such as the one below which has been adapted from the self inventory found in *How To Split or Share Your Job* is an important first step.

1. *Job satisfaction.* A real love of your work in general and your own job in particular are essential ingredients for getting you through the tedious process of turning your full-time job into a shared position. Once you've seen this process through to its conclusion and set a precedent in your organization by creating this arrangement, you'll feel obligated to stay on. So be sure, before you begin, that this job has long-term potential for you. If there are any negatives in the job as it now exists, come to terms with them now by deciding that the pluses far outweigh the minuses or that you would, after all, be better off with a different job entirely.
2. *Legitimacy of the need for reduced hours.* One of management's first criteria in reviewing your request is likely to be whether you have shown a compelling need for a pared down work schedule. Your employer will need to be convinced of the depth of your motivation in order for your request to be taken seriously. Be honest and direct about your feelings of commitment to being with your baby during the first crucial months and years of life, and be equally direct about your desire to continue in your professional capacity and your willingness to do more than your share to make the new arrangement work.
3. *Financial considerations.* Spend an intimate evening with your checkbook, and be certain that you can afford the half-time pay that comes with half-time work. It would be a hollow victory to succeed in having your job split, only to find six months later that your sub-zero bank balance demands that you return to full-time employment.
4. *Value as an employee.* If there is one factor that stands out as a key element in an organization's decision to convert a full-time job into a shared position or a permanent part-time position, it is the desire to use the new arrangement as a means of retaining a valued employee. An honest evaluation of your value to the organization will help give you a good initial assessment of your chances of success. If you have a hard-to-come-by skill or talent, if there is a

high training cost associated with your position, or if you have been with the company for a number of years and have made yourself an indispensable part of the team, the odds of success certainly shift to your side. If, on the other hand, you have only been with the organization for six months and have yet to establish your intrinsic value to the company, be prepared to make up for this deficit with the sales job of your life.

5. *Personal suitability for job sharing.* Now, rather than later, is the time to analyze your personal qualities as they relate to your ability to successfully share a job. Does your professional style tend to be cooperative or competitive? Are you willing to relinquish total control of your position, to share decision-making on a 50-50 basis with your partner? Or is your style so individualized that you would feel a partner was intruding? Would you welcome additional input, a second—and sometimes different—opinion, or would you find it an irritating nuisance?

   In the final analysis, you should find your personality scales tipped heavily in favor of an overall cooperative attitude in order for job sharing to be successful for you.
6. *Finding a partner.* Remember that sharing a job requires two people—and you are only one. You'll need to find a suitable partner, preferably before you make the initial approach to your employer about the possibility of splitting your job. It will be important to demonstrate that your team offers more skills, experience, and talents than one person can offer. Selling the organization on the idea that they'll be getting two qualified employees for the price of one is an important part of your overall strategy, and having the other qualified employee on line to begin with will decidedly strengthen your position.
7. *Acceptance of change.* Job sharing requires an ability to adapt to change, to be flexible when the situation calls for it. You'll need to be able to be open about the exact form the restructuring of your job takes, and to be able to accept new ways of doing things, if your job sharing venture is to succeed.
8. *Being prepared for the alternative.* Your employer may want to know whether you are so committed to only working part-time that you will leave the organization if your request is denied, or whether you intend to remain regardless. It would be wise to think this out beforehand, and be prepared with an answer that, without being threatening, clearly defines your position in this regard.

Choosing a Partner

The most successful pairing of partners almost always occurs between two people who already know and like each other. If there is such an individual already within your organization who has a solid reputation as a dependable, top notch employee, all the better. Ideally, your potential partner will have skills and abilities that complement your own.

If a ready-made partner fails to materialize, there are a number of places to look for your other half. Professional associations, other organizations that include positions similar to your own, local professional women's associations or other networking sources, and unions are all good bets for finding the person you need. A newspaper ad or an advertisement in your trade journal are also possibilities.

Chief among the qualities you will be looking for in a partner is compatibility. Mutual trust, absolute honesty, and a willingness to communicate are also high on the list. A good combination of skills will strengthen your value as a team. A positive sense of team competition may be a plus, too.

■ Job sharing requires an ability to adapt to change, to be flexible when the situation calls for it.

Once you have found someone who seems to be a likely prospect, invest in a number of in-depth discussions, both so that you can talk over the division of responsibilities and to get a feel of how well you would work together as a team. Now is the time to be frank and honest with yourselves and each other. Speak up about any questions or nagging doubts you have. Voice any and all concerns. Create a problem situation and see if you are able to work together to solve it. Discuss every detail of sharing the job, and get it all down on paper. Sleep on it, and talk it over again.

One of the initial ground rules for your discussions should be that if either of you feels for any reason that the partnership wouldn't work out, you should be free to say so without need for further explanation and put an end to the discussions then and there. Gut reactions can be every bit as accurate as logical reasons. If you sense that the two of you aren't going to be compatible, say so and then continue looking until you find someone you are totally comfortable with.

Choosing a partner is like entering a marriage—the contract can be broken, but it is a painful process at best. And remember that if your partner becomes dissatisfied and leaves, your job may be in jeopardy, too, if your employer insists on full-time coverage for the position and you are only willing to work half-time.

Management's attitude will have a decisive effect on the success of your job sharing venture. People, like all living things, need a favorable climate to grow and prosper. It will be worth your while to do whatever you can to win management—and particularly your immediate supervisor—over to your side. A supervisor can be, and often is, vital to the success of the job sharing experiment, no matter how qualified and dedicated the team. Happily, there are more and more reports of enthusiastic supervisors who make life easier, not harder, for the sharers.

"Our supervisor is very flexible," says Barbara Addis, who works as an occupational therapist in a veterans' hospital, "and feels that keeping experienced personnel on staff is important. She is strongly in favor of creative solutions to combining motherhood and working. My co-workers have been cooperative and helpful, too."

Communication

Open and ongoing communication is one of the most essential factors in the success of a shared position. As in any other situation, it requires both time and a committed effort for sharers to develop a comfortable, effective communication system. Honest communication is the only foundation upon which mutual trust and support can be built, so make good communication your number one shared priority. The longer you work together, the easier communication will become, until one day you realize that your communication system is working quite well without you having to give any particular thought to it.

The specific jobs and personalities of the sharers largely determine the exact method of communication that will work best. Some schedule an overlap time for face-to-face conferences. Others use the telephone, a daily log, or assignment calendar. For most job sharers, just talking regularly seems to be sufficient.

Be sure to keep up on communication with co-workers as well. Other staff members are most likely to react negatively to the job sharing arrangement if they feel out of touch with the sharers. The goodwill of your fellow employees is important, so don't let this area slide. If someone needs to go the extra mile to be cooperative and coordinate schedules, it will be the sharers who walk it.

Dealing with Problems

Particularly because job sharing is a relatively new, innovative approach to part-time employment, there are a number of problems that sharers may find themselves having to work through.

One of the chief obstacles to the success of the job sharing arrangement is the lack of legitimacy that is too often accorded to part-time workers. Part-timers still tend to be viewed as less committed and less career oriented than their full-time associates, regardless of the fact that study after study confirms that just the opposite is true. Old stereotypes die hard.

Negative attitudes and an overall hostile environment eventually brought attorney Helen Stewart's shared job to an end. Helen had been splitting her corporate position with another attorney, each of them working different days. "But I found that they expected me to stay late and work at home, plus I always felt they compared the amount of work I produced with my full-time co-workers. Sometimes emergencies would arise and I would have to come in on a 'day off.' Babysitting was hard to arrange with short notice. The main problem was my employers' attitude. I believe they resented my attempt to combine parenting and a career. I got a lot of sarcastic remarks about how I was taking it easy. Splitting a position or having a part-time worker posed real managerial problems for my employer. I left when the corporation decided to discontinue splitting the position."

Helen's solution to this difficult situation was to set up her own private law practice which, she says, has forced her to "develop a lot of new skills. I enjoy my current work, but I don't know yet how much money I will be able to make."

The appropriateness of reviewing the job sharers as individuals or as a team or both is often a gray area. This is one of those points that it is wise to clarify with your employer in advance.

Tenure is another cloudy issue. Will half-time employees receive a half year's or a full year's tenure credit? Will the position itself be limited to the tenure of the original two individuals involved, or will another person be hired if one team member decides to leave? Again, clarifying these issues before the fact can save problems later.

The allocation of fringe benefits should also be clearly specified in the beginning. Quite often the fringes provided to full-time employees are simply split in half with each sharer responsible for paying 50% of the cost of health, life, or other insurance. Vacation and sick days are usually divided in half between the team members. However, particularly if one sharer is married and has insurance coverage through her spouse, the partners may opt for one to take the full insurance coverage while the other gets a greater percentage of the sick and vacation days.

Be sure to clarify in the beginning what fringe benefits you are entitled to, and whether you and your partner have the freedom to divide them up as you wish.

Since the compatibility of the sharers is of paramount importance, it's a good idea to have the remaining employee be permitted to be part of the interviewing process if one of the team members leaves. Write this into your job sharing proposal, putting it in as a plus for the job sharing arrangement: "If one team member leaves for any reason, the other will be available to help screen for a replacement."

Sharers sometimes find that their part-time schedule translates into a loss of status and influence with co-workers. Sharers may find themselves excluded from decision-making, or one partner may be included when the other isn't.

Some full-time employees resent the sharers being given an equal voice since they only work part-time and may not be as familiar with the day-to-day needs and operation of the department. This is another area where ongoing communication with co-workers is essential.

Promotional opportunities are often sadly lacking for job sharers, partially because even professional part-timers continue to be seen as not especially serious about their work, and partially because a promotion into another position generally means having to work full time.

Occupational therapist Barbara Addis feels this in her situation, even though her immediate supervisor has been quite supportive of her job sharing arrangement.

"While on a part-time status, I continue to get routine step increases within my pay grade," Barbara comments, "and I also received an extra increase for quality performance. But I might not be considered for promotions and continuing education opportunities because of my part-time status."

Particularly because they are still so new and experimental, job sharing arrangements are often far from perfect, and don't always work out.

A major East Coast bank had two women job sharing for "six or seven months last year," but the program was cancelled "because neither woman had a commitment either to the bank or to her career," a bank spokesperson reports. "One of the sharers had been with the bank for a year, the other was hired to share the job."

This particular situation was loaded with pitfalls—an immediate supervisor who was perhaps less than enthusiastic, two sharers who did not choose each other, one a brand new employee and the other with the bank for only a year. The going is rough in such a situation. Sharers should be aware of any potential negatives in their particular situation and be especially diligent about doing whatever possible to neutralize them.

Many job sharers and others wanting part-time positions find that their most effective argument is the cost-effectiveness of the arrangement, i.e., two for the price of one, the reduction or elimination of benefits, and no overtime. Though part-timers should not have to make such sacrifices, until the future changes the choice is too often a part-time job without benefits or no part-time job.

Joan Ketterman, who works as a developmental disability specialist for Shelby County in Wisconsin originally converted her full-

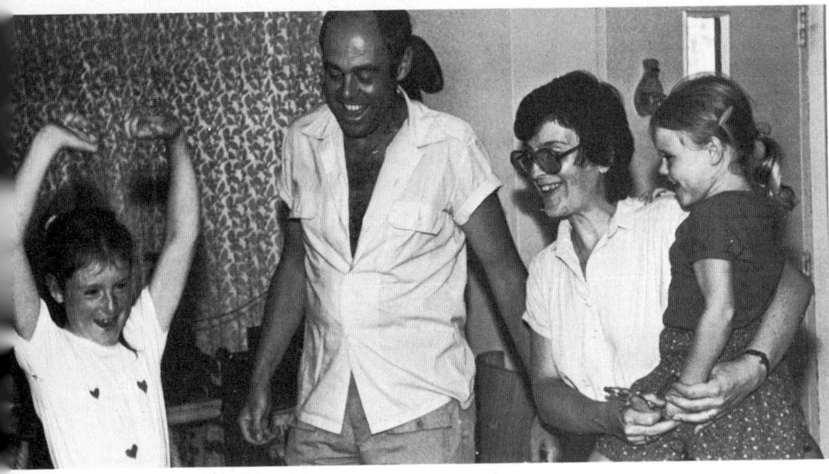

Librarian Darlene McKee is able to spend more time with her family because of job sharing with Lorna Ruder.

time job to a part-time position, and now job shares the thirty-five hour a week position with another woman, found herself in just such a situation.

"After my first child was born my boss was most cooperative in arranging my schedule to accommodate my desire to work part time. My co-workers pitched in to cover in emergencies when I wasn't there.

"But, in order to sell the county on this job sharing position, my co-worker had to sell it as cost effective since we work less than eighteen hours each, so we work without benefits.

Through persistence and determination, library assistant Darlene McKee created the first job sharing position at the Toronto Public Library.

"I had to get management and union to agree to job sharing formally in writing because we were attempting to unionize at the time. No one else is currently job sharing, although many have asked.

"I share a job with another (former nursing) mother, and we have had nearly all positive feedback. The branch head's only complaint is that she has to deal with two people instead of one. The mothers in the branch and management are all very positive."

Presenting a Written Proposal

When you plan to approach an employer with a job sharing proposal, it's a good idea to put everything in writing so both sides understand all aspects of the proposal. The following sample of a job sharing proposal is taken from the *Job Sharing Handbook*.

SAMPLE JOB SHARING PROPOSAL
To: Joyce Hanover, Manager of Flight Service
From: Sue Jones and Mary Devine
Subject: Job Sharing Proposal

This proposal represents a plan for implementing job sharing within the Flight Service Department. As with any new idea, it is important to start off by defining terms. A shared job is a form of permanent part-time employment in which two people jointly fulfill the responsibility for one full-time position or job title. Salary and fringe benefits are prorated according to time worked.

Mary Devine and Sue Jones would like to be considered as job sharing applicants for the position of Supervisor on Duty that is presently being advertised. We believe that this type of work arrangement would be ideal for the job and that, particularly in this case, the company would benefit in a number of ways. Some of the advantages include:

1. *A wider range of skills* than is possible with one full-time candidate. Our combined knowledge and experience spans more than nineteen years in progressively more responsible positions. As our résumés show, our skills range from organizing, coordinating and implementing training programs to supervising sizable staffs.
2. *Higher productivity.* Studies have shown that job sharers generally have more energy to devote to job duties and consequently are more productive. Absenteeism is also generally greatly reduced.
3. *Retention of trained personnel.* A great deal of time and money has already been invested by the company in our training and experience. A job sharing situation will enable us to continue to be a viable part of Acme Airlines during this period of our lives when we are unable to work full time.
4. *Job continuity.* Since we both agree to work full time if one partner becomes ill or leaves the position (at least until a new partner is identified), the job sharing arrangement will guarantee job continuity.

In sharing this position we suggest the following arrangements:

- As a team, Sue Jones and Mary Devine will jointly be accountable and share responsibility for the total job. Therefore, we would expect to be evaluated as a pair. If one partner does not work out or terminates, the other partner will take over the position on a full-time basis until a new partner can be found. The break-in training for a new partner will be conducted by the original remaining job sharer.
- We prefer a schedule that permits us maximum blocks of time on the job. Sue Jones will work all day Monday and Tuesday and Mary Devine will work all day Thursday and Friday. Staffing will be alternated on Wednesdays. We will jointly assume responsibility for changes in that schedule, including covering for one another during vacations and sick leave. Additionally, in time of unexpected company crisis, we agree to provide double coverage at our regular rate of pay. Out-of-town meetings will be handled in the same manner or negotiated against trading time off. Weekly staff meetings will be covered by the person on duty, who will brief the other.

- We propose a proration of insurance benefits, so that there will be a minimum of extra costs for Acme Airlines. For example Acme Airlines pays 50% toward a health policy for each job sharer or the equivalent of one full health policy which would have been provided a full-time employee. Each employee can then pay in an additional 50% in order to provide her own full health coverage.

Our proposal to share the position of Supervisor on Duty reflects the growing need on the part of many employees for alternatives to full-time work at some point in their career. Job sharing is a work arrangement which is being successfully utilized by many employers in a wide variety of classifications.

We have compiled information about shared jobs in other organizations. We have attached some background materials relating to some of the situations and are prepared to discuss the information we have gathered in more detail. Our research has shown job sharing to be an effective work concept. We hope you will allow us to show you how well we can make it work at Acme Airlines.

List of possible attachments:

1. Copy of airline's job sharing contract
2. List of other local companies where job sharing has been tried
3. Newspaper clippings about job sharing
4. Summaries of pilot-project findings
5. Selected reading recommendations on job sharing.

Job sharing proposals can and do get turned down. Judy Wunker submitted a detailed job sharing plan to her employer, who rejected it, but did arrange a three-hour a day part-time position for her. When the family moved from Indiana to North Carolina, "I found a job in my field working four hours a day," Judy says. "As always, getting hired part-time took a lot of sales talk on my part."

Job Sharing Teachers

Elementary school teachers probably form the largest single category of job sharers, according to *Job Sharing*. Teachers' tasks are clearly and easily divisible by both time and area of responsibility, making job sharing fairly simple to implement once the school's board and administration have been sold on the myriad benefits of such an arrangement.

As well as forming the largest single group of job sharers, teachers were the first profession to successfully implement job sharing. *Job Sharing in the Schools* reports:

In 1965, the Women's Educational and Industrial Union established a program in which it consulted with 15 Massachusetts school districts in Framingham and nearby towns and placed 120 carefully paired teams of teachers in their school districts. In 1965, Catalyst, a national research and educational service organization, in its publication "Part-time Teachers and How They Work," evaluated the program and found enthusiastic reactions from principals and parents. Both groups stressed the benefit of two different teachers, each concentrating on his or her own specialty, and the stimulation that occurs when a "new, fresh face comes in at noon to enliven the class." Initial fears about possible lack of communication between the partners, the staff, and the parents proved unfounded. Administrators often commented, "We are getting our money's worth and more from the part-time teachers."

The study reported that major preconceptions about part-time teaching and especially shared positions generally were mistaken. A larger survey (included in the Catalyst report) of 700 nationwide school districts, sponsored by the U.S. Department of Education, showed that superintendents who employed no part-time teachers expressed a wide range of objections to introducing such an innovation. In contrast, the 300 superintendents who did use part-time teachers favored the idea overwhelmingly. Many of the anticipated problems simply did not arise.

Job Sharing in the Schools also reports that the Hawaii state legislature established a three-year pilot job sharing program in 1978 because of the high unemployment rate among its teachers. Act 150 called for the conversion of a maximum of 100 full-time positions to be shared between tenured classroom teachers and unemployed teachers. At the end of the three-year period, seventy-five tenured teachers had agreed to the job sharing arrangement.

When the program was evaluated in 1980, the auditor found:

1. Job sharing is a feasible and desired employment option for teachers.
2. Job sharing increases the number of available teaching positions for unemployed teachers, but its actual impact in reducing the large number of unemployed teachers is minimal. The pilot test nature of the project, with its restrictions on program size, precludes it from having any significant effect on unemployment, but for those newly hired teachers participating in the project, job sharing has provided meaningful employment opportunities.
3. Job sharing has generally created a more stimulating environment for the tenured teachers in their professional capacities. Tenured teachers report an increase in job satisfaction, work productivity, and quality of work.

A study published in 1976 which covered a nine county area in California, as reported in *Job Sharing*, found that:

Job sharing is working well for teachers in Schaumburg Township according to Superintendent William Kritzmire.

Advantages of job sharing to the districts centered on the high quality of shared teaching, a result of great skill diversity within a single position and sharers' increased energy and enthusiasm. Sharing also allowed the retention of experienced older teachers and made possible some new hiring. Furthermore, the pairing of two teachers at different levels of the salary scale was perceived as a potential cost saving.

A Glowing Example

Dr. William Kritzmire, Superintendent of suburban Chicago's Schaumburg Township School District 54, the largest elementary school district in the state of Illinois with 750 teachers and 16,000 students, counts himself among the administrators who are extremely favorable to job sharing.

During the 1982–83 school year, Dr. Kritzmire had the first pair of job sharing teachers in Illinois in his school district and, midway through their first year, Dr. Kritzmire said that the pilot program was "totally successful."

Dr. Kritzmire is enthusiastic about job sharing from a number of different perspectives.

> The kids love it because there is an appeal system—there is another classroom teacher to go to. In the typical classroom setup, if a student gets into trouble early in the day, that day is ruined. But with job sharing teachers, he's got a second chance at noon when the new teacher comes in.
>
> The two teachers involved are really pleased, because one now has more time to spend with her small child, and the other has more time for herself.

> The school district is coming out ahead because each teacher is doing more than a half-time job. And because the teachers are getting to do what they want to do, we're getting more for our money. A happy employee is a productive employee.

There were few problems involved in implementing the program, according to Dr. Kritzmire.

"The teachers approached their principal with the idea, he was supportive and brought their request to me, and I took it to the board. They were delighted with the proposal. All it took was someone to put it together and present it. Job sharing in the schools is an idea whose time has come."

There were three contractual problems that had to be resolved before the job sharing program could be implemented in District 54. Dr. Kritzmire explains:

"We agreed that each year the teachers' shared job would count as a full year's tenure. Illinois law states that half-time people don't have tenure, but we felt that the teachers had to have some job security. Both of these teachers were already tenured, so it didn't present any real problem in this instance. We also agreed that each teacher would continue to gain seniority as if she were teaching full-time, and that both teachers would receive full benefits."

Benefits Abound

As in the case of this Illinois school district, it usually doesn't take long for a district's school board and administrative staff to become sold on the advantages of job sharing. School officials quickly find that they are getting more energetic and enthusiastic employees, the opportunity to take advantage of the diverse talents of two teachers instead of just one, and freedom from the need to hire substitutes since job sharing teachers almost always cover for each other.

Financial savings can result when an experienced teacher near the top of the pay scale is paired with a newer teacher who is earning less. The total of the two half salaries is less than the school district had been paying the more experienced teacher for full-time work.

Because most school districts expect one sharer to take over the class if the other sharer is absent, the district saves money by not having to hire a substitute, and the students benefit from greater teaching continuity.

As well as finding that they are less exhausted from the demands of teaching and therefore have more time and energy to put into their classroom responsibilities, job sharing teachers report that they often discover that the one-to-one relationship with their partner turns out to be a real bonus. Two good teachers will frequently inspire and stimulate each other, which encourages each one to be more creative and innovative in the classroom. Sharing the satisfactions and triumphs of teaching seems to double the rewards.

For the mother with a breastfeeding baby or toddler, the job sharing arrangement allows her to continue in the teaching profession with only minimal disruption to breastfeeding, and shortened hours of separation from the baby.

"Our son was sixteen months old and still nursing when I resumed my teaching duties on a half-time basis," says Arlinda McLaughlin, a Wyoming elementary school teacher. "The best part of the arrangement was that my husband was able to adjust his schedule so that he was with the baby for three of the five mornings I was teaching. This was precious time for him and the baby."

Barbara Lovley, who teaches high school home economics half time, was able to choose her own hours at school.

"Setting my own hours worked well," Barbara reports. "I set my time for when the children would usually be napping—then I have them when they are up! But once I set my schedule it is rigid and I must be there for class. This leaves little flexibility for demand nursing of a young infant. I have a sitter close to work, which shortens the length of time we are separated. And if for any reason my day needs to be longer, I can leave at lunch to nurse the baby."

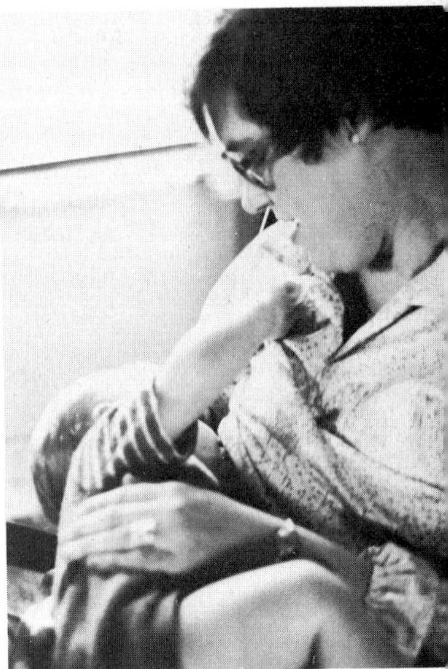

Barbara Lovley arranges her teaching schedule to allow time for plenty of quiet nursing sessions with Sammy.

Working as a Team

Compatibility is the first consideration in successfully matching a pair of teachers. And because compatibility, far more than any objective matching of teaching skills, is vital to the teachers' ability to function well together as a team, teachers need to be given the freedom to select their own partners.

"The administration should not be allowed to pair teachers," observes Superintendent Kritzmire. "Personality and compatibility are crucial in the initial choice, and the teachers should be allowed to make those decisions themselves. If they are not compatible, it could create real problems."

Winning the support of their co-workers is high on the list of priorities for most job sharers.

"My partner and I have made every effort to be active on committees, attend all staff meetings, and in every way cooperate with our co-workers so as not to make them feel we are getting special treatment from the school district," says Arlinda McLaughlin. "We have volunteered our services for many special projects. We felt it was necessary to help our employers and our co-workers develop a good attitude about our work arrangements. And, we obviously wanted to display a willing attitude. Consequently, everyone is very pleased with our arrangement, and the school district has granted part-time arrangements for other teachers now. The parents love it because their kids get a fresh teacher at noon, rested and ready to go with a whole new bag of ideas. I teach the reading and language arts block, and my partner, also a young mother, comes in at noon to complete the day. Since our school doesn't require us to have duty during our lunch hour, my partner and I confer each day at this time."

How to Initiate a Job Sharing Program

With the notable exception of the state of Hawaii, cited earlier in this chapter, and a scattering of states in the West, job sharing is almost always initiated in a school district at the request of a pair of teachers who want to split a teaching position. Much helpful information on doing this can be found in New Ways to Work's publication, *Job Sharing in the Schools.*

Teachers should be aware that school district policies concerning benefits, tenure regulations, and advancement procedures are not systemized and should be clearly defined and agreed upon.

Schaumburg Township School District Superintendent Kritzmire acknowledges that not all school boards will be as receptive to the idea of job sharing as his was. "Teachers may be told, 'It's not in the contract and we can't do anything that's not in the contract,' or that 'We can't try anything new.' " If either the superintendent or the school board stonewalls the idea, Dr. Kritzmire suggests getting a letter from the teachers' union granting permission for a pilot job sharing program in the district, or having the introduction of job sharing proposed by the union, perhaps as part of the contract negotiations.

An Answer for the Future

As school enrollments continue their steady decline across the country, administrators are increasingly beginning to see job sharing as a way of bringing in new teachers and avoiding layoffs. Job sharing is one answer to the problems of shrinking enrollment and the stagnant economy that began in the 1970s and continues to dominate the picture in the 1980s.

Says Superintendent Kritzmire: "Right now job sharing is on an on-demand basis in our district. But if it comes to the point that declining enrollment makes it apparent that we need job sharing to save jobs, it would be in our best interest, as well as the (teachers) union's, to actively promote job sharing. Now that jobs are scarce, why not pair teachers up? This will allow us to bring in new ones and keep the older ones."

Both Susan Novara and Barbara Lovley teach in school districts that are receptive to part-time teaching because it reduces the need for teacher layoffs.

"Because there have been many teachers laid off during the last couple of years, my employer and co-workers are happy with my job sharing arrangement since it saves one teaching position," Susan explains. "Each shared teaching position saves another full-time position."

"The school district offered half-time positions due to decreased enrollments," Barbara says. "Other co-workers with children are envious of this great chance I have, although many could not take the monetary setback. But I can compromise my career and salary to be with my children. They grow so fast. They need me, and I need them, too."

"I would like to see job sharing happen a lot," Dr. Kritzmire admits. "We've been talking about job sharing for years. It's not really particularly new or innovative. We've always hired half-time kindergarten teachers, and we've always said that we've gotten more than half-time service from them. Why are we so slow to make it available at all teaching levels?"

■ Chapter 7

Self-employment
Risks and rewards

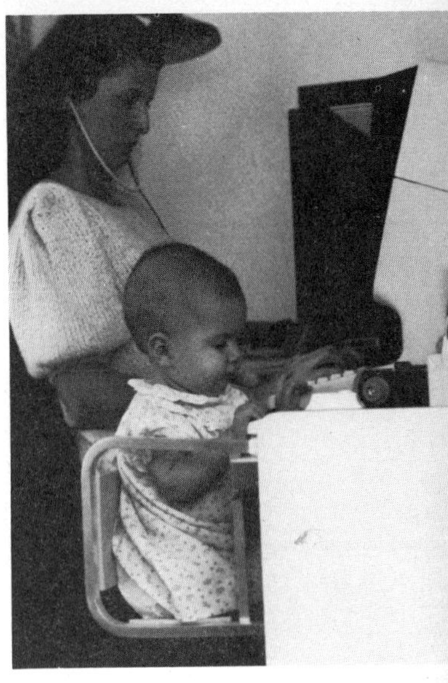

■ Trying to please the boss and meet the needs of a young family can leave a career woman-mother feeling as though she is spending her life running from one end of the ship to the other plugging up each new spot that springs a leak before the ship fills with water and sinks. She spends days racing off to the office trying to get caught up on her work, nights rushing back home where she attempts to make up for the time she lost during the day, and weekends being absolutely frustrated because she never has the satisfaction of feeling that she is doing a really good job either at home or at work.

For a growing number of women, the answer to trying to please herself and please the boss is to *become* the boss. By being in control of both her professional and personal lives, she finds that she is better able to mesh the demands of the two halves of her life into a more satisfying whole.

Practical Considerations

What is to be gained by combining home and work under one roof? Plenty, according to those who have done it.

First, there is the obvious advantage of not having to go any further than your own dining room or spare bedroom to get to work.

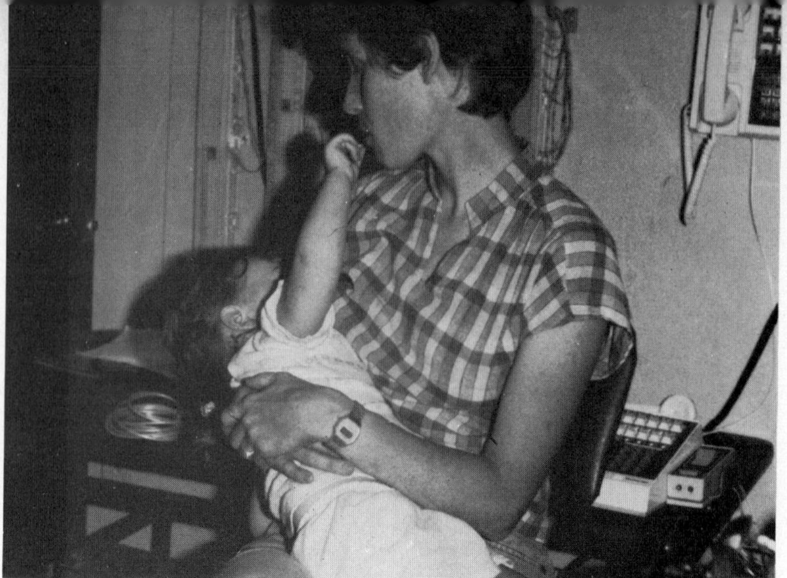

Miriam Hawkins, self-employed, takes a break from her janitorial duties to nurse Rachelle.

You'll save travel expenses and travel time, as well as achieving the more altruistic goals of conserving our natural resources and doing your small part to unclog the highways and reduce air pollution.

There are any number of tax advantages and tax write-offs available in the U.S.A. to those who are self-employed. You'll find at tax time Uncle Sam smiles with a certain degree of kindness on those who own their own business. This means that you'll be able to keep more of what you earn, or that you can earn less and still have more spendable income than is usually possible when you are employed by someone else. By starting your business in your own home, you'll save the expense of additional rent and utilities. Why not make one roof do the work of two?

It's more difficult to put a price tag on having the freedom to create your own business, to do your work to your own very exacting specifications, but many entrepreneurs say that this is an even more important reward than the monetary gains of being self-employed. If you especially enjoy doing something, and find great satisfaction in doing it particularly well, there will be emotional rewards aplenty for you in owning your own business.

For the career woman-mother with a nursing baby to consider, working at home brings the ability to breastfeed and mother the baby uninterrupted by long hours spent in the office away from the baby. If the baby has one of those up-and-down nights, you'll probably have the option of sleeping in the next morning. If he comes down with a cold, you won't have to worry about missing a day's work to stay home and take care of him. If he's teething or going through a particularly demanding phase, or for any other reason finds parting from you difficult, you won't have to face having to listen to him cry when you leave him with the sitter. And there's the added luxury of being able to take the morning's first phone call or get the work started while still in your bathrobe!

Working for Yourself

Self-employment

When striking out on your own in the business world, it is important to keep your start-up expenses as low as possible. Independent business people who dig themselves into a financial hole they can't possibly get out of keep personal bankruptcy courts busy 365 days a year. On the other hand, if the business is successful, you may end up earning more money than you could have by working for someone else.

As Juanita Jacobs says, "My income was reduced, but as the business grows the gap is closing. The business provides an income potential I could never have received as a teacher."

Most people who decide to go it alone generally create a home business out of an already existing professional skill, hobby, or craft, and already have all or most of the equipment they will need.

"Home-based entrepreneurs are springing up everywhere because it's cheap to get started, there is no overhead, no investment in capital equipment, and the women can still be at home with the kids," says sociologist Louis Ferman, co-director of the Institute of Labor and Industrial Relations at the University of Michigan. "It's a testing ground, a way to try your hand at a business and see if you can make a go of it. It's a very strong trend in the country right now."

But in addition to the tools of the trade, there are a number of other expenses that need to be calculated before making the decision to hang out your shingle. In *Working for Yourself,* Geoff Hewitt offers this sobering but realistic advice.

> It is a mistake to start your plans for business independence by tallying imaginary profits. Financial considerations, unless you have unlimited wealth, must include the worst contingencies. A compelling reason for selecting a business that you already enjoy on a "hobby" basis is that presumably, you have much of the necessary equipment and the know-how to reduce expensive purchases and costly fumbling. Such experience will help convince your local banker of your potential in a chosen field and improve your chances of receiving a loan.
>
> Insurance is a costly item, but it is a deductible business expense, and you should carry a realistic insurance policy to cover your business in case of fire, theft, and all potential liabilities.
>
> Be prepared, in making a financial assessment, to calculate all the "hidden costs." These include taxes (federal income, state income, real estate, property, school, road, sales, capital gains, and who knows what else), necessary licenses and permits, alterations of existing structures, tools, maintenance, construction of new structures and how these will affect taxes, electricity, gas, oil, mailing, travel, telephone, and extra help.

What professional expenses will you incur? Will you need a lawyer to check your plans and to help with deeds, taxes, and contracts? A good accountant may be necessary. When in doubt, figure that you will need such professional services, and then phone around to learn who can help you most favorably. Try to select lawyers and accountants and insurance agents from among personal friends, who already have an interest in your well-being. To retain such friendships, be sure your "understandings" are written out on paper.

Whether you're going to be working at home or somewhere else, your new schedule and your new financial realities will require new energies of you and of your family. The more you involve your family in every stage of planning and actual work, the more easily transitions will occur.

It is a mistake to enter any new situation with preconceptions about "how it's going to be," even though we all seem to be habitual victims of this sort of romanticizing. Plan carefully, then stay loose and adaptable!

Small businesses take an average of three years to show a profit, so plan accordingly. Prompt payment from your clients is vital to remaining solvent. Remember to promote yourself. Your name and address should be included on anything you produce. If you are providing a service be sure to always have a card. Satisfied customers—who know how to tell their friends to find you—are one of your best forms of advertisements.

Most home-based business people find it important to have a specific place at home set aside as a work area. It will help keep you organized, and you'll learn to "think business" when you're there.

One final word of caution: Before you launch your own business, whatever it is, be sure that you enjoy doing it because you'll be doing it a lot. "One of the biggest problems is that work never ends," admits Anita Untersee. Or, as Geraldine Usery, quoted in *Working for Yourself,* puts it, "You go self-employed and the hours will be a lot longer. So you better like what you do!"

The statistics all show that those who are self-employed work longer hours than do their counterparts who work for someone else. But when you are your own boss, longer hours or not, you at least have the flexibility to work the hours that suit you, whether those are days, nights, weekends, or, in all probability, some combination of all three. For the woman who is combining a career and motherhood, this flexibility is what makes it possible for her to mother her own baby in her own way in the manner that she feels is best.

■ Carla Bombere, Graphic Artist

With my first baby, I thought that mothering was all I'd ever want to do. Then about nine months after his birth I found myself really missing doing artwork.

My solution was to start doing free-lance work out of my home. This allowed me to fulfill my own needs and still be accessible to my son, and later to my second baby as well.

I am able to take the kids along to see clients, or leave them with Grandma occasionally. When the baby needs holding all day, I am able to stay up at night or get up very early the next morning to do my artwork. I also have a babysitter come to help entertain the kids when I am particularly busy.

Many of the people I work with, such as typesetters and photographers, also work from home so they can be with their kids.

I don't take jobs in the city, and a customer who is convenient and pays promptly is more valued than the one with the big fancy job that I would have to travel far for and who might take three months to pay me.

I probably earn only a third of my potential since I only work fifteen or twenty hours a week. But this is a good foundation for a business I can expand as the kids get older, and it has the potential for making me much more money than a straight salary would pay.

I feel that working has enhanced my self-image. Being an artist is a very important part of my make-up, but being a mother is something I'd never want to let pass me by. ■

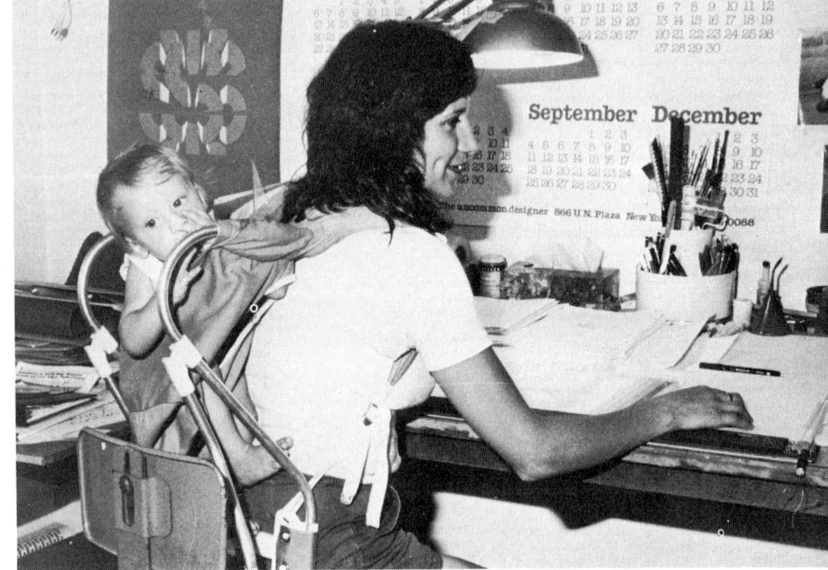

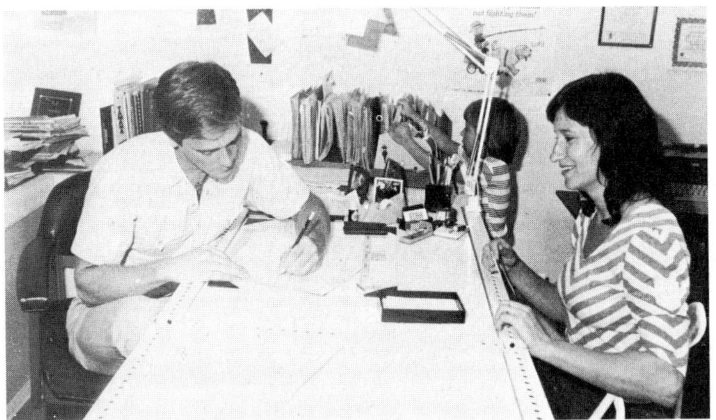

A Musical Mother

Professional musician Diane Dollak has managed to remain very active professionally—self-employed piano teacher, church organist, accompanist, solo performer—while raising five children.

"My work is in many ways flexible," she says. "I can say no to new students or refuse a particular accompanying job. I have generally made it a practice to teach less and not plan a major solo performance while I have a small baby. When my last child was born two years ago I found myself having a hard time managing since he was so much more difficult than the others had been. The spring after he was born, four senior students graduated (one went off to Julliard and another to Curtis) and I simply didn't fill those spots for more than a year. I took on very few outside jobs until I felt that I could handle things. Dealing with the older children seemed to me to be the bigger problem when time, patience, and energy were short; the baby demanded and got what he needed."

Like many of the other women whose nursing babies are very much a part of their working lives, Diane found people to be quite accepting of the total situation.

"I suppose some church people thought it was a little fanatical to be bringing a baby with me to rehearsals for six to eight months, but I never received any direct criticism. Parents of my piano students might have thought it was a little offbeat when my toddler stepped up for a nursing, but they kept coming for lessons. One adult student was moved to breastfeed her third child after bottle feeding the first two. Actually, I don't think I've ever lost a student because of all this madness! I do suppose I would have done much more in the way of improving my own performance skills, but I'm not sorry I made the trade for my family. I really have pretty much managed to have my cake and eat it, too. I am sometimes tired and often feel the stress of trying to do a little too much. But the things you do expand to fill your day no matter how much or how little you do.

"A real problem I've noted is that the baby often seeks my attention while I'm teaching by coming over to nurse. An infant is one thing, but a standing-up toddler with shoes is another! (I did it anyway.) This was more of a problem in the morning when the older children weren't around to play with the baby. When he was twenty months old I made arrangements with a neighborhood mother to watch Jordan for the hours I taught in the mornings. In the afternoon my own children are in charge of their brother on specified days.

"It is a real problem to be present, yet unavailable. It is difficult for the children to understand that when I am teaching I am not available for conversation, but I can give a greeting, a hug, a kiss, a wave, a smile, a nurse. . . .

"I have to be careful not to overextend myself because I get snappy with the children when they interrupt practice time if I'm really under pressure and can't afford the interruptions. It is the older children I feel I need more time with since they're at school all day and I don't get time with them until evening—and then they're busy. Perhaps this happens to everyone with larger families as the children grow older and get involved in more activities."

Creative Solutions

Susan Edwards, a designer, began silk-screening at home when she became pregnant with her first baby. "Having waited so long to have a baby, I was able to spend a lot of time exploring job opportunities. When I found I was pregnant, I left the place I had been working and pursued my hobby of silk-screening full time, setting my own hours. I worked at home and took my baby with me on deliveries, and never had any problems until she was old enough to 'help!' "

Laura Strasberg was already working at home as a quiltmaker when her baby was born. But home-based business or not, Laura found that in her situation quiltmaking would have to be put aside for a while.

"Once my baby was born, it became obvious that she needed me around the clock. Even though I was already working at home, I saw that I wouldn't be able to work the six hours a day that I used to—or even four or one. She was breastfeeding constantly, and was not able to amuse herself in a crib or playpen or even in an infant seat watching me. I couldn't sew at the machine with her in a carrier, so I could only work when she was asleep or with her father. Babysitters didn't work well until she was six months old or so, and then only for an hour a few times a week.

"I finally gave up quiltmaking for a year, until she was two and a half," Laura explains. "My career as a designer and quiltmaker does not depend on constant exposure, so I feel I can give it as much or as little time as I want to. In fact, I feel my work will be improved after a time away from it."

For Laura, career and baby posed a real conflict, and baby clearly came first. "It was very difficult for me to do both. The work was on my mind even when I wasn't doing it. I was constantly frustrated that I couldn't find more time to work. It was difficult to combine the work with the mothering. And I am first a mother—everything else can come later."

Phyllis Carlyle works two evenings a week at a store as a bridal consultant, and designs and sews wedding gowns, hats, and veils at

■ Isabelle Dubois-McCaughey, self-employed potter

I really wanted to have another baby, but already had a successful business going that I didn't want to give up. I found that I could do both. When my baby was really little, I only worked about three mornings a week, and had a playpen for her so she wouldn't be crawling around in the clay dust (pottery studios are notoriously dirty!). When she got older I put away the playpen and turned the whole studio into a playroom, except for the space I needed, and she has grown up around "work in progress" and is really careful.

It has almost all worked well, especially my being there all of the time. It also works well for the older children, since I am home when they get home from school, which they really like. The only bad part is when I *have* to get an order out, and Theresa wants/needs my attention for the whole day.

At times I feel like working when she feels like needing me, and I have to have a talk with myself about priorities. But by working as I do, I get to be with Theresa and she gets to be with me. I can also (almost always) take the time for other things that non-working mothers can do, such as attending morning Bible study, baby showers, and so on.

My pottery is a very creative activity for me that I had been doing before the baby came, and I knew I would not want to give it up for any length of time. It *is* me, in many ways. It is not just a job which I could have given up. I have hired other people to help me, and I frequently hire other mothers of young children to do production type work, and the kids come to work with their mothers. In this way, I can continue to work when I choose as my business grows, and still be with my little girl. Kindergarten will come all too soon. ■

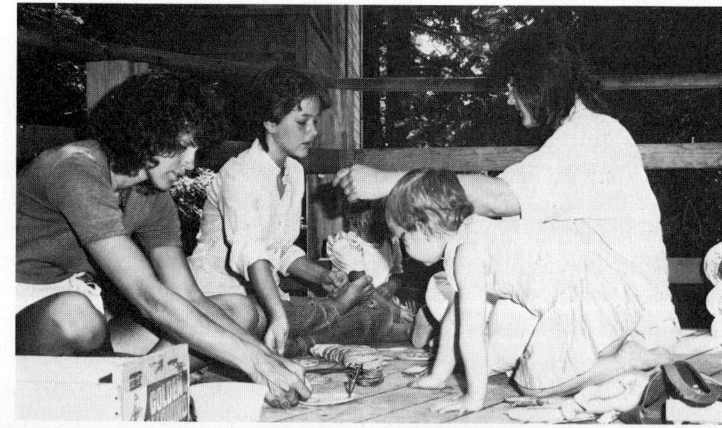

home. "I used to sew in the evenings when my husband Don was home or Kevin was sleeping," Phyllis reports. "However, Kevin is now a busy, active crawler, so when he was eight months old I started taking him to a Mother's Day Out group two mornings a week. This way I can get in a solid seven hours of work, and we have more evenings together as a family."

Tutoring

As a group, teachers probably have the easiest time making the switch to working for themselves out of their home. There always seems to be a pool of students waiting to learn whatever the teacher happens to be teaching, and parents and students alike are usually quite happy to go to the teacher's house or have the teacher come to them.

Shelagh Peterson, Lisa Castrignano, Jane Pollak, and Deborah Chase-Cargill are all teachers who have found self-employment to be the answer to combining motherhood and a career.

Shelagh Peterson of Canada returned to teaching ten days after her first baby was born. "I am sure this resulted in my failure at breastfeeding. I wanted to nurse my second child, and felt I could not work full time and nurse. So I now tutor in the evenings and will supply teach later on."

Shelagh chooses to go to her students' homes "so as not to bother my own children. My husband usually looks after the children (three years and six months) while I am gone. I try to limit my sessions to an hour in length, and have occasionally had trouble explaining to some students that I must leave after one hour so I can go home to nurse Kathryn."

Though pleased overall, Shelagh has found both pluses and minuses to her arrangement. "I feel that Kathryn has grown closer to her father, and that I feel more relaxed when I return to her. Tutoring has kept me in touch with teaching, but it disrupts our family life at night."

Lisa Castrignano, an English teacher who is living in Italy, teaches English to doctors from a nearby hospital.

"As of now, I bring my year-old daughter with me to two of the three people I teach," Lisa says. "The third, a psychiatrist, prefers that I come alone, so I meet my husband after my previous lesson and he takes care of the baby from 5:00 to 7:00 P.M. three days a week."

Lisa finds it quite a challenge to cope with an active toddler while teaching, and has also had to adjust to the uncertainty of the income that tutoring provides.

"My daughter often makes a great deal of noise while I am teaching, or demands my attention, so I've been forced to turn down another doctor whom I had promised to teach. While the baby enjoys interacting with many people, I think she feels confined when I teach in an office. She is used to having the run of our house, which is quite spacious.

"One major disadvantage of tutoring is that I now have no steady source of income. Students often cancel at the last minute without valid reason. But the positive side of this is that if the baby is sick or I can't make a lesson, I can reschedule or cancel it."

Motherhood Adds Depth

Artist Meryl Butler Perry not only kept her baby with her while continuing to teach and paint part-time, but, as she explains it, "I developed new and different directions as a result of being a mother that have given my career a richness and depth that I probably would not have experienced otherwise. Naturally, I haven't painted as many paintings as I might have, but that is a small price to pay. And the paintings I have done are mostly of Christy, and filled with love."

When Christy, who is now five years old, was a newborn, Meryl brought her along when she taught art classes, keeping her in a baby carrier. "I also painted a number of portrait commissions with her in the baby carrier.

"My students, all women, loved having a baby there and would beg to hold her. I nursed her on my right side just before class so that during class, if she wanted to nurse, I could hold her in my left arm to nurse on that side and still have my right hand free for demonstrating.

"Teaching art classes with a baby/toddler/preschooler has forced me to use my brain for creative problem solving and to find a way to fill everyone's needs at once. One of the creative solutions I have come up with is to teach children's art classes so that Christy could be included."

Even with all of the adjustments she has made in order to accommodate her daughter's needs, Meryl says guilt still shadows her. "I feel guilty if I'm not being 'supermom,' but I also feel guilty if I'm not doing something related to my profession. My solution has been to divide my time between mothering and my career and let everything else, like housework and social engagements, fall by the wayside. I pay people to do the things that I don't mind delegating to others, like housework, yard work, errands, and secretarial duties. Actually, I suspect that I get to spend more one-on-one time with my daughter than the average homemaker who doesn't work outside the home. Even if I had to pay my 'helpers' all of my income (which I don't), it would still be worth it to have someone else do the

■ Jane Pollak, art teacher

I began teaching art classes at the Jewish Center across the street from our apartment after my baby was born. I now run an art school in my home for first through third graders.

Students come to me for one hour after school. I have a high school sitter come in on the days that I teach. She either helps with the set-up or the baby, depending on the situation. If the baby cries during class, the sitter brings her to me and I put her in my backpack.

I've found dinnertime to be very hectic since my classes are from 4:00 to 5:00 P.M., and so I have recently decided to cut back my teaching from three afternoons a week to two.

When my first child was born, my salary was eliminated and I received only occasional amounts of money—all small. However, eight years ago it was easier to live on less, and we had been banking my salary anyway so it wasn't sorely needed. Now, with inflation and three children, things are a bit tougher, but I am contributing a bit more and I look forward to struggling a bit less.

At this point I realize it would be difficult to re-enter the job market. But what I have come to realize is that I am capable of creating my own job and my own future. I am so aware of how precious babyhood is. Luckily I realized early on that mothering a baby doesn't last forever—in fact, it seems to be over before you know it. Understanding this and knowing that I would be capable of creating my own job situation allowed me the freedom to enjoy what I have in its appropriate time without guilt or fear of losing a career. ■

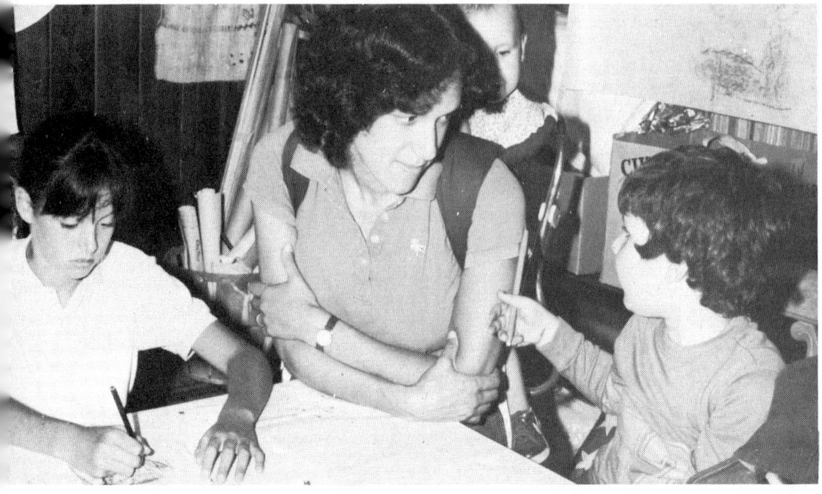

things I'd rather not do so that I can spend my time doing the two things that are most important to me—being a mother and an artist."

Deborah Chase-Cargill, a ballet teacher, transformed her basement into a dance school so she could continue teaching without having to be separated from her son.

"Our home has always been the center of our life," Deborah explains. "Our son was born in our family bed with the help and love of two midwives and my husband. Needless to say, it was the high point of our lives. We felt it was very important never to be separated from our newborn son. Therefore, it was a natural decision that I continue my work as a ballet teacher in our home. We equipped the basement with barres, mirrors, and the other necessities.

"I have my career which I have trained for since I was a child and also hold a college degree in. And most important, my son is always nearby. Since my business is my own, I schedule students according to Jamie's needs. When he was an infant, I taught for two and a half hours, had a half-hour 'nursing break,' and finished my day with another two and a half hours of classes. Now that he is a toddler and nursing less frequently, I teach for five hours, four days a week. Either my mother or sister-in-law cares for Jamie while I am with students.

"Another facet of my work is the choreography I do for the local high school and civic theaters. It has never been a problem to take Jamie to rehearsals. I have used my backpack frequently and there are always free hands belonging to people who are not involved in the scene that is being rehearsed. Jamie is very much at home on the stage already.

"For our family this has been an excellent alternative to the full-time mother/career woman dilemma. I have not had to sacrifice my principles on mothering or nursing. And neither have I had to give up my work which satisfies my soul and creative energies and is a necessity to our financial solvency."

Going It Alone

For a single parent who is left to struggle alone with both the financial and emotional burdens of raising a baby, the options are fewer and the problems greater. No solution ever feels like a good one in this situation, since earning enough money to get by means taking time away from the baby, and taking time away from the baby feels like a double deprivation since there is only one parent to help meet his needs instead of two.

Sharon Turner who has raised her daughter, now four and half

Sharon Turner gets lots of help from her daughter Amrit in her home sprout business.

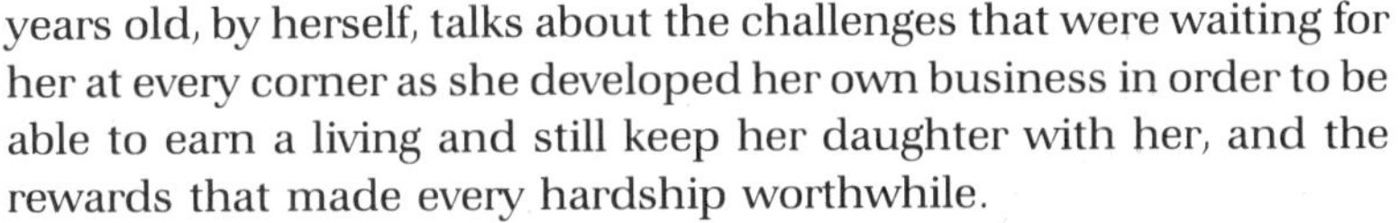

years old, by herself, talks about the challenges that were waiting for her at every corner as she developed her own business in order to be able to earn a living and still keep her daughter with her, and the rewards that made every hardship worthwhile.

"I had quit my job as a social worker when I was seven months pregnant, before I separated from my husband. I was on welfare until the baby was four months old. At that point I decided I could not live on welfare funds alone, and decided I had to work to support the two of us.

"First I did housework and took the baby with me, but that was really hard. Then I slowly developed a sprout business. I started growing alfalfa sprouts in my home and selling them to restaurants, health food stores, and grocery stores. When my daughter was a baby, I worked either with her on my back, or while she was sleeping. As she grew, I was able to work while she played in an area close to me in the basement.

"I can work my own hours and days and set my own schedule. It feels as though I work eighty hours a week, but that's because working, child care, meals, and laundry are all interspersed.

"I take my daughter with me if she is not in school, or I trade child care with another mother, which is probably the best trick I've learned. The people I sell sprouts to have been very accepting of a baby or child coming along on deliveries, although I try to avoid bringing her on sales calls.

"My biggest problems were feelings of loneliness and total exhaustion. My baby wanted to be carried all the time and nursed every two hours, so I had to do a lot of my work at night. There was very little income to live on until the business grew.

"But the baby made it all worthwhile. I adore her and have no regrets for the hardships. Being with her when she was small was the most important thing in the world to me."

A Change of Plans

Like many other career women-mothers, Alice Baumeister thought she would return to work after her baby was born. But as soon as she held her newborn daughter in her arms, she knew that a change of plans was in the making.

"After Jenny was born, it became increasingly apparent to us that returning to my previous job, even on a part-time basis, was not an ideal situation. I wouldn't make enough money after expenses to make it worthwhile, and we didn't like the idea of having someone else raise our child. I just couldn't bring myself to be away from her for eight or nine hours a day."

Alice is now self-employed as an international wholesale supplier and says the change "hasn't hurt a bit. I'm my own boss, so if Jenny doesn't feel well or needs some extra attention, I just take the day off. I am able to run my own business—which is steadily growing—and take care of my family the way I want to. I feel that I have the perfect situation and the perfect business. I'll be able to take as much time off for my next babies as I want/need to, without jeopardizing our income from the business."

Office Skills

Typists also find it fairly easy to move their skills from the office to the home front. Not only do secretary-typists find they can almost always earn as much or more by working from home, but many enjoy the feeling of being the person in charge rather than the subordinate to others as they often are in an office setting. The freedom to set their own hours and accept or reject work as they choose are privileges few office-bound workers ever get.

While some home secretary-typists limit their work to typing, others branch out into bookkeeping, editing, copywriting, and graphics. Nearly all typists require that work be picked up and delivered by the customer, a special advantage for the woman who has a baby and doesn't want to be bothered having to constantly gather up his things to rush out to deliver a job.

Typists use a number of effective methods to advertise their services—newspapers, mailings to small businesses, the local chamber of commerce. Several typists who live near a university report having great success with college students who always need a term paper or thesis typed. Resumé preparation and mailing labels and envelopes are other possibilities.

Nancy Larson, who has five children and has worked as a home typist for five years, got started because, "I knew someone who knew someone who wanted four hours of typing a week done from home.

After that I decided I could type for other people, too. I called other typists for their overload, got a book manuscript to do, and began putting my business card up at all of the universities. It's the universities that give me most of my business. It doesn't seem to matter how far they have to drive to get to me. Once they find a good typist they really cling. I give my customers personalized attention that they can't get from a downtown secretarial service. And none of them seem to mind my five kids running around—it's all part of the package."

Nancy suggests calling around to find out what the going rate in a particular area is, and to charge a little less than a secretarial service. She says the average 1983 secretarial rate is $10.00 an hour, $12.00 for an IBM selectric. Work on a word processor runs $20.00 to $25.00 an hour.

Nancy says she averages three to four hours of work a day, "but some weeks I don't work at all, and other weeks we eat at fast food restaurants every night and my kids wonder if they will ever see clean clothes again."

▪ As soon as she held her newborn daughter in her arms, she knew that a change of plans was in the making.

Nancy publishes a newsletter, *Words at a Stroke,* for free-lance typists, secretarial, and word processing services. Subscription is available by writing to *Words at a Stroke,* P.O. Box 647, Clayton, CA 94517.

Toby Speed was a secretary who quit her office job before her baby was born. When the baby was eight months old and the family was in need of additional income, Toby opened up a home typing business.

"Seventy-five percent of my work consists of typing depositions and hearings for a court reporter," Toby says. "The other twenty-five percent includes correspondence and operative reports for a doctor. My work is delivered to me and picked up. I take on only as much as I can comfortably handle, working about twenty hours a week now that the baby is two years old. I type mornings, afternoons, evenings, and weekends, in between caring for Vanessa, cooking, keeping house, walking in the sunshine, seeing friends, and so on. I charge by the hour for one client, by the page for another, whichever they prefer.

"This business took a lot of determination on my part to start," Toby admits. "I had very little money and no contacts. Through heavy direct mail advertising, an article about me in a local paper (that I wrote), and signs all around town, I was able to get customers. The money barely trickled in for months and it was very discouraging. But at last my work paid off and I was able to make up for my losses, buy my own office equipment, and begin to earn a fair profit.

"It has all worked out terrifically for the baby. Sometimes I take too much work and become very anxious, and I start to ignore some of my daughter's needs for my time. But she sets me straight right away—she simply won't let me type! Then I realize that it's time to cut back, or at least stop for the moment and go for a walk.

"I feel that a home business is the best answer to combining working and mothering. It is dangerous to get caught in the money trap idea and think you need a certain amount to live well. It is amazing how much income you can give up and still be happy—or happier than you were before. The children appreciate a mother's presence more than we know."

Other Skills

Women with a variety of professional skills have also gone into business for themselves.

Michele Moldenhauer, a medical technician, switched from working part-time to working free lance out of her home.

"With my part-time job, I think they were pretty considerate and understanding," Michele recalls. "One time my husband brought the baby to me to nurse because I was uncomfortable. On at least two occasions when I had to stay late, I brought the baby to the lab, nursed, then completed my work.

"But staying late was often a problem," Michele admits. "It was difficult to make the transition back to being home, coping with the children's needs, and trying to fix dinner. Finding a dependable babysitter to come to my home also created a lot of stress from time to time.

"It is much easier to free lance at home with a babysitter coming in. This way I am free to join the baby whenever he needs me, instead of having a sitter give him a bottle while I'm away at work. I feel I'm able to do the best for my children while keeping in touch with my field of interest, and helping to supplement the family income."

Priscilla Hanz has found a variety of jobs that keep her and her youngest child, Laurel, together—cake-decorating, restaurant inspections, teaching and demonstrating microwave cooking, starting a catering business, and opening a restaurant.

"Laurel always went along on restaurant inspections, unless the weather was bad or it was late at night," Priscilla recalls. "She made a great cover—most of the employees watched her instead of me, which made it easier for me to observe and take notes.

"I could occasionally take her when I conducted a microwave cooking class. I had one store that really liked it when she came along because she knew how to use the microwave, too. It was a great sales pitch!"

Priscilla feels lucky to have found such an interesting variety of things to do during the years she had a small child in tow, but realizes that, "Laurel was and is easygoing, healthy, and well-behaved. If she had had a different type of personality, it might not have worked as well."

Laurie Carroll has found janitorial work to be, overall, a good way to mix motherhood and a career.

"Nine years ago, when my first baby was about a year and a half old, my husband was asked if we would take over maintenance at a local bank. We agreed, since we could do it in the evenings and take our daughter with us. Our reputation grew, and without any advertising, we had more work than my husband could do in the evenings while working days as a carpenter. So it became my business and as our family grew—we now have three children—the children came along. In order to accommodate the children, I always bid jobs on a per week basis rather than hourly so that I can take long nursing breaks, eat supper, read stories—in general be a mother—while still being fair to my employers.

"I have always helped the children understand, according to their limitations, that this is work, and we must follow the management's rules. Before I bid a job, I check to see that there is an area where the children can play safely and happily. I will not clean doctors' offices because of contamination, or places with machines or chemicals that could be harmful to the children. My children are well behaved, follow directions, and get along well with each other so I know I can trust them in an office environment. Whether this is just their nature or partly because of the structure of their lives, I'm not sure—but they're great.

■ "I feel that a home business is the best answer to combining working and mothering."

"Sometimes after backpacking a twenty-pound baby while cleaning a bank and rushing off to get the seven-year-old to bed before 9:00 P.M., I get very crabby and tend to become irritated over small things. Sometimes I wonder if they might not be better off with a babysitter, and me with a 'regular' job that I could punch in and out of. But we have no loving grannies in our family, Daddy wasn't ready to take on children after putting in a ten hour day, and Mary Poppins was busy, so child care fell to me.

"For us, the money does not buy luxuries, it is essential. Sometimes I resent the situation very much, but at least I feel I have given the older children a very good, realistic role model. We need to work to keep our family together.

"Custodial work was not my first choice of 'careers.' It is not very stimulating, nor does it impart status. But it is flexible, and my schedule can be arranged around the needs of my children—nursing, naps, Brownie meetings, Christmas programs. Despite the backaches and frayed nerves, it has been worth it in the long run."

A Family Affair

A few women merge marriage and a career by owning and operating a business with their husbands. This "business marriage" usually has the delightful advantage of eliminating all objections from the "boss" about bringing the baby to work.

A couple quoted in *Working for Yourself* offer would-be husband and wife teams a piece of sage advice: "The fights are worse, but the help is cheaper!"

Kriste Kendall and her husband especially enjoy owning a bookstore because it enables them to work together as a family in the shop, and provides "the flexibility that makes it possible for us to bring our baby to work with us. We can go to the doctor when necessary, hire extra help when we need it, hire a sitter if we need to. But we've mostly had Caitlin here in the shop with us all of the time since she was two-and-a-half days old," Kriste reports.

"Believe me, breastfeeding is extremely helpful in such a situation. We keep a small refrigerator at the shop, as well as diapers, clothes, crib, playpen, backpack, front carrier, and a stroller. The customers enjoyed sharing our pregnancy, and are now enjoying the ever-changing stages of Caitlin's growth as an infant and toddler. I even began a mothers' group through contacts made behind the counter."

Kriste says she takes Caitlin home every afternoon to meet her older son when he comes home from school, and get dinner preparations underway. "Those are the advantages of being your own boss!"

Beverly Mitchell works at home as an architect, while her husband takes over most of the on-site duties of their architectural firm. "I rearranged job priorities with my husband to allow me to spend more time at home doing behind-the-scenes type work," Beverly explains. "I wanted to be able to breastfeed the children (now three and a half and one and a half) and be available to them, so I work part-time as needed at home. I work approximately twenty hours a week in an office in a separate part of the house. I draft and design, do bookkeeping and general office work. Occasionally I go to a job site, particularly when we are planning a new project where design input is needed or the desirability of the project is in question."

Beverly finds that the advantage of her arrangement is that, "I am able to be with the children a great deal. If they are sick or fretful, my work can always be put off until a better time, and in a pinch my husband can pick up the slack. Bob is also home a lot, so the children see both of their parents all day long, doing other than sex-stereotype jobs with enthusiasm."

The Mitchells have a woman who lives in to ease the workload around the house. "She devotes a great deal of her time to housework and often watches one child while I do something special, such as a library group or a nursery school co-op, with the other child. The children are secure, and she likes them very much and is kind and gentle. She takes many household chores away from me so that I can be with the children more."

Beverly says that she is tired a lot, a common complaint among working mothers who are carrying the double load of child care and career. "I work many evenings in order to be able to spend as many day hours with my children as possible, so I don't get as much rest as I probably need. But I am able to spend a lot of time with them and still feel that I am contributing to the family business, and can be close to my husband and his work. Our family, all four of us, are able to be together a great deal."

Karen Duchac worked for a Certified Public Accountant before her baby was born, and then quit to work for her husband, also a CPA, out of their home. She finds that her working arrangement almost always works well. "I get to spend more time with my children than I would otherwise. I only use outside help one day a week now, and it's working out nicely. There are times, however, when I must leave unexpectedly to see a client and may have trouble getting someone in to care for my children.

"I'm very glad I have taken this time to spend with my children," Karen says, "and intend to stay home and work until they don't really need me here."

■ "I rearranged job priorities to spend more time at home. . . . I wanted to be able to breastfeed."

Sharon Redman, who makes church organs with her husband, originally began keeping her baby with her while she worked because there wasn't any other choice.

"We were starting a business of building pipe organs when I became pregnant," Sharon explains. "There was no money for a babysitter and there were no nearby relatives to babysit free. We just sort of 'slid' into the arrangement. Discovering that the baby needed me happened after the obvious practical arrangements had been made.

"We spent the first year using our garage as a workshop. Then after moving our workplace into an industrial building, we still kept an office in a bedroom in our home so that I can type and pay bills anytime it is convenient. We use a call-forwarding system for the workshop phone so that I can answer our business number at home."

Sharon did find some inevitable conflicts in her dual role, but feels that overall it has been a good way to combine motherhood and a career.

"The babies, all four of them, got my total attention when they needed it. I did not have any problem with breastfeeding. Breastfeeding was the excuse for such bizarre (to others) working arrangements. I have also worked at the shop with whichever was the current baby there in a playpen, and taken them out of town with us when we're installing an organ in a church.

"I am sometimes irritable with the conflicts of all of the things that need to be done. But if I weren't having a problem juggling home and business, I'd be out making more problems by joining clubs, volunteering, and so on. I think that any problems I've had are more due to my personality than to working. The most helpful phrase is the one that comes from La Leche League: family first. This has resolved most problems for me.

"Even though at first we kept the babies with us because it was the practical thing to do, we later both realized the importance of one primary caretaker for a young baby. Naturally, we feel that our 'method' is the reason we have such intelligent, independent, loving children!"

Sharon offers these hints to husbands and wives who are considering going into business together.

- Be sure that both of you want this arrangement.
- Both of you need to be self-starters. One spouse shouldn't have to be in the position of having to beg (or nag) the other to get work done.
- While work time needs to be flexible to accommodate the baby's needs, the mother has to realize that she has to get the work done sometime.
- Remember to consider the feelings of other employees and customers when it comes to the baby nursing or crying.
- Don't have arguments in front of the employees, especially about the baby.
- If you're working at home, try to take full advantage of the baby's nap schedule.

Anita Untersee thought she would take her baby to her husband's photography studio to work, but changed her mind after Anna was born.

"Whenever I heard 'babies are a full-time job' I couldn't believe it," Anita admits, "so I had always planned to take her with me to the studio while I worked. My dream scenario was that she would peacefully nap while I wheeled and dealed on the phone.

"In reality, I found that she needs very little sleep, and by the time I got all of her gear together and drove for half an hour to get to work, I got nothing done anyway. It made more sense to work at home and have our secretary come to me.

"I handle bookkeeping, estimates, and client contacts over the phone from home. Usually I can get in an hour or so in the morning

■ Miriam and Phil Hawkins, Janitorial Team

We tried leaving our first baby with Grandma while we worked, but that proved unsatisfactory for everyone. So we took him with us. When he was small, he slept in a car seat near us, watched from a walker or a stroller, or was held by one of us while we worked. Later we took puzzles and toys and he played in the hallway near where we were. As he got older he liked to play with building blocks on the floor near us. I made playmats for him to put his blocks and other toys on. The playmats are a real life-saver. Now at seven and a half, he is able to read or do homework. He also has some jobs of his own which we pay him to do—he shelves paper towels or toilet paper, picks up paper clips and staples that the vacuum won't get, and occasionally does other small jobs.

We've never left our second child, but I work less than I did with the first. When I go to work I put her in the baby carrier or the stroller, or let her sleep nearby in her car seat. Now that she is walking, we explore the building together and she gets into very little trouble. Most buildings have safe places where very little damage could be done. I usually try to work there if I work, and let her be free to roam about.

There are drawbacks to such a system of all of us working together. We have to work more slowly; we take more breaks; we stop and play a lot. Some nights we are all tired and crabby, but on those nights we make a promise of a reward as soon as we are finished working. Sometimes we have to clean up our own messes.

But we feel that our children will grow up with a better concept of our work, and we like having breaks and meals together instead of alone. My husband feels that his family comes before a career. Eventually we want to get into another kind of work, or find a way to live with less work and less money. But we like working as a family, and any change we make will have to accommodate everyone. ■

while Anna naps, another hour or so in snatches while she wriggles and plays on the floor, and another hour if I'm lucky while she sleeps in the afternoon. The phone rings almost constantly, so I use call-forwarding to the office when I need some peace and quiet.

"People have a hard time taking you seriously when there is a baby laughing or crying in the background," Anita points out, "and I'm often distracted and can't give Anna the attention I'd like to. But my job and contact with the outside world make me feel that I am still an interesting and vital person.

"One of the biggest problems," Anita says, voicing the reality that faces nearly all home-based business people, "is that the work never ends. It's always there."

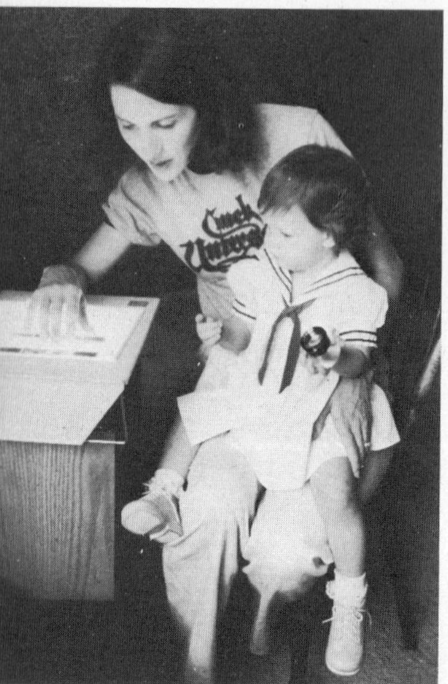

Anita Untersee checks photo proof sheets with daughter Anna on her lap.

Avoiding Problems

Opting for self-employment eliminates many problems, but it creates some others, as Susie Crayton, who along with her husband owns and operates "Crayton de Signs," points out.

"Because my husband and I are self-employed, we encounter different problems than two people who work outside the home. There are interruptions from friends and neighbors (because we are home and/or available). We had to set definite schedules for ourselves and our work. We had to learn to relax on days that were not the traditional weekend. It was kind of hard to do, especially since both of us were raised with the five-day workweek and two day weekend.

"One of the difficulties of self-employment that we had to deal with involved making a concerted effort to talk about other things besides business. Sometimes it was easier to see more clearly the 'working partner' than the lover, wife, and mother or the lover, husband, and father. When the kids were really young, we would go on hikes and walks, for rides in cars, and go out to eat when we could. We play all kinds of games, both inside and out.

"As we see the children maturing so fast, we find it easier to let them take on more responsibilities and find ourselves being surprised by their insight, especially when it pertains to our emotional disposition. Quite often they encourage us to plan a day 'away' at the ocean or the mountains so we can all look forward to a day later in the week when we will all be able to relax.

"Setting work schedules at home with a small baby, under crawling age, is fairly easy. Time for work may be snatched between feedings and at naps. After the baby starts crawling, it is more difficult. We have found that rearranging the household so that dangers to the baby are decreased helps immensely. Interesting manipulative toys, many homemade, help provide entertainment.

"Because we use tools and wood in our production, the kids always love to get a piece of scrap wood and a crayon or piece of chalk. When they reach about two years, we let them work with large nails and hammers from a toy tool box.

"When warm weather comes, we move the work outside. Playing is always within our eyesight.

"Because we are self-employed it has been easier to adjust to times when baby has a rough day—or one of the kids is sick. I am able to earn money at something I am good at, but there are always days when the baby-child needs mom. And mom is there."

Cashing in on Crafts

In this age of plasticized, homogenized everything, crafts-people are finding a new, appreciative market—and cashing in on it. Nearly everyone, it seems, is yearning to own something unique and individual, something that was made by a person who cared instead of churned out automatically by a mass of metal.

Ironically, the rise in working women has undoubtedly provided a sizable boost to the burgeoning crafts market. Without the time to make handmade items themselves, working women are purchasing other people's crafts, both for their own families and for gift-giving occasions.

Creative women everywhere are finding that for them the solution to the career vs. motherhood dilemma is to turn a hobby, craft, or creative skill into a moneymaker. In line with the first priority in setting up a home business, this usually calls for very little in terms of cash outlay. Sometimes the home business contributes significantly to the family income. In other cases, it is far more important as a creative outlet than a moneymaker. Either way, the woman involved is happier, and more fulfilled as a person because of the work she is doing.

A Business of Your Own

If you have a craft or artistic skill, you may want to look into the feasibility of turning your hobby into an income producing business. The minimal capital outlay, plus the freedom to work from home and be your own boss, and the ability to earn money by doing something that you thoroughly enjoy, make this an attractive option for many women.

To succeed at handcrafts, you'll need to market yourself as well as your products. Be sure that every item you make has your name and address on it, or one of your business cards attached to it. If your business is going to grow, satisfied customers have to know

■ Patricia Holliday, Psychologist

When Tiffany was born, I worked at a private outpatient clinic, seeing clients in psychotherapy. Since I had worked there for three years, and had rarely been sick, I had accumulated thirty days of paid sick leave. So I took fifteen days and stayed home three weeks, and then stretched some of my remaining time by working half-time for five or six more weeks. I would hand-express and leave milk frozen for Tiffany for the four hours I would be gone. When I went back to work full time I still had a few hours of sick leave left, and I would take two hours of sick leave a day, giving me a three-hour lunch break so that I could go home, nurse Tiffany, take a nap, eat lunch, nurse her again, and go back to work for another three hours. Actually, I rarely got my nap, preferring to play with Tiffany. The Chief of Psychology at the clinic asked me at the time how long I would need to do this; I told him I honestly didn't know (being a first-time mother, I really didn't!). When I saw I was going to run out of sick leave, my husband and I sat down and talked about alternatives. I really had begun to feel that it was wrong to be away from Tiffany if I was just sitting around the office, with no clients, as occasionally happened. So we decided that it was time to take the plunge and open up my own office.

I've been in private practice for nine months now. It has worked out very well. I feel breastfeeding helped me to cope with the anxiety of resigning a salaried job and getting used to the uncertainties and fluctuations of a private practice. Tiffany and I still have our lunches together, and I now work only four six-hour days a week. In fact, my husband is now looking into opening his own structural engineering business in the hopes that some day he will be able to quit his forty to fifty hour a week job to be home more with Tiffany and the other children we hope to have.

Part of what has worked out so well was finding a babysitter to come to our home. We felt it was very important to find someone who would continue to work for us for all the years we needed her, because we wanted Tiffany to form a close relationship with her.

I find that my own opinions on child rearing have changed so dras-

tically. Attending La Leche League meetings has opened my eyes to a much easier, more enjoyable way of having babies and raising children. I never imagined in my wildest dreams that raising a baby could be such a pure form of intense pleasure so much of the time.

The unlimited nursing, the backpacks, holding her a lot, spending almost all of our free time together, taking her with us almost anywhere we go, all of these ways seem to have made her such a happy, calm, contented baby. I am sure I am much more reluctant to leave her when I am not working, because I have already been away. I find that I am not willing to put her in church nurseries or to leave her with a babysitter she doesn't know and love, but our church and friends have been accepting of having her come along.

I really appreciate LLL because through its efforts and information, Tiffany and my husband and I have experienced the most wonderful, most enjoyable months, better than we had ever dreamed possible. ■

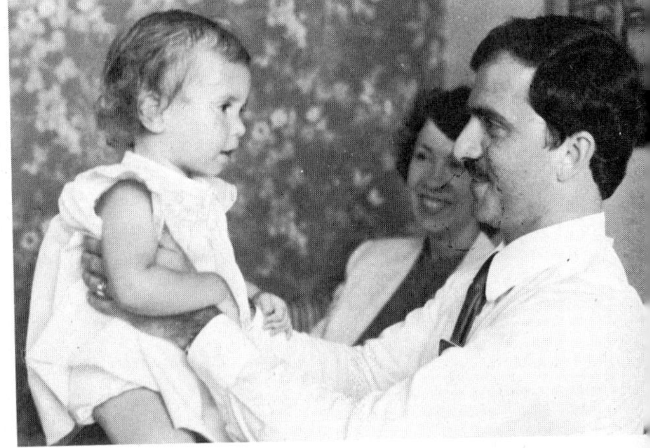

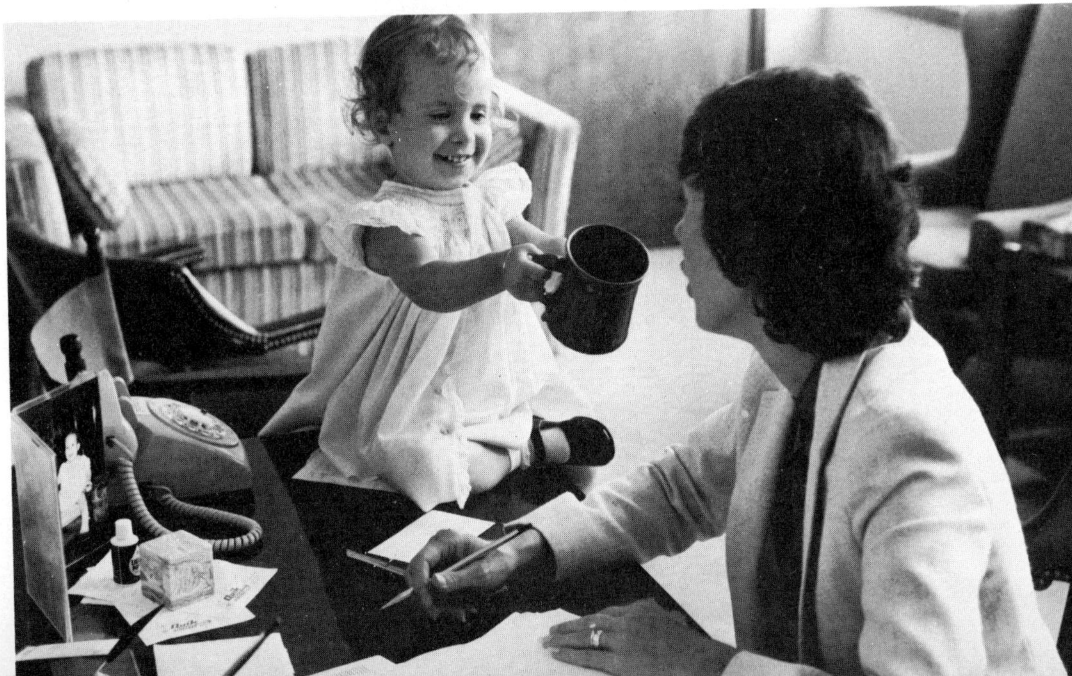

how to contact you to place a repeat order or refer friends and neighbors to you when they want to purchase your product.

You can sell your merchandise either wholesale, retail, or on consignment, or a combination of all three. When selling wholesale, you'll need to price your product according to the cost of the materials and whatever you figure your time to be worth. The person who is retailing the merchandise adds on enough to cover the cost of distribution plus a profit for himself.

Often, retailers will double the wholesale price, so in order to make wholesale selling a viable option, it is usually necessary to sell to the retailer in a large enough quantity that you can afford to take a lesser profit per item. Otherwise, by the time the retailer adds on his mark up, your merchandise has been priced right out of the market. Being relieved of distribution problems and having a steady bulk purchaser should compensate for the lower profit per item.

Retailing your own merchandise gives you a larger profit margin since both the wholesale and retail profit stay with you, but it also brings the added work and expense of selling as well as producing your own work. Flea markets, craft fairs, and a broad base of satisfied customers who bring repeat business and a steady stream of referrals are the best retail markets.

Selling on consignment is also an option worth considering. With consignment selling, a retailer agrees to display your merchandise and handle sales in exchange for a percentage of the profits, but he does not pay you until your merchandise is actually sold, and has the right to return all unsold merchandise to you. This system relieves you of the responsibility for distribution, but it may also mean that your goods are tied up for long periods before you see any money for them. You are entirely dependent on the consignment retailer to promote and properly display your work, and any items that are broken or soiled while in the store will be returned to you as a total loss. Check carefully before agreeing to sell on consignment. Ask to see how and where your merchandise will be displayed, and consider how carefully you feel it will be handled to protect it from damage.

A Word of Caution

But before you count on feeding and clothing your family with the proceeds from your handiwork, there are some sobering points to consider.

The first order of business is to do some careful calculations, figuring the cost of your materials, your time to produce each item, any other production expenses, your anticipated sales price, and how many items per week or month you can reasonably expect to sell. Remember to include gasoline expenses to attend flea markets and craft fairs, or to go from place to place looking for people to sell your merchandise on consignment or on a retail basis. The resulting figure will represent your net profit.

Most of us tend to be starry-eyed optimists, particularly when it comes to something we have made and love, so take your projected net profit figure and cut it in half. Would this amount of money, or less, be enough to make your efforts worthwhile, and would it produce at least the minimum amount of income you feel you should realize?

Remember that a craft is never likely to produce a really substantial income, and it will probably take two or three years to learn where your best potential markets are and to get yourself known in the community. Turning a hobby into a profit-making venture is a feasible alternative only in cases where you can afford to get by on little or no profit for several months to a couple of years.

Be aware, too, that once you turn your hobby into a business, it may no longer be the source of relaxation and pleasure for you that it was when you did it purely for personal satisfaction.

You will want to be sure that the combined effort of producing and marketing your craft item does not become so great a physical and psychological burden that it defeats your original purpose by leaving you too tense and preoccupied to enjoy your time with your baby.

The Real Challenge

Whatever kind of work you do, whatever number of hours you work, striking a comfortable balance between work and family life is the most important job of all. Without that balance, which will require ongoing readjustment as work and family needs change, neither work nor home life will be as fully satisfying as they should be.

Be alert to the changing needs of your baby/toddler, be sure the dialogue with your husband is ongoing and honest. And don't make the mistake of neglecting to give adequate thought to your own state of well-being, as well. Short tempers, frequent arguments, sleepless nights, or a chronically upset baby are red flags that should not be ignored.

The whole premise behind seeking an alternative to the forty-hour workweek is to cash in on the flexibility it provides. Take advantage of it. Turn down a new assignment, readjust your hours, start taking an afternoon nap with the baby, add extra household help, redivide household and child care responsibilities with your husband. Keep rearranging and restructuring until all aspects of home and work life are again in balance. Maintaining this delicate balance amid the ever changing needs of a growing family and the unceasing demands of your chosen career is the most challenging job of all.

Chapter 8

Other Options
Multiple choices for redesigning your career

If your job is such that neither permanent part-time nor job sharing would be feasible, you still have one more option for restructuring your current job—flextime. Flextime is not yet a commonplace option to the standard workweek, but even so, it may be the answer for *you*.

Flextime May Be Right for You

Flextime is a system whereby the employee works a full eight-hour day, but each employee is free to adjust his starting and quitting times as he wishes. Often companies with a flextime program have a core time—commonly from about 10:00 A.M. until about 3:00 P.M.—when all employees are required to be present. Other than that, each employee is free to start his day early or late, according to his own preference.

While this system is less than ideal for the woman with a small nursing baby because she must still be away at work a full eight hours each day, it may have some real merit where an older toddler or preschooler is concerned.

At the very least, flextime would permit the day to get started in a less harried fashion, especially if the baby/toddler is one who likes to sleep in past 6:00 or 7:00 A.M. With the option of not having to arrive at work until 10:00 A.M., or even later, there is time to begin the day at a more leisurely pace with your little one, and perhaps even start a load of laundry or get a crock pot dinner underway so that the evening can be more relaxed.

In the best of circumstances, a flextime work schedule can minimize the time the baby/toddler needs to be left with a caretaker. If the mother is able to work from 11:00 A.M. until 7:00 P.M. and the father has a job that allows him to be home at 3:00 or 4:00 P.M., the baby only needs to be left in someone else's care for four to five hours a day instead of the nine or ten hours that would otherwise be necessary.

■ Some of the most innovative organizations have offices equipped with space age technology, high powered executives—and playpens.

Computer systems analyst Cindy Karl and her husband worked out a combination part-time/flextime arrangement that necessitated only a minimal amount of child care for their two preschool age children.

"I work from 8:00 A.M. until 12:00 noon, twenty hours a week," Cindy explains. "My husband works from 10:00 A.M. until 6:30 P.M., so we only need to make child-care arrangements for about two and a half hours a day. My husband's boss is very happy about this arrangement because this way he can get more computer time in on off hours." Cindy works for the federal government and says that, "Several women have worked part-time for a number of years in my office, so my schedule isn't any big deal. But my experience with other employers is that they want you full time or not at all. The biggest problem I've had is that sometimes my job requires traveling, which I won't do while I'm nursing."

Of their arrangement, Cindy says, "The children love it because they get lots of mommy and daddy time, plus seeing just enough of another environment to make things interesting."

For couples who have a preschool in the community with extended hours, it may be possible for the mother to drop the child off on her way to work, and the father to pick him up on his way home. If the husband spends the two or three hours before his wife comes home playing with the child and getting dinner on the table, the whole family can relax together in the evening.

Eric Rambusch, Director of Human Resources for the Reuben H. Donnelley Company, reports that when a woman from another division had a baby and didn't want to work full time, she was hired as a thirty-hour a week personnel manager for their office. "We already had flextime in our division, so she just makes her own schedule."

Flextime arrangements are theoretically possible in almost any job setting, but according to Stanley T. Nollen, Associate Professor of

Business Economics at Georgetown University, who has conducted extensive studies of alternative work patterns, flextime is currently most often found in finance and insurance companies, and less likely to be found in manufacturing firms.

An even more accommodating program than the basic flextime is the variable day where each employee may work more or less than eight hours in a given day, as long as the total hours worked in a specified period (usually one or two weeks) amounts to the regular workweek of thirty-five to forty hours. In a situation where the father or other relative has one or more days off during the week, the mother may choose to work three twelve or thirteen hour days per week. Not every job lends itself to such scheduling and not every woman could work such long hours in a single day, but for certain families it could minimize the need for outside child care.

The burgeoning computer field is one area that lends itself particularly well to variable starting and quitting time. Beth Lindberg, a lead computer operator, made arrangements to work three twelve hour days, feeling that the drawbacks of such long days were more than compensated by the larger blocks of time she has available to be with her children.

"As a single parent by choice, it was important to me to be able to spend as much time with my children as possible. Supporting myself and two children, I must earn a full-time salary. I was offered a forty hour salary for thirty-six hours, working three twelve hour days. Those three days are rough, but I have four full days off every week. The long days mean that the children are *very* eager to see me, but I feel less pressure than with a nine-to-five Monday through Friday job. This schedule allows four days off for excursions, story hour at the library, cultural jaunts, minimal (by choice) housekeeping, and plenty of time for just being together as a family."

Beth, who returned to work when her second baby was nine weeks old, also enjoyed the freedom to nurse the baby often during off days, and was able to maintain her milk supply by nursing in the morning, again in the evening, and during the night on the days she worked.

Mother and Job and Baby Make Three

Some of the most innovative organizations in the country have offices equipped with space age technology, sophisticated equipment, high powered executives—and playpens.

When a career woman-mother is just too valuable to lose, progressive employers offer the woman the ultimate carrot—come back to work and bring the baby with you.

Suburban Chicago's *Daily Herald* ran a story about a top executive from a major oil company who intended to quit her job and stay home and breastfeed her baby after she gave birth.

> Her supervisors, however, were not anxious to lose the services of a valuable employee, not even to allow her to take a long leave of absence. Instead, they moved her into a secluded private office, and urged her to bring the baby to work with her. She did, with few disruptions in her schedule or the company's.

Actress Lynn Redgrave sued CBS for the right to nurse her baby on the set. Iowa firefighter Linda Eaton* sued for the right to have her baby brought to her at the firehouse to be nursed. "Good Morning America" co-host Joan Lunden* was two steps ahead of the game. When her first baby was born during the summer of 1980, she negotiated a new contract with ABC specifying that the network would furnish her office with necessary baby equipment, and provide a nurse for the baby whenever she traveled on the job.

Joan Lunden's determination to breastfeed and to mother her baby herself in spite of her demanding, high-powered career, is a highly visible symbol of a growing national trend: the refusal of women to make an either/or choice between a baby and a career. Though few women have the advantage of a six-figure income and a studio contract, women in a variety of job classifications and professional fields are doing just what Joan Lunden did. They are insisting that if they come to work, so does the baby.

Joan Lunden insisted that her daughter Jamie come with her to work at ABC-TV's "Good Morning America."

How It Works

Nurse Patricia Wendt was working twenty-two hours a week with the federal Women, Infants, and Children's (WIC) nutrition program when her baby was born.

"I didn't want to try to force her into a schedule or give her a bottle just because I wanted to work, so I arranged to take her to work with me," Patricia explains.

"I had my own office, and when I returned from my seven-week maternity leave with the baby, they had set up a bassinet and a rocking chair for Katie and me. All of our clients are low-income pregnant or breastfeeding women and their children. Katie would sit in my lap or on my desk in her car seat. I sometimes nursed her while I did clients' health histories.

"My employer was very supportive and encouraging, as were my co-workers, all of whom were women. They enjoyed having Katie there and were glad to entertain her if she got fussy while I was particularly busy. They knew it was important to me to have her there, and they wanted to keep me with the program. They also felt

*See chapter 17 for more information on Joan Lunden and Linda Eaton

■ Sally Strosahl, clinical psychologist

I wanted to return to work after my baby was born, but I did not want to leave him nor did I want our nursing to be interrupted. So bringing him to work with me seemed like the ideal situation.

I am a family therapist at a mental health center and we deal with treatment of child abuse cases. As part of our program, we have a child care area for families to use when they are receiving counseling. I hired a private sitter who looked after my son there. The other children are watched by agency staff members.

Andy was home with me in the mornings, then we went to work together in the afternoons. I would take nursing breaks between counseling appointments, and he often joined me during staff meetings where he would play quietly or nurse to sleep. At suppertime my husband would come to the center to pick Andy up after I had nursed him, and take him home for the evening. I would be home in time for his bedtime nursing.

The director of our agency was very supportive and tolerant of the inconveniences. She believed that since our job involved working with families in stress, it was important that we make the needs of our own families a priority in order to have the emotional resources to deal with our caseload. As long as we put in the required amount of work, she agreed to flexible hours.

But no situation is perfect, and there were several problems I had to deal with. Two of the male staff members expressed discomfort when I nursed during staff meetings. I think some people did not feel it was "professional." I also found that it was hard to share myself between the baby and the clients. I had to separate the roles clearly.

I believe Andy benefited from the security of spending a lot of time with both parents, and being with the other loving adults at work. The stimulation of the other children at the center was good, he progressed very quickly, and he's at ease with lots of people. However, his schedule was disrupted—he couldn't nap easily with the noise at the center—and he was exposed to some aggressive behavior which we didn't want. So at the age of one year we made different arrangements, having the sitter take him to her house in the afternoon. By then we felt he could handle being separated from me for four hour periods. ■

that we were a good mother-child model for our low-income mothers who knew little about stimulating their babies, were not accustomed to breastfeeding, and had never heard of a baby going to work."

Although Meri Pohutsky-Hofmann works forty hours a week as the director of a runaway shelter, she is able to take her five-month-old baby to work with her.

"Running a program for homeless youth in a home environment makes it easy to bring my baby to work," she says. "I have a playpen, swing, and walker in my office for the baby, and can easily stop and nurse her whenever she needs it. When I have an administrative meeting, I usually bring the baby with me.

"Both my employers and co-workers have been very supportive of my setup. The baby has even been a positive influence on the clients—they seem to be more responsive to therapy and counseling after spending time with Molly."

Except in the most unusual of situations it is neither possible nor practical to bring a baby to work indefinitely, and Meri is wisely planning ahead for the time when a change will be in order.

"Once Molly is walking, I will alter my schedule to work afternoons and enroll her in a nursery school."

Similarly, Canadian June Friesen found that being a houseparent in a boys' group home was a good way to keep her three children with her while earning a living.

"My husband wanted to return to the university and we needed a way to support ourselves," June explains. "Being houseparents provides us with an income until he decides what is next for him. It also provides us with a home, giving us a chance to decide where we want to settle before buying our own home.

"Our situation means trying to provide a home-like atmosphere for four teenage boys. We can't stop them if they want to run, but if they become violent or disruptive they are placed elsewhere. They come to live with us of their own choice, with the approval of their social worker and parents.

"We find that it takes a while to establish rapport and that they don't easily confide in us. The home's board of directors sees our three children as an advantage, as a way of reaching the boys.

"I am available to Matt, sixteen months, just as I would be in our own home. He is getting to know others outside of our immediate family, and that is fun to watch. The teenagers are sometimes hard on our six-year-old, perhaps feeling that we treat him like a baby.

"This situation is a long way from the registered nursing I was trained for," June admits, "but my husband Rick and I feel that my going to work outside of the home and leaving the children is not an option we would consider. Rick would take any job before that happened.

"When our youngest reaches three or four and his father can watch him, we may look into my returning to some nursing related job. But we can't see holding down two full-time jobs and managing house, children, church, and our other interests. Beyond providing necessities, money is not a priority for us."

Dolorosa Welch went to work in a nursery—for plants, that is—and took her baby with her until he was over a year old.

"I started part-time, and then my hours were increased to full time," she recalls. "I set up a playpen for the baby and every time he even whimpered my employer insisted that I go take care of him. My co-workers supported what I was doing and went out of their way to be helpful. It was an ideal situation."

Chiropractic assistant Anna Gomes didn't ask to bring her baby to work. "The doctors I worked for suggested it themselves," she explains.

"Prior to the baby's birth we had decided that my husband would care for the baby. He was home anyway, preparing for a business of our own. But when Danny was about a week old, the doctor that I worked for called and suggested that I bring the baby to work with me. He completely agreed with my belief in the importance of breastfeeding, and knew that having the baby at work would certainly make it easier. He also knew that I would be happier not to have to leave the baby.

■ **"My husband and I feel that my going to work outside the home and leaving the children is not an option we would consider."**

"The arrangement worked well because my job is mostly paperwork and it is flexible. The rest of the office staff is like a family, and Danny was enjoyed by one and all. They were absolutely fantastic and I will always appreciate their attitude."

Anna continued to bring Danny to work with her until he was about six months old.

"In the beginning he slept nearly all of the time, but by the age of five months he had started staying awake a lot and I felt badly about leaving him to himself so much of the time, so I began leaving him at home with his dad. But even so, I was able to nurse him until he was a year old."

Nurse-practitioner Kathy Rousset has taken all four of her children to work with her when they were babies—the first two in a hospital and a private doctor's office, the last two with the same group of obstetricians.

"My employers seem satisfied with this arrangement—after all, they let me do it a second time. My patient load is equal to or greater than the other nurse-practitioners, and I have yet to receive a complaint from a client. My co-workers are all very supportive. They have enjoyed the babies and are happy to assist if I am busy and the baby starts to fuss. As far as I know there have been no complaints that I am receiving 'special treatment.'

"I have found that I cannot concentrate well after the baby

reaches about ten months of age. I don't want the baby to get in danger, and I don't want him to get in the way of the other staff people. So once each one has reached that point, he joins the older siblings with a babysitter.

"Since my first child was born nine years ago, I have always worked part-time. Because nursing always has a need for workers, I could ask for and get concessions to the forty-hour week. I was divorced after having my first two children, and was very grateful that I had maintained a career. I could and did support them by working four days a week.

"I feel that I am a good example of both breastfeeding and mothering for the pregnant women who watch me function in the office. I hope that my example encourages other women to take their children with them if they are going to work."

Leslie Ann Kuss has been a cook for a college fraternity for the past seven years, and takes her children with her.

> I worked up until the day I went into labor with my first baby, and returned to work four months later after the summer vacation was over. When I went back, Melissa went with me. Three years later, Leanne was born during my summer vacation, and began coming to work with me in the fall when she was two months old.
>
> I cook breakfast and dinner, so we are at the fraternity house for two hours in the morning and several hours in the afternoon. We're home by 8:15 A.M. after cooking breakfast, so we have the morning for activities (kindergarten for Melissa), then lunch, rest time, and back to work. We eat our meals at the fraternity house, or bring them home, which saves both money and cooking and clean up time at home.
>
> My daughters both learned to be helpers at an early age. They were tearing lettuce by eighteen months, and they love kneading their own rolls for dinner and stirring anything and everything.
>
> There is no television, so the girls have really learned to play well together. The fraternity house's floor plan is one that enables me to easily keep an eye on them. I supplied outlet plugs and safety gates when the girls were younger, and regularly check to see that nothing dangerous has been left around. "The guys," as Melissa calls them, are very good about helping me keep the area safe and clean, and they helped me rearrange the pantry so that it is safe for the children.
>
> I work anywhere from twenty to thirty hours a week, and I am paid by the meal rather than the hour. I spend more time at work now than I did before the girls were born, but I am easily able to take a break whenever one of them needs me.
>
> Of course, there are disadvantages, not the least of which is having to move two sleeping girls wrapped in quilts from bed to car to couch in the morning. I guess they are used to it though, because neither one wakes up. But I sure hate to do it on cold, rainy mornings.
>
> This job enables me to make enough money to meet our needs, and actually I probably wouldn't really net more money working elsewhere

> because I would have to pay for child care for two children. But, most important, I haven't had to leave a baby or child at home. I have never had to worry that my child might be missing me or might want to nurse, and I've never had to pump my milk. I am glad that I have been able to be there for all of the problems, all of the joys, and all of the firsts.

Celia Vayro thought she would have to resign from her position as coordinator for a teacher-training program for native Indians when her first child was born.

"But my supervisors convinced me that I could continue my job by working part-time and bringing the baby with me on most occasions," she reports. "My work included counseling about fifteen adult students, supervising and instructing student teachers, and running an off-campus teacher training program.

"In the first year I received half pay for what amounted to more than half-time work, about thirty-two hours a week. After that year, my supervisors made sure I was paid a full wage, even though my baby was frequently with me, because they knew that I was doing the job carefully and thoroughly.

"My husband took over a considerable portion of the child care after the baby was about a year old," Celia recalls. "By then she was becoming disruptive at meetings. But overall I found few objections either to the baby or to nursing."

▪ "My supervisors convinced me that I could continue my job working part-time and bringing the baby with me . . . ."

Linda Smith, mother of three children who has a degree in physical education, made a career out of teaching a variety of classes, always with the stipulation written into her contract that she could bring the baby along.

"I would not leave a baby to take any kind of job," she says. "I've taught many kinds of courses for different organizations over the years—childbirth, parenting, children's exercise and gymnastics, diet management, and dance—and I've always specified in the contract that my child would accompany me at all times. I simply would not accept a position that necessitated my leaving a child before that child was fully ready and could participate in the decision. Being a La Leche League member for twelve years gave me a firm set of priorities."

Linda has met with a variety of reactions from prospective employers and students over the years.

"The person hiring me for a county sponsored parent discussion group thought I was a little strange, but when I made it obvious to him that leaving my child at home was not an option that I would consider, I guess he decided that they needed me anyway. The same for my current physical education job. The principal appeared to accept my stipulations when I made them with confidence and without hesitation. The childbirth students I taught at home sometimes made mention of the baby I often nursed to sleep during class, but never in a negative way. The parents who have a child at home understand the separation anxiety of a two-year-old, and the first-timers see a parenting model."

Linda also recalls the time she was leading a parent discussion group where the policy was to have the mothers separate from their eighteen-month-old children during the discussion time. An aide was provided to babysit for all of the toddlers, but Linda did not encourage the mothers to send their children off, and she gave the aide instructions that no child was to be allowed to cry—any upset toddler was to be brought to his mother. "My boss admitted later that my way worked better for everyone."

Nikki Ann Ravey and Molly Jaeger-Begent share a unique situation. Nikki, the mother of four children ranging in age from sixteen years to seven months, owns Southwest Printing. Her youngest child, Katherine, "was born on Thursday morning at 8:17 A.M. and I did the payroll the next Monday morning. I did not work full time for several weeks, but I was in the office every day," Nikki recalls.

Nikki keeps Katherine's baby bed in her office, and feels that bringing the baby to work or providing on-site day care are workable options that more employers should pursue.

These are no idle words on Nikki's part since she did just that when one of her own employees gave birth eight months ago. Nikki agreed to have Molly Jaeger-Begent divide her work between home and office, and encouraged Molly to set up a portable crib in her office for the baby to use during the two hours a morning they are at work.

"I'm extremely lucky to have an employer who was willing to let me modify my workday to accommodate my baby," Molly admits. "And the baby has enjoyed the attention of my co-workers, who like him a great deal."

Like most other working-nursing mothers, Nikki has found it difficult at times to juggle the simultaneous demands of job and baby.

"My workday at the office with the baby is very broken, but is far better than not being there at all," Nikki says. "If the baby had not had colic for the first four and half months it would have been a lot easier. My time has been the most frustrating thing. It seems to have gotten better now that Katherine is older, or maybe I have just gotten used to it.

"Being with mother is great. Having to wait for mother when she is busy with employees or customers is not. When you're working, the baby does not have 100 percent of mother's attention. You don't have as much freedom and flexibility as a mother at home does, so you just arrange things the best you can. You nurse before an ap-

■ Cheryl Pledger, advertising sales representative

I work for my brother-in-law two mornings a week. I take both of the children with me, as well as a tote bag filled with toys, books, paper and pencils, and a non-messy nutritious snack. They are now five and two years old, and super little working partners. I have not met a single person who was put off by my children being with me. In fact, most have obviously enjoyed them.

On one occasion the only time I could meet with a man was in the afternoon. I had a sleepy little girl with me who would not be put off till a more convenient time. So while he and I talked business, I discreetly nursed her to sleep. Thank goodness he turned out to be the father of breastfed children.

My brother-in-law is totally satisfied with my production since even after only one year my share of the business has shown a profit, with even better prospects for next year. ■

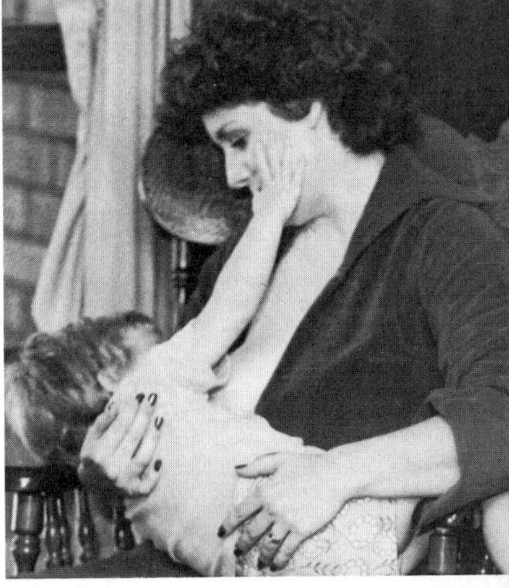

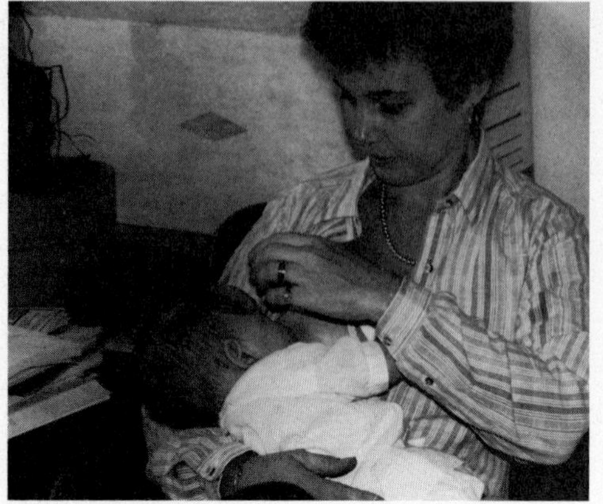
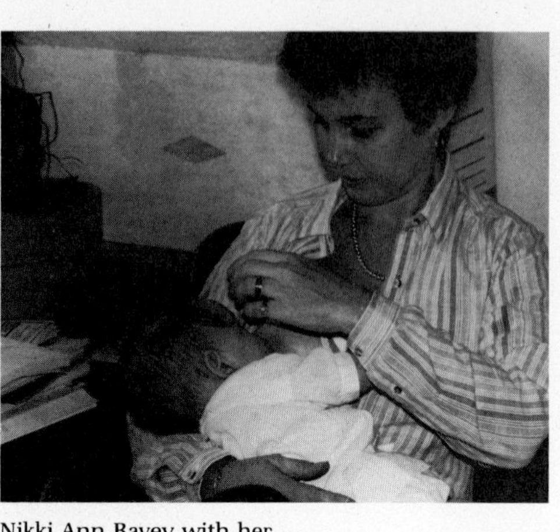

Nikki Ann Ravey with her youngest child, Katherine Ann, and Molly Jaeger-Begent, with her son, B.J. (opposite page), handle business as usual with their "working babies."

pointment even if it's not time, and hope the baby will be good while you are gone."

Like Nikki Ravey, Debbie Daunt Everett, who is co-owner of a bridal shop, has a "working baby" with a crib near her desk, and a playpen and toys adorning her office.

Meghan, now nine months old, is at work forty hours a week with her mother. "As she grew more mobile and vocal at about seven months, I hired a babysitter to watch her here in my office about half-time so that I could get my work done and still be with my baby," Debbie reports.

"I feel that I lose some credibility with my office looking like a nursery, but generally the reaction to the arrangement has been positive.

"Two of my employees are expecting babies this spring. They will both be taking a minimum maternity leave because their babies will be 'working babies,' too. But we will have to find a larger nursery—my office will be too crowded!"

Legal assistant Madeleine Holmberg, too, knew that the only way she would continue to work would be if she could bring her baby with her.

"For me, it was never really a choice between leaving her with someone else while I worked or quitting. I knew that if there wasn't a way to keep her with me, I would stay home. I wanted to be with her, and didn't want to miss out on the developmental changes that occur so quickly in the first year."

Madeleine, whose baby is now a year old, was fortunate to have a nearly perfect situation that easily permitted the addition of a baby to the office decor.

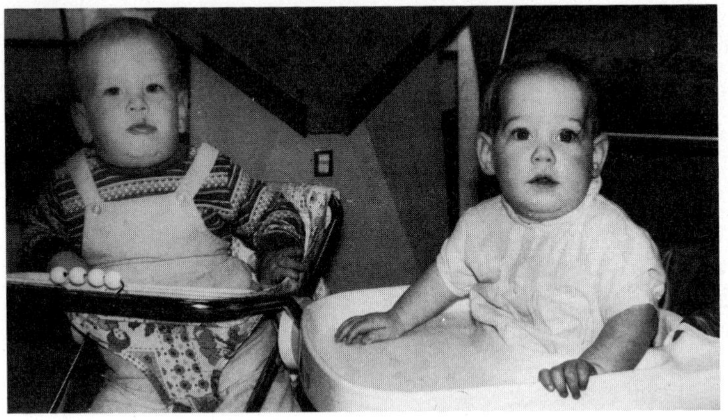

Our office is in a large house overlooking the Columbia River, so it has all of the amenities of home. The baby even has her own room with a crib in it. I have set up "play stations" all around the house, and she entertains herself fairly well. We take lots of time-outs, but she is good about understanding when Mom is busy, and will usually find something to do. She can even play outside on nice days.

The baby was very colicky the first four months and cried quite a lot. I had to walk her to keep her happy, so I carried her in a front baby carrier while I typed and answered the phone. Sometimes it got pretty hectic when clients came to the door while I was trying to nurse her, but we got through it.

My employer has been completely supportive which, of course, is an absolute necessity. He and the baby have a very special relationship. Of course, there are days when the whole situation must be frustrating for him, as it sometimes is for me, but as long as we can get the necessary work done he is very patient. We work in criminal law and our clientele are mostly working class people. So far no one has ever objected to seeing toys and a baby in the office. Mostly, it brings a lot of smiles.

Nansi Casper, another secretary who works twenty hours a week and brings her three-month-old baby to work with her, found that her biggest problem was her own anxiety.

"The biggest problem I had was my own nervousness. When Nikki got fussy or began crying, I would get nervous because I was worried that I wasn't getting enough work done or that I was annoying other workers in the suite of offices. It seemed that the more I tried to calm her down, the more she cried. She obviously sensed my nervousness and we were caught in a vicious circle. There were several times in the beginning when I had to leave the office and take her home.

"I have calmed down considerably now, mostly due to the support of my employer and the lack of complaints from other workers. Now I am usually able to deal with the fussy times just as I would at home. When she gets unhappy I simply put her in the carrier and we go for a walk—outside if the weather is nice, down the hall if it is raining. She either goes to sleep or calms down enough to go back to the office and nurse before dozing off.

"I find that instead of working at a steady pace throughout the morning, I work at a fast and furious pace when Nikki is asleep and at a slow and relaxed pace when she is awake. I have found that I am so much happier about being at work when my daughter is with me. I often find myself humming or singing. I am also learning to type one-handed!

"I feel very blessed to have such an understanding employer. There are so few of them out there, and so many mothers who must work."

Melanie Williams-Pollock felt that having to pay for day care wouldn't make it financially worthwhile to work, so she decided to look for a job that would enable her to keep baby Nathaniel with her. What she found was a job as a youth worker in charge of a community service program for juveniles.

"I could put in as many or as few hours as I was able, and could do most of my work at home. Whenever I had to go to the office, I took Nathaniel with me. He also comes along for meetings and appointments. I have the full support of everyone I work with. They all enjoy the diversion whenever I bring Nathaniel to the office, and they even have a big box of toys for him. No one minds when I nurse him, even though he is now past two. The only problems I have encountered have been small ones, such as teaching Nathaniel to leave the photocopier and other office equipment alone."

Half and Half

When the workplace can't or won't accommodate the baby full time, it may be possible to divide work between home and office, or bring the baby to work for part of the workday.

Computer systems engineer Victoria Winters arranged to split her work between home and office after her baby was born.

"I go into the office three mornings a week, and do the rest of my work from home," she explains. "The company put a computer terminal in my home and I had an extra phone line installed. I still work forty hours a week, but I can choose the times I work—when the baby naps or in the evening when my husband can care for him or when he is asleep.

"At first it was hard to discipline myself to sit down and do my work at home," she admits, "and I found myself feeling somewhat isolated from my co-workers. But everyone has been very positive about my working from home. My bosses were unsure at first about how it would work out, but it has gone very well. Now other people have inquired about working from home, too."

Karen Fields, a dietician who is the Administrator of Health Programs for a health department, also works forty hours a week but brings her baby to work with her for part of the day.

"I now work from 6:00 A.M. until 3:00 P.M. instead of my old schedule of 8:00 A.M. to 5:00 P.M.," she says. "Five-month-old Kristin comes to work with me until 10:00 A.M. when she goes to her grandmother's. I go over to feed her at lunchtime, and then I am off for the day at 3:00 P.M. With this system, she is only away from me for four hours a day. My husband has changed to a four-day week, so he keeps her on Fridays and they come to visit me at 'hungry times.'

"I have found that it is difficult to get as much done when Kristin is with me, but I just work harder and faster when she isn't with me. My employer has said that the arrangement is fine as long as the quality of my program is maintained and the employees get enough supervision."

■ "I feel very blessed to have such an understanding employer. There are so few of them out there and so many mothers who must work."

For Lori Estreicher, employment outside of the home came as a result of her husband losing his job when their daughter was twelve months old.

"He was out of work for nearly a year," Lori explains. "During that time the director of a rape crisis center offered me a job as her assistant twenty hours a week. I agreed to take the job if I could work at home or bring my daughter to the office with me. Though we desperately needed the money, maintaining the stability of our family was my highest priority. I did not want to resent having to leave the baby."

But taking the baby to work proved to be unrealistic in her situation, Lori said, "so instead I worked a flexible schedule. At first I left for work just before the baby's nap and returned two hours later when she woke up. I took care of typing and phone calls at home in the evening, and tried to schedule all meetings in the evenings or on weekends. I refused to go on day trips out of town.

"In return for all of these conditions I put on the job, I made a point of always being available. I stayed an extra hour or two if necessary, and worked longer hours than my job required. I was always willing to go above and beyond what was expected of me."

If her husband wasn't able to be home with the baby, the baby went to work with Lori. "I couldn't tolerate leaving her with anyone else besides my husband. Police, hospital employees, just about everybody enjoyed seeing the baby the times I brought her with me.

"My employer and co-workers 'tolerated' the situation, probably because they respected me and understood our financial situation. But I don't think they ever understood my need to be near the baby and my insistence on not using day care. When my husband found a job they asked me to stay, but it would have meant using a babysitter fifteen hours a week. I refused to do that and quit."

Bringing an Office Job Home

Modern technology is now in the process of doing a remarkable thing. It is enabling us to move *backwards,* back to the days before the Industrial Revolution when people earned their livings by working at home.

The 1880s home-based blacksmith and carpenter are gone, but the 1980s data processor and computer operator who work from home are here to stay. Perhaps one of the most unnoticed marvels of the computer age is that it is making it technologically possible for large numbers of people to bring an office job home.

For the mother of an infant or preschooler, this Industrial Revolution in reverse allows the career woman-mother to combine the office and the nursery under one roof—her own.

About 200,000 home computers were in use in late 1980, according to *Worksteads* by Jeremy Joan Hughes, "many of them plugged into data banks that include the United Press International news service, airline schedules, and a 10,000 item catalog shopping service that takes computer orders." Such innovations increase almost by the hour, bringing the work-at-home option closer to reality for a broader segment of the work force. Word processing, accounting, insurance analysis, and processing of insurance claims are just some of the fields being opened up for home computer terminals. As computer and communications costs continue to decrease, the home-based computer operator will become more and more commonplace.

Although the technology to make such work-at-home opportunities readily available is still evolving, there are a number of corporations that already have such programs in place, and many more companies anticipate setting up home-based computer operators in the coming years.

Control Data Corporation,* one of the country's most talked about leaders in the area of non-traditional work options, has an Alternative Work Sites program employing about 100 persons, primarily computer analysts, who work entirely from home or divide their work between home and office.

Other companies across the country, most of them on a smaller scale, are also experimenting with the work-at-home option for computer operators.

*See chapter 16 for more information on Control Data Corporation

For the employer, although implementing a home-based work program requires some farsighted planning and innovative thinking, the long-range benefits are considerable.

- Overhead can be substantially reduced by having employees work in their own homes, instead of having to provide heat, light, and expensive office space for them to work in a central location.
- Considerable savings can be realized by having the home-based employees use the computer in off-peak hours.
- Disabled employees who can be set up with a computer terminal at home can be paid their regular salary for work performed, instead of costly workman's compensation or disability payments. The loss of productivity while the job remains vacant or the training costs involved in hiring a new employee are eliminated completely.
- Worker morale and productivity may be improved through the work-at-home arrangement. The worker in such a situation is acting much like an independent contractor, and as such is motivated to do his best to protect and enhance his professional reputation.

But like any other new field, there are some uncharted territories that the potential home-based worker should be aware of before accepting such a job.

Supervising at-home workers is a relatively new management concept, so you'll want to be sure expectations concerning the amount of work you will do and the time in which you are expected to do it are clearly understood in advance. An at-home word processor or computer terminal can function as a time clock, automatically recording the amount of time the employee spends on line. As long as the employer is agreeable to having the work done in blocks of time that suit the baby's schedule, this is a workable arrangement for the mother with a baby or toddler.

The other option in managing home-based computer operators is to pay the employee on a per project basis. Again, this is an arrangement that can work quite well for the mother of a baby or young child, as long as the amount of work and the deadline imposed for completing it are compatible with meeting the needs of the baby/toddler. Women in such situations often find themselves sitting at the terminal well into the night or early in the morning while the baby is sleeping, but for the woman who chooses this option, the luxury of working from home during these important years more than compensates for the sometimes bizarre working hours.

Another point to clarify with your employer is the question of liability. You will want to know who is responsible for broken equipment, and whether you can deduct your home office as a business expense. Currently, employers are tending to regard the employee's home as an extension of the office, making the employer responsible for equipment repair and job-related accidents on the same basis as if the employee were working in the office.

One word of caution if you are thinking about working out of your home on a computer for a company. The field is new enough that sometimes such projects are cancelled or temporarily shut down. Continental Bank in Chicago had a home computer operator program, but discontinued it in 1982 "until more cost effective technology becomes available," said bank spokesperson Madalene Thompson. "We consider it a very successful pilot and expect to do it again in a year or two."

Temporary Work

If you can afford to get by without a regular weekly paycheck, working for an agency that provides companies with temporary help is a good option for the mother with a baby or young child. Working on a temporary basis will allow you to accept work or not, as your family (and perhaps financial) needs dictate. You're free to turn down a job the week the baby has a cold, without fear of any repercussions. At other times when the baby/toddler is feeling particularly sociable and you have child care arrangements you are comfortable with, you can accept one long term or a string of short term temporary positions. When the wind shifts again (as it inevitably will) and your little one makes it clear he wants to be with you, you can say no to job offers until he is again agreeable to being left with a sitter.

Approximately two-thirds of all temporary positions are for clerical jobs, according to JoAnne Alter in *A Part-Time Career for a Full-Time You,* so you'll stand the best chance of finding temporary work if your skills lie in the area of typist, secretary, receptionist, or bookkeeper. Health care agencies, one of the fastest-growing fields in the country, also offer good opportunities for temporary work.

One great fringe benefit of working on a temporary basis, as JoAnne Alter points out, is that it provides "an excellent earn-while-you-learn situation. Having the chance to practice operating sophisticated new office equipment or to upgrade skills you already possess makes temporary work one of the best training opportunities around. Working at different companies or in various fields can give you broad experience and exposure to many kinds of businesses." This, in turn, will considerably broaden your contacts and range of skills, providing you with a decisive advantage should you want to look for a permanent part-time, shared, flextime, or full-time position in the future.

Free-Lance Opportunities

Again, if a regular paycheck in a fixed amount isn't a necessity in your situation, free-lancing may be an option to consider. Although free-lancing and being self-employed are in many respects two sides of the same coin, free-lancing usually involves working steadily, although independently, for several of the same clients. An engineer might work on a free-lance basis for two or three engineering firms, providing extra manpower for large assignments or during occasional peak periods. A graphic designer might be called on a number of times every year to complete assignments from the same three or four publishers or printers. Those who are self-employed may or may not rely on a steady stream of repeat business from the same sources.

Some women, deciding that they are not willing to be separated from their babies the forty or more hours a week required when working full time for someone else, have arranged to work on a free-lance basis for their former employer.

Insurance underwriter Barbara Albert, though she is technically self-employed, has only one client, her former employer.

"I work basically two seven-hour days a week," Barbara explains. "There are weeks when I go in an additional day, but this is rare. Usually, if I cannot meet a deadline I bring the work home. When I accumulate seven extra hours, I bill the company for an additional day. If for some reason I need to be home on a 'work' day, I can easily switch days.

"My employer's attitude about this arrangement has been excellent. We both have to bend a little. My supervisors know that I will come through when they need me. I'll rearrange my schedule, if at all possible, to be in the office for meetings. I'll bring work home with me if I need to. In return, if I must stay at home because my child or the babysitter is sick, they are understanding.

"Most of my co-workers are also accepting of the situation, although some look askance when I leave promptly at 4:30 P.M. to catch my train so that I can be home in time for my babysitter to leave. But I have had this arrangement for over four years now, so most of them treat it quite matter-of-factly.

"My income has obviously been cut substantially by the arrangement," Barbara admits, "because I only work two days a week now. But my job is at the same level. It's not like taking a traditional part-time, lower paying job."

Reesa Abrams,* a management consultant who produces quality software for computer hardware manufacturers, works out of her home as a consultant to Digital Equipment Corporation. Digital installed a computer in Reesa's home in order to allow her to continue in her career while being a full-time mother.

*See chapter 17 for more information on Reesa Abrams

"I signed my contract with Digital three days after the baby was born," Reesa reports. "We are now in our second contract and negotiating a third. I take her with me when I travel one day a month, and arrange my schedule so that she is never with a sitter for more than three hours at a time.

"She always went into the office with me, too, usually two days a month, until she started crawling and it became unsafe.

"All in all, I think this has been a good arrangement," Reesa concludes. "I didn't have to give up a peaking career (a twenty-year investment), and yet the baby and I are able to spend as much time together as we want."

Debbie Armstrong, a physical therapist who worked full time at St. Joseph's Hospital in Arkansas before her baby was born, contracted with the hospital's Home Health Department when her baby was five months old, and now provides physical therapy to patients in their own homes. The new arrangement gave her the freedom to make her own hours, and to reschedule appointments any time her baby is ill.

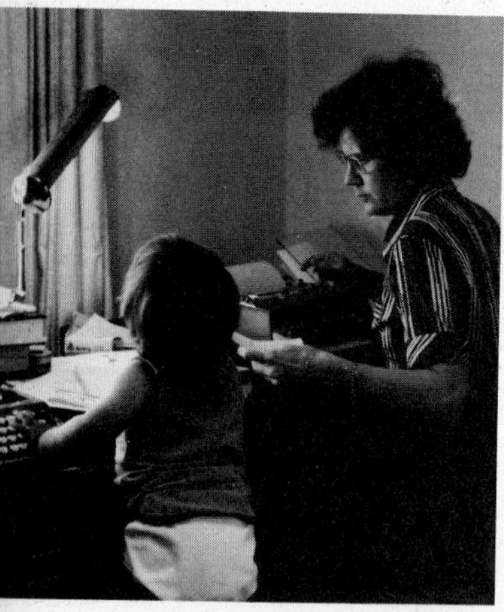

Ellen Davies, law librarian, works at home so she can be available to her youngest son Stefan.

Law librarian Ellen Davies credits fate with the creation of her at-home work situation.

"Fate, in the form of a job transfer, sent us to a new town shortly after the baby's arrival. There was no room for an office in the courthouse, so I made special arrangements with my boss (a single parent) to work out of an office in my home. My job was to write a procedures manual for the library system, which could easily be done at home."

So Ellen set up an office in her home, hired a sitter to care for the baby, and went to work. "When he cried or was hungry, I came out of the office and nursed him. I saw the baby at break time and during my lunch hour, as well as for his 'nursing calls.' "

Like many other people who set up a satellite office at home, Ellen discovered she felt a sense of isolation from her co-workers. She also experienced fatigue, especially when she had to be up at night with the baby. And there were times that she was torn between work and the baby, so much so that she felt a choice was in order.

"Sometimes I felt myself torn in half between my baby's crying and work deadlines. But working for those four months after the baby's arrival was a good transition for me. I went from 'super career woman' to accepting motherhood as an alternate career."

Jae Asancheyev, who was living in France when she had her first baby, was offered a very flexible part-time schedule by her employer as an incentive to come back to work after her baby was born.

"My employer consented to an arrangement as rare as it was liberal—a half salary for a half day of work. Come when you want,

■ Katie Costanzo, Fire Protection Engineer

When I was seven months pregnant, I gave my two weeks' notice. The company I worked for received a large fire sprinkler contract about then, and by mutual agreement I was given the job and the necessary equipment to work as a subcontractor out of my home. Since finishing that job, this same company has sent me most of their design work. Now that I have my office set up at home, I could also find work through other fire sprinkler companies.

I've found this arrangement very conducive to being able to care for my baby, now fourteen months old, and still keep a hand in my profession.

Because I have been free to arrange my work schedule around my child's schedule, it has worked well for everyone. I work at home in our third bedroom, usually while she sleeps or plays quietly nearby. When she has been sick I have usually been free to skip working for a few days to take care of her.

The people I am working for are very sympathetic unless I get too far behind in my work. If I say I will have so much completed by a certain date, they expect it to be done. I have found that I can work much more efficiently at home than I did in a business office. ■

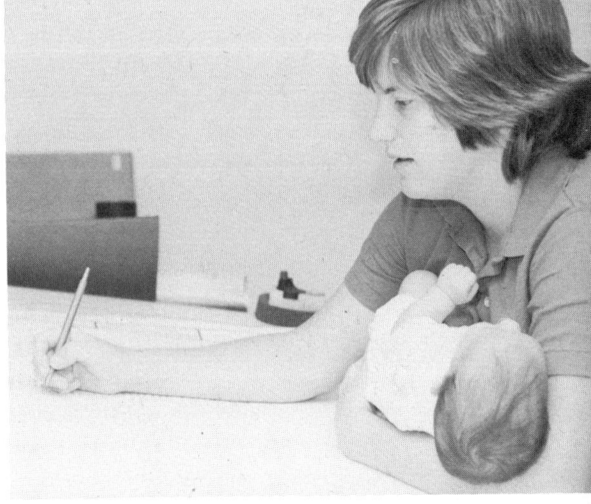

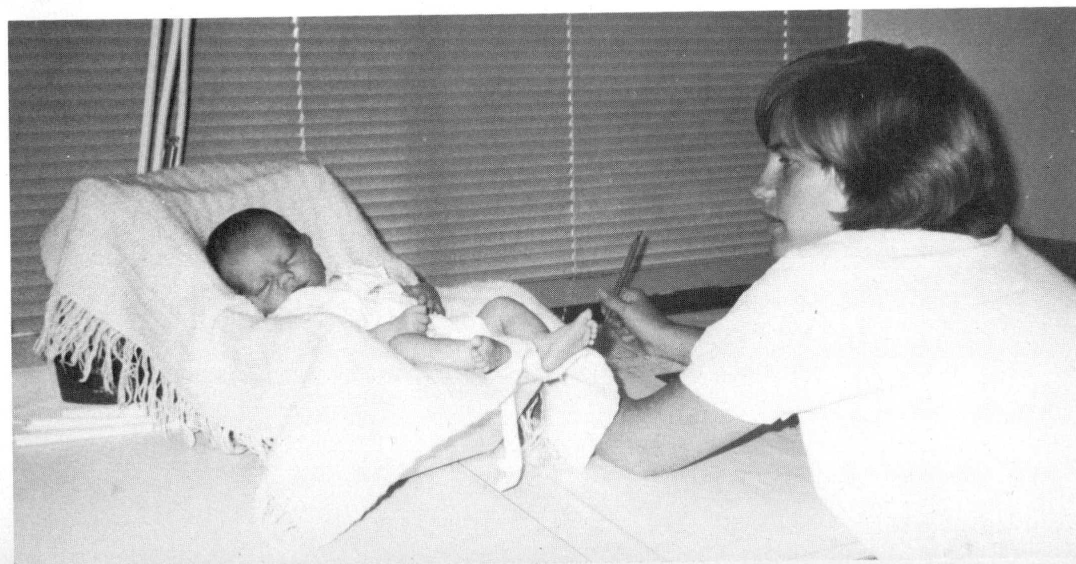

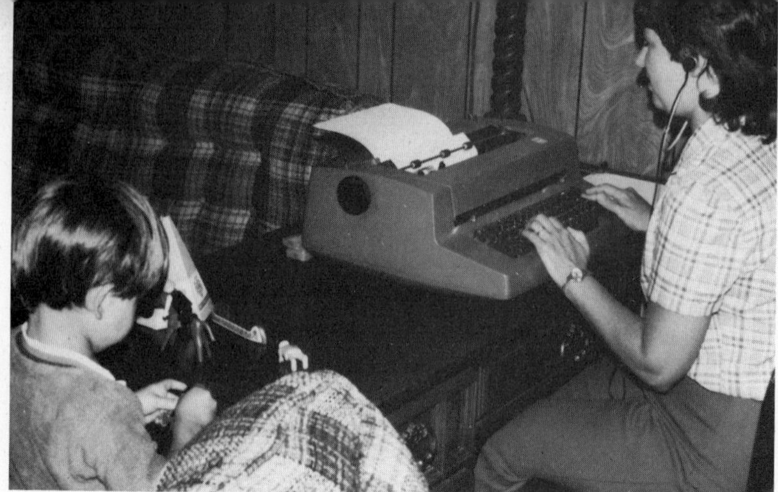

Carol Lee handles her medical transcribing business from home while caring for her three children.

work out whatever schedule suits you—per day, week, month. But after the baby was born I realized that the baby was there all day long, and that if I left her, someone else would be receiving all those smiles which were mine. Also, it took just one phone call to a prospective sitter to realize that nobody loved her as I did. So I called my employer at the end of the eight-week postnatal leave and said I was sorry, but there was no part of the day when I felt I could come down to the office."

But instead of being the end, that decision turned out to be the beginning of an entirely new and much more satisfying working arrangement for Jae.

"After I explained that I was not available to come to anyone's office, a client of my employer's proposed that I accept a consulting job and work for him from my home. I acquired a computer terminal like the one used at the client's office and installed it in the kitchen. Working involved spending one or two days a month using this machine with the baby on my lap or the floor, plus a few extra phone calls. I spent an average of one day a month at their office with the baby."

Jae continued with this setup for four years and says that, "The overall advantage was an unquestionably high ratio of income for the time worked. This is the reward and result of having acquired a great deal of specific knowledge, and a good relationship with the customer who needed me not so much for actual hours of work, but more as someone he could talk to on a consulting basis about problems he encountered."

As more employers and creative entrepreneurs come to understand the cost effectiveness of having employees work from their own homes, this option is becoming available in a wider range of fields.

Carol Lee, who has three small children, found a job situation that enabled her to bring her hospital typing job home. She spotted

an ad in the newspaper for medical transcribers to do work at home, called for an interview, and was hired. Not only did this allow her to work and be at home with her children, but it gave her the flexibility to work as much or as little as she chose.

"The company I work for provides a typewriter, dictaphone, and all of my supplies," Carol explains. "On Monday, Wednesday, and Friday afternoons they pick up and deliver cassette tapes to me from hospitals all over the city. If I want extra work, I can call in and request a Tuesday or Thursday delivery as well."

Carol says that the system worked perfectly when the baby was small. "I typed during the day when he napped, and in the evening when my husband and the other kids were around to amuse him. When he was very small I put his infant seat beside me while I typed so he could see me all the time. Of course, I was free to stop and nurse him anytime."

Carol has found the entire arrangement to be full of pluses. "I do exactly the same work at home that I did in the hospital, only now I can work as many or as few hours as I want to. I make much more money than I did doing the same work in a hospital. I miss being around other adults, but otherwise this is the ideal job when you have small children."

This innovative system is obviously working well for the company, too. "The company has about 200 typists in the Philadelphia area alone," Carol says, "and they have recently opened offices in Houston, Detroit, Los Angeles, New Orleans, and other large cities across the country."

Leslie Bateman, who has a master's degree and most of the work on her doctorate completed, is another career woman-mother who used her determination and ingenuity to redesign a job in order to continue working for the same employer, but from home.

"When our daughter was born in 1975, my husband was in graduate school. ('But what if it takes you two or three years to conceive?'

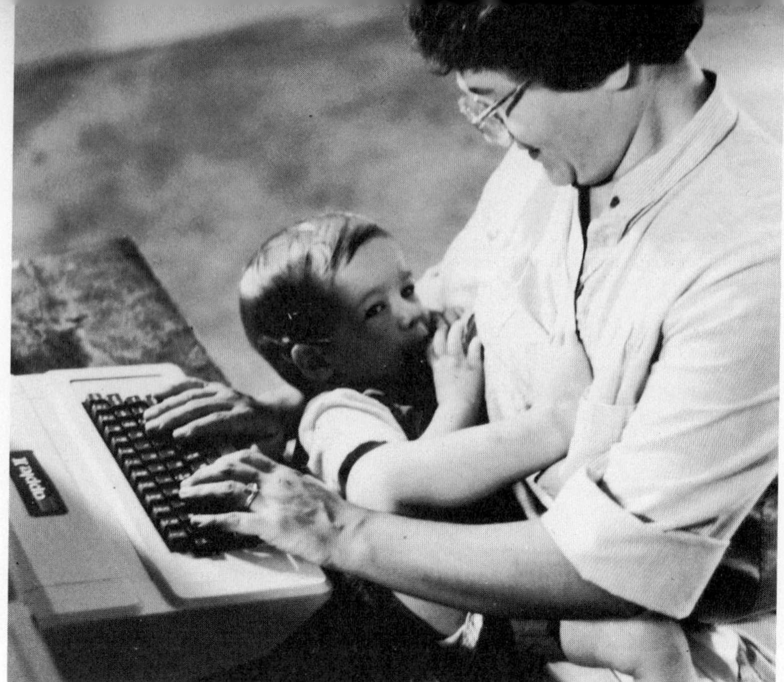

Leslie Bateman, who works on a course development project from home, finds she can nurse her son Timmy as she works on the computer.

asked the gynecologist eleven months before the baby was born.) I was teaching and my husband's tuition was a 'perk' of my job at the college. I returned to work when Kathy was two months old. My husband arranged his schedule to care for her two days a week, a neighbor the other three. Kathy was breastfed for a year, thanks in part to my boss who had nursed her own two children and was as flexible with my schedule as administratively possible. My husband graduated and got a job when Kathy was sixteen months old, and I cut back to teaching two days a week and began working at home doing course development projects for my former boss.

"I have a second baby, now ten months old, and a contract from my former boss for a one-year course development project. I have a large sewing table in the dining room to hold the computer and some materials; the rest are under the table. (Luckily the baby is a scooter and I can distract him before he gets to the papers that are within his reach!) I write when he naps, proofread and run the printer when he is playing. I can, and often do, run the printer with one hand while holding and nursing him. As soon as my husband is off to work and my daughter catches the bus, I start writing and keep it up until the baby wakes up."

This setup has proved to be a good one for Leslie and her family. "Everything seems to be going fine," she says, "but when deadlines approach and the baby is having a fussy day, things get hectic!

"I could easily be making four times as much money," Leslic admits, "but money isn't everything. I wouldn't have missed the baby's first year for anything."

Arrangements such as these minimize the risks associated with being self-employed, while enabling the mother to be with her baby most, if not all, of the time, while still continuing to earn a living and keep up her professional skills.

Those who opt for free-lance or self-employment quickly realize that there are minuses as well as pluses to contend with. When you work for yourself, you forgo the luxury of leaving the office at 5:00 P.M. and forgetting about work until nine the next morning. You will work yourself harder than any boss could if you are an entrepreneur and any time you are not actually working you are thinking about a current project, the next job, a new prospect. . . . Perhaps one of the greatest challenges of being self-employed is rounding up enough discipline to put work completely out of your mind when you need to be resting, enjoying the baby, or just getting a psychological breath of fresh air.

Benefits for Society

Although the advantages for society of having work-at-home options available to a greater number of people have been talked about, they have not yet received the serious attention they deserve. Knowing that the typical worker commutes an average of eighteen miles per round trip to work, the next gasoline shortage may spur industry, labor, and government to combine forces and put some serious effort into making electronic cottages commonplace. Unclogging the highways and reducing automobile-induced air pollution would also have advantageous ripple effects. Many families would find they could get along with one car instead of two if one or more family members worked from home, and the one car would certainly last longer and need fewer repairs if the daily commute to work were eliminated.

Harder to measure but of incalculable importance is the humanization of work that is an inevitable byproduct of the ability to work at home. For families with infants or preschool children, the need for child care services, with the possible exception of an occasional sitter during peak periods, would be eliminated. A woman who works from home is free to care for and love her child as only she can, even though she is working at a terminal several hours a day. For the man who chooses the work-at-home option, there is a new-found opportunity to participate in the day-to-day joys and triumphs of the preschool years, so long denied to men who left for work at dawn and returned home long after the children's day had drawn to a close. No amount of Saturdays at the park or the zoo can compare with the bonding that occurs through day-to-day interaction with a growing baby.

The freedom to choose to work at home, whether at a computer terminal, a drafting board, or a potter's wheel, permits the complete integration of home and work, family life and work life, minimizing the need to choose one over the other and maximizing the potential for a satisfying, balanced blend of self-fulfillment through work and soul-satisfying relationships with those we love.

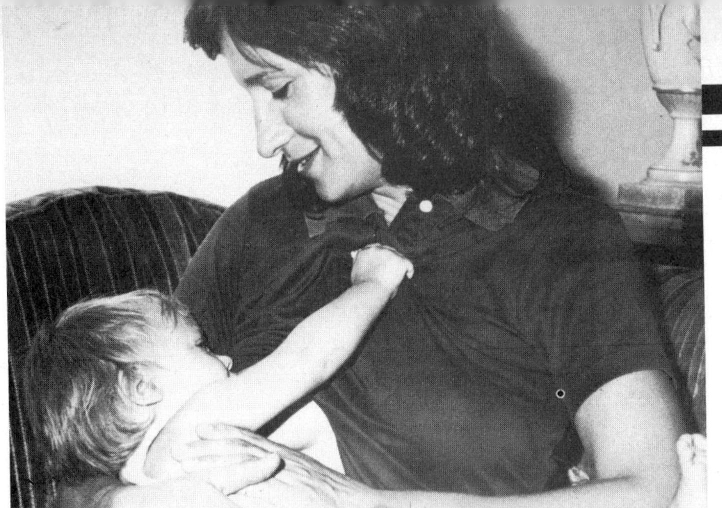

Part 3

The Reduced Workweek: Making it happen

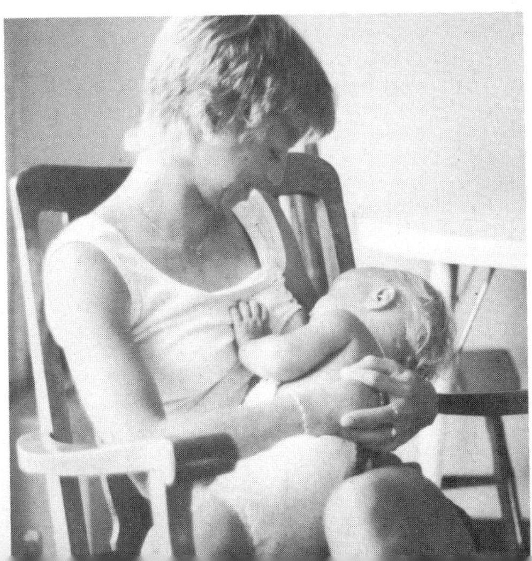

Chapter 9

Approaching Your Employer

Making it easy to say yes

Your abdomen is expanding, your due date is drawing closer, and you now realize with your head what your heart has known for some time. You don't want to leave your baby in someone else's care for ten or more hours a day during the crucial first months and years of his life. But you don't want to give up your job either.

It's time for a talk with your boss.

But this is no casual request you will be making. You will be asking him or her to restructure a job, institute a new policy, handle more paperwork, and develop different supervisory techniques. This presentation may well make arguing a case before the Supreme Court look like a stroll down Sesame Street. The burden of proof rests with you. Before agreeing to a modified working arrangement, your employer has to be convinced that he or she stands to gain through the arrangement you are proposing. Even if you perceive your employer to be a family-oriented person who would be sympathetic to your need to be able to mother your baby, he or she is a businessperson first and foremost, and as such will have to see where the benefits to the company are in the arrangement you are proposing before agreeing to give it a try.

The key to succeeding in having your job restructured was neatly summed up by FOCUS' Nancy Inui: You have to make it easy for them to say yes. Presenting all of the advantages of the arrangement from the employer's point of view and showing how any potential disadvantages will be avoided or compensated for should form the backbone of your presentation. Carefully think through the changes that will occur as a result of the restructuring. Anticipate and be prepared to respond to all of the disadvantages to the arrangement that your employer might bring up.

"You have to think this through from the employer's point of view and anticipate all of his questions," Ms. Inui advises. "Be very articulate and be very prepared. Don't make the mistake of bringing this up until you have had time to thoroughly prepare. You'll have to show significant advantages for the employer. Otherwise, it will look like a second class approach to the job."

"You want to talk to the employer about his or her concerns, not why you want to reduce your work hours," adds New Ways to Work's Barney Olmsted.

Nancy Inui of FOCUS

Both Nancy Inui and Dr. Diane Rothberg of the Association of Part-Time Professionals agree that it is not particularly important whether you have a written presentation to give to your employer, but you should have careful notes to work from as you make your case. You don't want to get sidetracked or flustered and forget to list some important advantages that could make the difference between winning the new arrangement or not.

If you have a specialized hard-to-find skill, or if the company has invested a great deal of time and money training you for your position, the odds of winning a modified working arrangement have just shifted heavily in your favor. The company then has a vested interest in keeping you on board and will be much more likely to be willing to work with you to come to terms on a reduced schedule that will be satisfactory to all.

For those who are not in such an enviable situation, "a lot of the success has to do with the salesmanship of the person making the proposal, and the reasonableness of the person receiving the proposal," Ms. Inui explains. "If you're talking to someone who just can't see anything less than a sixty-hour week, you're talking about a whole different view of life and the best proposal in the world doesn't stand a chance of success."

During the interview remember that you will be doing two things at once: selling yourself and selling a new idea, cautions Barney Olmsted. "Employers have a natural resistance to changing a situation which is satisfactory to them."

"Whether or not your boss is sympathetic to your desire to have more time with your baby depends on whether he feels women should be able to mix a career and a family, or whether he feels all women should stay home and raise their kids," says Ms. Olmsted.

Be specific about your plans, and be willing to work with your employer to find a workable compromise, suggests Mary Lou Maxie of New York's Buck Consulting, Inc.

"You need to start talking to your boss far enough in advance that arrangements can be made," Ms. Maxie says. "Give him or her enough time to start shuffling people. Your boss may want someone to work with you for several weeks before you leave so that person can become familiar with your job.

"Be specific. Know exactly what you are talking about. Present an exact timetable. 'I will be leaving on such-and-such a date and will be back three days a week on such-and-such a date.' "

A pleasant smile and a willing attitude will go a long way in this situation, the experts agree. "Don't be demanding," Ms. Maxie cautions. "You'll just be closing the door and putting your employer's back up against the wall. Smile. Be very nice. Go at it with a positive attitude. Remember that trying to work things out is advantageous for both you and the employer."

"We require the employee to show how the job will be restructured when he or she requests to move to less than full time," says Marion Gardner-Saxe of the First National Bank of Boston. "Usually it means that the professional will do only what is really worth her time, and that the rest will be absorbed by secretaries or administrators."

Ms. Gardner-Saxe reports that all of the part-time positions at the bank are working out well because "there were clearly defined goals and expectations on both sides. These women are not new to the bank, they know their jobs well, and they are valuable to the organization."

Any modified working arrangement means change and some companies, even in this fast-paced world, seem to pride themselves on being almost immune to change or innovation. Go easy, cause as few waves as possible, and remember that your first job is to make it easy for them to say yes.

A Plan of Action

Long before you make a presentation to your boss, you will want to carefully assess your company's previous experience with and attitude toward less-than-full-time working arrangements.

- The first order of business is to determine whether anyone else in the company has ever worked reduced hours, and if so what the rationale was for granting the request. Find out if the arrangement created any problems or if there were any negative repercussions so that you can be prepared with solutions when your employer points them out.

- Determine which people in the organization would be most agreeable to the change you are proposing, and which ones are most likely to oppose it. Line up as much support on your side as possible, and do whatever is reasonable or possible to win over or at least dilute the objections of the opposition. A well-thought-out and carefully executed strategy may have a decisive impact on the final outcome of your proposal.
- Assess the organization's attitude toward less-than-full-time employees. If their experience has been good, build on it. If they view part-timers as second class employees who are not serious about their jobs or their commitment to the company, you'll need to be prepared to show otherwise. Do your homework carefully in this area, because the burden of proof rests entirely with you.
- Come armed with examples of companies who have successfully employed part-timers, and check to see if there are any firms in your immediate area with good things to say about the quality and productivity of part-timers on their staff. Use the resource list in the back of this book for the names and addresses of national alternative work organizations that can be helpful to you.

The attitude of your immediate supervisor is likely to be of crucial importance. If he or she feels your plans are unworkable, or that the changes you are proposing will create management problems, the supervisor is likely to kill the idea before it has a chance to go any further.

No one wants extra work. You stand a greatly improved chance of winning your supervisor over if you can show that your arrangement won't place any additional burden on him or her, that it won't make his or her job any more complicated or time-consuming. Remind your boss that what would be time-consuming is training and supervising a new employee. Show that he or she will be time and money ahead to keep you instead of hiring someone new.

In its survey of 374 corporations, Catalyst asked who within a company was responsible for drafting the policies and practices. Sixty-five percent of the companies checked "Personnel Manager or Department," while another twenty-three percent checked "Senior Management Committee." This is important information to keep in mind as you plan your strategy for instituting change in your place of employment.

Job Security

There are prices to be paid for the luxury of part-time work, and one of them may be job security.

"It's better than it used to be, but working part-time is still a danger," says Barney Olmsted. "During the recession a lot of companies went back to the 'get rid of the part-timers' thinking. If you are in the professional classifications, there is less concern. A lot is determined by the organization's structure and attitude."

"Across the board, part-timers are more vulnerable," agrees Dr. Diane Rothberg. "They are considered more expendable."

"This situation won't change until we get more career-oriented part-timers in there," observes Ms. Olmsted.

Forewarned is forearmed. When negotiating a part-time schedule, if at all possible get your agreement in writing and try for a clause stating that your job security will not be affected by your part-time status.

Fringe Benefits

When moving to a less than full-time schedule, fringe benefits become another area of negotiation with your employer.

Historically, because part-timers were viewed as casual workers who worked sporadically in non-professional jobs as their mood or financial circumstances dictated, fringe benefits were almost never included. Most part-timers were students, seasonal workers, married women whose husbands had full-time jobs with full benefits, or unskilled workers who were viewed as not having a commitment to work in general or to a specific job in particular. Fringe benefits were not perceived as being particularly important to these workers, and as a group they did not press for them. A study conducted in 1972 revealed that the only fringe benefit received by most part-timers was vacation time. Some employers made a point of hiring part-timers specifically because they could avoid paying costly fringe benefits.

By the late 1970s, the picture had changed dramatically. The influx of women into the labor market, along with the enormous swelling they created among the ranks of professional part-time employees, made fringe benefits for less than full-time workers a suddenly important issue. Part-time or not, these women felt they were entitled to a proportion of the fringe benefits that would be given as a matter of course to a full-time employee in the same position. Because fringe benefits can account for 20% to 35% of the total salary package, they are a matter of considerable economic importance.

Today, studies indicate, more than half of all part-time employees receive fringe benefits, with the percentage of professional part-timers who are included in the benefits package probably much higher.

Some employers object to paying fringe benefits to part-timers on the basis that it is proportionately too costly. But in most instances, this is not the case.

"Mandatory benefits such as Social Security taxes only cost the employer more if there are two people sharing the job whose combined salaries exceed the base," explains Dr. Diane Rothberg, president of the Association of Part-Time Professionals. "Unemployment insurance varies from state to state, and may cost the employer more for a part-timer in some cases."

■ Restructuring a full-time job into a shared position is usually a time-consuming process.

Other than that, it is a fairly simple matter to prorate fringe benefits. Job sharers can easily divide the fringes, each paying half the cost of their health and life insurance, and splitting the vacation and sick days.

For other part-timers, the fringes can be prorated according to the number of hours worked. "More and more part-timers are getting the same fringe benefits as full-timers, on a prorated basis," Dr. Rothberg comments.

Retirement benefits and credit for years of service are other areas that should be clarified with your employer.

In some cases, most notably the health care field, part-time employees are paid a higher hourly rate in lieu of fringe benefits.

"We'd like to see employers begin to view the benefits as being attached to the position," says Barney Olmsted of New Ways To Work. "We hope that people will push hard on retaining health benefits. Married women are often covered by their spouses so it's not an issue for them, but those part-timers who need health insurance coverage should be entitled to get it from the employer, at least on a prorated basis." For part-timers who are single or for some other reason are not covered by a spouse's health care plan, health care coverage is an important issue. During these economically difficult times when more and more women are being thrown into the work force as the family's primary wage earner, health insurance for part-time employees has become a major concern. Once health coverage is offered as a matter of course to part-timers, those who do not need it may opt for a higher wage or other benefits.

As more professional part-timers use their positions as leverage to gain concessions from employers in the area of fringe benefits, fringes will become increasingly available to part-timers across the board. Unions may also jump in to begin filling the void in this area.

"There has been some movement on the part of unions to take up issues related to the part-time worker as more women enter the unions," Diane Rothberg observes. "Unions could use this as an opportunity to build more membership, by working for more fringe benefits for part-time workers."

Once again, the federal government is clearly the best employer in terms of fringe benefits provided for part-timers. All federal employees who work sixteen or more hours a week are entitled to fringe benefits on a prorated basis.

One company cited in *The Job Sharing Handbook* provides full health and dental benefits to all part-time employees because "cost analysis indicates that reduced absenteeism and savings on overtime offset that expense."

"The inclusion of part-timers into fringe benefits packages is a definite trend," Barney Olmsted notes.

Part-time employees need not be shy about requesting a reasonable percentage of the benefits provided for the company's full-time employees. As more professional part-timers push for benefits, particularly health insurance, either because they need it or because they feel that the position itself merits having benefits included as part of the salary package, the full range of fringe benefits will become increasingly available to all part-timers.

Proposing a Shared Job

If you have decided on job sharing as the best alternative to the forty hour workweek, the advice from the experts is to start early because restructuring a full-time job into a shared position is usually a time-consuming process. New Ways to Work's *How to Split or Share Your Job* reports that, "The experience of people who have tried to convince their organization to allow job sharing has demonstrated that it is most often a slow, arduous process, averaging around six to eight months. It requires a lot of patience, determination, and commitment on the part of potential job sharers."

You will be points ahead if both you and your partner are already employed by the company. That makes both of you known quantities, and increases the chances that the employer will opt for the inconvenience of splitting a job rather than losing one or both of you as valued employees.

Both you and your partner should apply for the job together, pointing out that the company will be receiving the talents of two for the price of one, that you can reduce or eliminate absenteeism by covering for each other, that there will be two of you to cope with time pressures and deadlines, that you have anticipated and solved any potential problems, and that your complementary personalities and skills will enable you to function well together as a team.

"You may want to impress the employer with your similar backgrounds and interchangeable skills, or you may wish to stress the wide range of skills and experience the two of you will bring to the position, Barney Olmsted and Suzanne Smith suggest in *The Job Sharing Handbook*.

Whatever alternative arrangements you are seeking, it is important to leave the employer with the feeling, as JoAnne Alter points out in *A Part-Time Career for a Full-Time You*, that "rather than being a source of continuing confusion and disorganization, you will offer stability and competence."

If your best efforts have failed to win your employer over to your side, suggest that he or she allow your alternative work arrangement for a six-month trial period. This minimizes the risks involved, while maximizing your opportunity to demonstrate that your proposed reduced schedule will work.

If approval for your plan is granted reluctantly, you'll need to go an extra five miles to dispel the doubts surrounding your arrangement. The burden of proof, and the ultimate responsibility for making the restructured job a success, almost always rests with the employee. Remember that in this situation the supervisor has to cope with two new employees and one new way to work.

The Time Is Right

Even though your request for less than a full-time schedule may make you feel like a lone crusader trying to fight off the villains of apathy and resistance to progress, the tide of social change is on your side. As more and more women acquire specialized skills and move into positions of responsibility and influence, and as more and more of these women opt to start a family during the peak years of their careers, the simple economics of the situation dictates that alternative work options will become increasingly commonplace throughout the next decade.

These women want to maintain their careers without sacrificing their babies in the process, and companies can ill afford to lose the investment they have in their professional female staff members. With time, the concessions won by these professional women will trickle down and benefit women in nearly every occupational and skill category. Nearly all of the work alternatives experts agree that the option to choose a reduced workweek will be offered as a matter of course within the next generation.

With it will come the freedom to find fulfillment and satisfaction in the career of molding personalities and shaping destinies. As this new generation of career women-mothers is discovering, no silver gavel or string of promotions can compete with the lifetime smile that is etched on their hearts because someone calls them mother.

Chapter 10

Maternity Leave
Historical perspectives, legal directives

Career women, and especially career women who establish themselves before even starting a family instead of after the youngest child is safely off to school all day, are such a relatively new phenomenon that the business world has been largely at a loss when faced with a pregnant professional employee who wants to continue working in some capacity after her baby is born.

Gone are the days when women dropped out of the work force the day they got married. In the not so distant past, those few independent souls who continued working after the ring was on their finger were expected to quit promptly as soon as a pregnancy was confirmed, certainly before they started to "show." Why it was so important not to work and "show" at the same time is unclear, although it probably had a lot to do with the prevailing feeling, particularly among men, that all women belonged at home, especially pregnant ones.

As pregnant professional employees began turning up with more and more frequency in the late 60s and early 70s, employers handled the situation on a very individualized basis. Some made it clear that the woman was no longer welcome (in 1964, 40% of all employers terminated pregnant employees), while others provided generous maternity leaves and encouraged the new mother to stay at home as long as she felt she needed to before returning to work. Many women, partly out of fear of losing their jobs, and partly to prove they were still the best corporate men in the organization even though they had just given birth, were back at their desks almost within moments after the umbilical cord was cut.

Maternity leave was largely a free-for-all in the U.S.A. until 1978 when the federal government stepped in with the Pregnancy Disability Act which mandated that pregnancy must be treated like any other medical disability. Women giving birth had to be given the same leave time as employees with other disabilities, which usually translated into six to eight weeks of paid leave, with a guarantee that the woman's job and salary would be held for her. As the law now stands, those who want to extend their time off by taking an unpaid leave or using accumulated vacation time, do so at their own risk. In such cases, the law no longer protects their job or salary.

For women who may have felt compelled to leave week-old infants to rush back to work in order to protect their jobs, the act was a godsend. For women whose employers had formerly provided generous compensation and long term leaves, the act deprived them of the important time needed to bond with their infants and become comfortable with the new demands and challenges of motherhood.

"The law did help some women, but it didn't help a whole bunch of others," explains Pat Ibbs, associate editor of *Spencer Reports,* an employee benefits publication for Fortune 1000 companies. Before the passage of the Pregnancy Disability Act, many employers were much more liberal concerning maternity leave, with many willing to give long unpaid leaves of absence, she adds.

But with the passage of the act, "They had to worry about discrimination problems against men if they treated women employees differently." The law requires that pregnancy be treated exactly like any other medical disability. "If an employer extends disability leave for one employee," such as a woman giving birth, "he would have to extend it for all," Ms. Ibbs explains.

John Galvin of the Women's Bureau, Bureau of Labor Statistics, confirms that most companies are now doing no more and no less than what is required by law.

"My impression is that most companies tend to follow the law," he observes. "They say, 'I've complied with the law, so that's all I have to do.' "

But the birth of a baby is *not* like other medical disabilities. In fact, as women glowing with pride while they hold their newborn babies well know, it is not a disability at all. As Meg Wheatley and Marcie Schorr Hirsch put it in *Managing Your Maternity Leave,* "Maternity leave has become such a problematic issue because of the way pregnancy has been defined in America. Legally, and in most eyes substantively, pregnancy is considered a disability, no different from any other medical problem. By lumping pregnancy and maternity leave in with all other medical disabilities, organizations have been relieved of thinking through arrangements and options that would more appropriately fill the needs of new parents and their babies. And the pregnant worker is left in the difficult position of finding ways to express the physical and emotional demands of her condition. . . . Nearly all women find that the benefits provided by their employers fall far short of their needs. They are left to their own devices, either to return to work too early for their own and their child's welfare, or to negotiate an individualized leave plan. . . ."

■ The birth of a baby is not like other medical disabilities.

Sharyn Stolzenbach, a psychiatric registered nurse, found herself in just such a situation. She was given only a thirty day leave, plus accumulated sick leave, vacation, and holidays which totaled seven weeks. "Because of the short leave allowed, I had to work right up until I went into labor—or otherwise my position would not be held for me if my time off exceeded the seven weeks. I, of course, wanted my time off to be spent with the baby rather than waiting at home to go into labor. Never again! No job is worth the amount of physical and psychological stress it takes to work until the last moment. I was tired before my nineteen hour labor began."

Veronica Peregrim Gliniak, a project engineer with a large international corporation, was not happy being forced to return to work full time after fourteen weeks of leave (admittedly a generous leave by most standards). "My husband did not have a job after graduation in June, and was not getting a good response to his resumé at the time my employer notified me that I must return to work or lose my job," she explains.

"I resented having to return to work so early, and I was very fatigued. My work projects were changed, requiring more out of town overnight travel. In effect, the company was saying either 'we don't want you' or 'prove yourself—prove you can be a mother and still hold this position.' "

A flight attendant with a major airline, who asked to remain unidentified, found her employer equally unwilling to recognize the needs of a mother and newborn infant.

"My employer could care less about accommodating nursing mothers," she reports. "Even with an allergist's letter saying my son had an allergic reaction to formula, their attitude was, 'no leaves for breastfeeding, no matter what' and 'it's not in your union's contract that nursing mothers must be accommodated, so if you want your job, back to work.' I think they would like senior flight attendants to quit in disgust so they could keep junior flight attendants working at the cheapest rate of pay. My co-workers, many of whom were or are nursing mothers, have been sympathetic and supportive, even though many did say they gave up nursing sooner than they wanted to because of the difficulties of schedules and the sheer exhaustion both from new baby pressures and jet lag."

The Winds of Change

Happily, there are some glimmers of light at the end of the tunnel. Some progressive companies have accurately assessed the situation, and are offering child care leaves to parents who want additional time beyond six weeks to be with their babies full time.

American Telephone and Telegraph instituted a child care leave in 1979 which entitles natural or adoptive parents—both mothers and fathers—of infant children to a six-month unpaid leave. The company guarantees a job with the same rank and pay when the leave is over and the employee returns to work.

The Reuben H. Donnelley Company, a subsidiary of Dunn and Bradstreet with 18,000 employees in the United States and 25,000 employees worldwide, provides its employees with the option of a six-month unpaid personal leave on request. The leave can be taken for any reason, and "child rearing is as good a reason as any for a personal leave," explains Eric Rambusch, Director of Human Resources.

Rambusch adds that Reuben H. Donnelley's personal leave policy "just evolved. We don't have maternity disability or child rearing leave policies. They are treated like any other medical disability or personal leave."

The policy has been in effect for about six years, and, like AT&T, Donnelley guarantees a comparable job at a comparable salary upon the employee's return.

"You can't hold a specific job for six months in an office environment," Rambusch explains, "but we do guarantee that the same or a comparable job will be available when they come back."

While it would be nice to think that these changes were being made out of concern for the welfare of the mother and her new baby, and in some cases this is no doubt the case, hard economic realities are behind policy changes in most cases. As a bank executive quoted in *Managing Your Maternity Leave* says, "When enough good women leave because your policies are not compatible with their needs, you change—and we did."

Clearly, the direction of change is in favor of being more responsive to the needs of new mothers and their infants. As more and more women request provisions for extended leaves, and companies are faced with the choice of accommodating the women or losing their valued employees, policies will emerge that will give recognition to the fact that many employees—whether it's a new mother with an infant to love and care for, or a male in his 40s who needs a lengthy breather for reasons of his own—need the option of taking several months of leave when their personal circumstances dictate.

Once again, the U.S. government is among the leaders when it comes to providing generous leaves which are particularly well-suited to the needs of a woman with a new baby.

"The federal policy is one of the best in the country," says John Galvin of the Bureau of Labor Statistics. "There is no maternity leave as such in the federal government, but women can take advance annual leave, saved annual leave, sick leave, advance sick leave, or leave without pay."

The arrangements are subject to the agency head's approval, "but having a baby would be a priority situation," Galvin reports. "Government personnel policies are broad enough to cover a variety of needs."

"Most employers, as long as someone else can cover the job or the job can be left 'on hold,' will allow the mother to take a few more months as a leave of absence with a guarantee that her job will be there when she returns," says Mary Lou Maxie of New York's Buck Consulting, Inc.

Mary Lou Maxie

This holds true most often at the professional and managerial level for people with training or specialized skills who would be somewhat difficult to replace. "Most employers are willing to cooperate as long as it doesn't disrupt things. They know that this way they will have an employee who is happy, who is eager to come back when she is ready, instead of resenting the fact that she has to be there when she doesn't want to be," Ms. Maxie adds.

And when these women are ready to come back to work, many employers are willing to let them come back two or three days a week instead of five, at least for a while, Ms. Maxie reports. "They know that the mother is going to feel better if she doesn't just disappear from the baby's life except for weekends."

Professional career women, due to a combination of factors, are blazing the trail when it comes to asking for and receiving child care leaves. Most are in their 30s before having a baby, with many years spent establishing themselves in their professions. Companies are willing to bend in order to retain these women, even if it means granting several months of unpaid leave. Most of these women are married to men who also earn substantial salaries, making it economically feasible for them to take several months off without pay. As concessions are granted to these women, company policies will evolve which will benefit all women in the organization.

Generally speaking, the longer you have been with your employer and the harder you would be to replace, the better your chances are of winning an extended maternity leave, if such provisions do not already exist.

Check first to see exactly what your company's policy is concerning the kind of leave you would like to take. Even if your findings are discouraging, make your request anyway.

"There can be a great difference between a company's printed word and their actual policy," observes Pat Ibbs of *Spencer Reports,* especially where valued employees are concerned.

Companies that tend to be especially generous are large, progressive firms, or smaller, family-oriented companies that feel women need and deserve time off with a new baby, according to Mary Lou Maxie.

It is best to start early, soon after you realize you are pregnant, to assess the company's policy, Ms. Maxie advises. That way you'll have time to negotiate an individual agreement if necessary, and the employer will have time to make necessary adjustments and shifts in personnel. If special arrangements are being made for you, be sure to get it in writing so you are assured that your job will be waiting for you when you return.

The doors to the right to an extended maternity leave are beginning to crack open, and as more and more women request this option, the resistance on the other side will continue to lessen. The ultimate gain is well worth the effort involved.

As Meg Wheatley and Marcie Shorr Hirsch put it, "Your time at home now is a rare opportunity, never to come again, to get to know two fascinating people—you, as a mother, and your wonderful new baby."

Chapter 11

Starting from Scratch

Finding a new job with modified hours

Your best chance of getting an extended maternity leave or adapting a job to fit a modified working schedule is to stay with your current employer. If you are already a valued full-time employee, you are far more likely to be able to win some modifications than if you applied for a new job as an unknown quantity.

But if your present job precludes anything less than forty hours a week and/or does not permit as long of a maternity leave as you would like to have, don't despair. There are plenty of places to look where the odds of finding a modified work schedule will be more in your favor.

Where to Look

The United States government outshines all other public and private enterprises as the country's most progressive and innovative employer. If you are starting from scratch, a government job offers the best prospects for a professional position requiring less than forty hours a week. As the country's largest employer, Uncle Sam hires in every imaginable field at every conceivable skill level, so, whatever your talent, there is probably a need for it by the federal government.

Many state and even some local governments are following suit by specifying that certain positions must be made available on a part-time or shared basis. Keep knocking on government doors until you find the one that opens. As JoAnne Alter says, "In any bureaucracy, one office frequently has no idea what the next office is doing. If you have no success with the centralized personnel office, ask what state, county, or municipal agencies you might contact directly, and get in touch with them."

According to a report from Catalyst, "Large companies were more likely (48%) than small companies (26%) to offer flexible working hours and to favor flexible working hours. And large scale companies were more likely to favor flexible workplaces than small scale companies. (40% as opposed to 27%) . . . Large scale companies were more likely to offer leave without pay with position assured upon return (72%) than were small scale companies (55%)."

If you are a teacher, you are in the right place at the right time to land a shared position. Job sharing is particularly well suited to the classroom situation where the position is easily divisible by time and task, and progressive school systems are at last beginning to capitalize on their ability to get the talents and energy of two teachers for the price of one.

As school populations continue to decline, many people in the education field think that job sharing will become an increasingly common way to reduce the number of layoffs that would otherwise be necessary.

"Teachers and social workers were the first to get part-time options," says Barney Olmsted, "because many employees were females who had family responsibilities." A second impetus, particularly for teachers, was that "The economy began to dry up there earlier. The crunch hit the teachers in the early 70s. They've had the pressure on longer." Ms. Olmsted points out. The advantage for any job seeker in these two professions is that, "There are already role models and policy models. You don't have to start from scratch."

"Alternatives are most likely to be found in workplaces that are responsive to the needs of their employees," says Ms. Olmsted. She advises looking for a particular management style for a good indication of the company's receptiveness to part-time professionals. "Remember that organizations have personalities, too."

In her study of job sharing, Gretl Meier reports that "Generally, teams are employed by relatively small institutions." Forty-one percent of the job sharing teams in her study worked in organizations of 100 or fewer employees. Almost one-third worked in companies with 100 to 500 employees. Job sharing is still in its infancy, as evidenced by the fact that 41% of the respondents said that there were no other job sharers in their organization.

Ms. Meier also found that, "Although all but a small percentage

■ Lynda Dunal, Occupational Therapist

When Patrick was five months old, I began to look for part-time work. I wanted to continue nursing my baby, but I wanted to get back into the work force as an occupational therapist. I do enjoy it and I missed it while I was staying home full time. By looking for a new job, I was able to find one to suit both my baby and myself.

I found that in a position with the Community Occupational Therapist Association (COTA). I work a twenty-five hour week and I have the freedom to set my own hours.

There are more than fifty occupational therapists working for COTA and many are mothers. My boss has been very supportive of my needs, and of the challenges that face a new mother returning to the work force. I had to cancel one or two meetings when the baby was sick, and the other staff members were very understanding—they have children, too.

I particularly enjoy my flexible part-time status because I was able to go home and nurse Patrick at noon until he was ready to take solids and stretch out the time between nursings. I am able to stay home with him when he is sick. I can pick him up early in the afternoon, and I can take an occasional day off to spend with him. ■

of job sharers are employed by non-profit institutions, it is important to note that 26% of these are in the private sector, with public institutions, education, and government accounting for the rest."

Don't overlook your professional organization, trade association, or union when looking for an alternative working arrangement. Many jobs, especially the really desirable ones, never make it to the want ad pages. They are filled by word of mouth, often on the basis of a personal recommendation. Those currently employed in your field are likely to have the most up-to-date and accurate information about job openings that may fit your needs.

Remember that each of us knows 300 or more people. This is no time to be shy. Tell everyone you know that you are looking for a modified working arrangement. Be specific about your skills and strong points, and ask who they know who might be able to help you. The merchandise that is most prominently displayed is usually the first to be sold. Advertise yourself through all of your friends and associates.

To Tell or Not to Tell

When submitting resumés cold to firms that have advertised full-time openings, all of the experts agree that it's best not to indicate at the beginning that you are looking for reduced hours. The first prerequisite is to convince the company that they need your skills. Once they are sure they want you, you can talk about working less than forty hours a week.

"Part-time is a red flag," warns FOCUS' Nancy Inui. You are ahead to sell yourself positively during the interview, generating enough interest in the things you have to offer the company that they'll be willing to listen to your need to work less than full time."

"Apply for the job just like any other candidate," advises Dr. Diane Rothberg. "Don't mark part-time on your resumé. You'll never get in the door."

Find out everything you can about the job, advises Dr. Rothberg. Know how it can be split or shared or done on less than a full-time basis. Talking to a long-term employee in the company can provide important inside information that may help you in presenting your case.

"It may also be helpful to look at the company's annual report," Barney Olmsted and Suzanne Smith suggest in *The Job Sharing Handbook*. "It can give you a sense of what the organization is like. If all of the photographs are of buildings and machinery, you get a certain feeling about the company's priorities."

If you are applying for a job and don't already have a baby or one on the way, speak to prospective employers about the possibility of reduced hours anyway, so that if you should decide to start a family at some time in the future you'll know what you will be up against. If a hard-to-find skill gives you the upper hand in an employment situation, you may wish to have a written agreement that the company will work out a reduced workweek with you if you request it following the birth of a baby.

If your skills are less in demand and you would be unlikely to win such a concession up front, it will still be to your advantage to get a feel of how receptive a particular company would be to a future request for part-time work. Such information may influence your decision about which job offer to accept. At the very least, it will let you know ahead of time how much or how little difficulty you can expect.

If you have sold a company on hiring you, but they are still skeptical about a part-time arrangement, offer to work for three months without obligation. Then prove yourself and the viability of the arrangement.

■ Tell everyone you know that you are looking for a modified working arrangement.

Margaret Risk-Bryan works as an editor on a free-lance basis for the same publications department where she was employed part-time before she became pregnant with her second baby. Margaret originally took this particular job with an eye toward having a second child and being able to continue working for this company on a free-lance basis.

"My employer was willing to talk about a future at-home working arrangement at the time I was interviewed for the job," Margaret explains. "Complications developed during the pregnancy, and I had to stay in bed for four months. My employer agreed that I should begin working at home during that time.

"Now, when there is editing to be done, I pick up the work at the office (taking my baby along with me) and bring it home. I work at a desk in the family room in between doing things for my family. Fortunately, it is the kind of work that can be done in snatches of time, without requiring undivided attention for sustained periods."

As an added bonus, Margaret says she has had "nothing but positive cooperation" from her associates.

Susan McTigue* decided to "retire" from her full-time position as a museum curator and administrator to become a full-time mother before her first child was born. "I felt some guilt and regret at leaving my job, but I had no intention of letting someone else raise my baby. However, I felt it would be demoralizing and wasteful to completely walk away from a field I love and for which I spent so many years being educated, so I began a small, *very* part-time business at home framing and selling original engravings."

*See chapter 17 for more information on Susan McTigue

Susan's husband converted a large basement closet into a work area. Susan explains, "I rarely spend more than a few hours a week at this job, and fortunately my husband's income is such that my small business does not have to be financially successful. While it hasn't produced much income, it has provided me with a great deal of pleasure and allowed me to maintain at least some contacts in the art world. I feel that I am weaving a thread between my past professional career and the future one I will pursue when my children are older."

Although the work she is doing now is more of a creative outlet than a professional commitment, Susan observes, "The lifestyle I have chosen has made me a happier person, with no regrets about trading in my art career for my new career as mother."

Looking for any job is hard work; looking for a professional part-time position is harder still. "Hang in there," advises Barney Olmsted. "It doesn't come easily, but it does come. Don't take the first turn down as the end of the line."

Blazing a Trail

After all, what you're doing is trail-blazing and trail-blazing, by definition, involves creating a path where none existed before. Wrong turns and dead ends are often part of the process. But, for those who persevere, so is success.

Part 4

Beyond Career: Achieving harmony at home

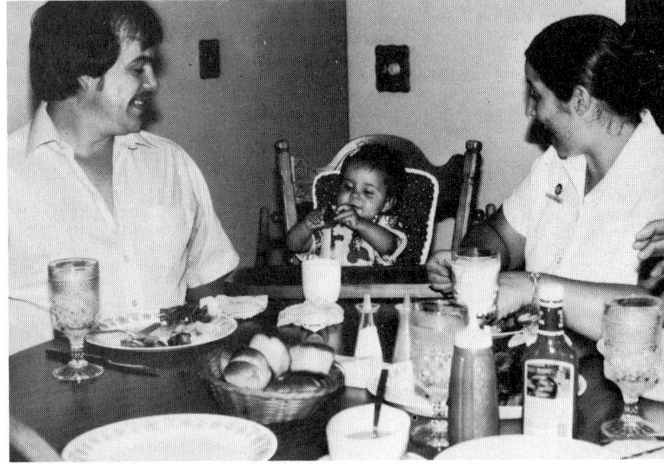

Chapter 12

The New Father
Partner in his child's future

An interesting thing happened on the day mother walked out the door to go to work. On the way down the front walk she brushed shoulders with dad, who had come home to claim his rightful place in the mainstream of family life.

With his wife now gainfully employed and young children at home to be cared for, there was suddenly a great void on the home front. With grandma hundreds of miles away, and in many cases holding down a job of her own, it fell to dad to fill that void.

But these husbands and fathers, many of whom had been raised by a typical 1950s father whose chief involvement with his children had been to pay the bills and administer the discipline, happily seized this opportunity to become full partners in the rearing of their children.

The women's liberation movement of the 1960s not only freed women to find fulfillment outside the home, but it also liberated men from the burden of bearing complete responsibility for the family's financial well-being. As women began contributing to the family income, it relieved some of the pressure on men, who began to realize they wouldn't be jeopardizing hearth and home if they dropped back a notch in the corporate race.

When fathers like John Pledger develop a closer relationship with their children, the whole family reaps the rewards.

With wives sharing the financial burden and husbands pitching in to help with child care and household responsibilities, many of the rigid sex stereotypes of the last century began to soften. As women discovered what life outside of the home had to offer, men began to see what they had been missing by being away from home so much.

Glenn Collins, in a *New York Times* article titled "New Perspectives on Father and His Role," quotes Dr. James Herzog of the Harvard University School of Medicine as saying that the concept of father as merely a secondary caretaker is a relatively new development. Dr. John Demos, professor of history at Brandeis University, is quoted in the same article as saying that in Colonial times "Once infants were past the age of breastfeeding, fathers spent most of their time in the presence of their children. It is a picture, above all, of active, encompassing fatherhood, woven into the whole fabric of domestic and productive life."

The article goes on to point out that "throughout the 1800s, virtually all human relationships were shaped by a vast system of what modern sociologists would call sex role stereotyping. Women and men were thought to occupy different spheres appropriate to entirely different characters."

The article concludes by quoting Dr. John Munder Ross, clinical associate professor of psychiatry at Downstate Medical Center in New York, as saying, "A more involved style of fathering is catching on because it is an expression of basic, gut emotion that fathers have always felt as well as the social forces that have made it necessary."

Working As a Team

As we analyzed the information from the hundreds of women who shared their experiences with us for this book, one fact became increasingly evident: These dual career couples are truly sharing, working together as a team, to make a home and raise their children. For these families, there is no concept of it being "his job" to go out and earn a living and "her job" to stay home and wash dishes and raise the kids. With both spouses employed outside of the home, both spouses pitch in *at* home. And the wonderful dividend, as we heard over and over again, is that by being real participants in their children's lives, fathers are reaping a joy and satisfaction in parenting that had for so long been available only to mothers.

"My husband has become deeply involved in our son's care," explains college professor Merike Tamm. "He is very glad I am working because it gives him more time to be with Aleksander. He has said that if I hadn't gone to work he would not have developed such a close relationship with, and would not have learned so much about, his son."

"My daughter and my husband have been able to develop a great closeness due to his really taking care of her," observes Patricia Street, a part-time secretary with the California State Legislature.

Clinical microbiologist Linda Caplan, whose husband often cares for their two preschoolers while she works, reports, "Having their father provide for their total care on weekends is a wonderful way to strengthen their relationship and to give him a realistic picture of parenting."

Nurse Sharon O'Shaughnessy, who has a nine-and-a-half-month-old baby, observes, "Our son and his father are very close. They have a beautiful relationship."

▪ These couples are truly working together as a team to make a home and raise their children.

Attorney Susan Miele sums up her feelings this way: "One of the biggest benefits of my returning to work has been the amount of time the baby gets to be with her father *alone*. Somehow, when I'm around, I'm always 'in charge,' when it comes to child care. This way, they both really pay attention to each other. My husband is European and speaks only Italian to the baby—she's becoming bilingual already."

"My working has given my husband more child care responsibilities, which has brought the three of us closer," says Nancy Wolkenhauer who is employed by Amtrak.

Lenna Foster, who has a fourteen-month-old son, says, "Deklin is really getting close to his dad. I went back to work when he was twelve months old, so I think he was ready for the separation. It's also been great for his dad; their relationship is really blossoming."

"Kathryn has grown closer to her father," echoes teacher Shelagh Peterson, who does tutoring in the evenings.

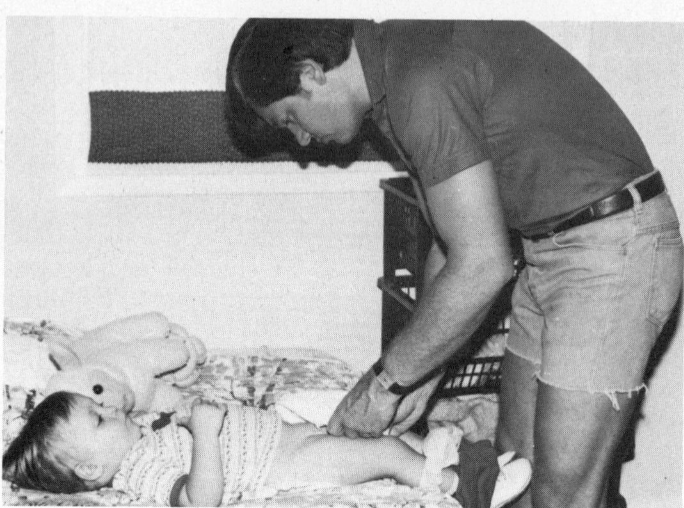

Fathers are becoming real participants in their children's lives: (l to r) Paul Stolzenbach enjoys bathtime with daughter Kendra; Don Carlyle changes son Kevin's diaper; Michael Lupia offers a bite of banana to his father, Tom; D'Arcy Dunal visits the park with his son, Patrick.

"My husband takes care of our son on Saturdays and on Monday evenings," says bridal consultant Phyllis Carlyle, "and father and son have a most precious relationship."

"Taking responsibility for our son on a regular basis has been good for the relationship between my husband and son," reports nurse Carol Smith.

An article titled "Superwomen Find They Need A Little Help" by Anita Shreve confirms what these women already know—that the support and active participation on the home front by the father is vital to the success of a two career family. Ms. Shreve continues:

> It is clear that, across the country, the definition of "father" is beginning to change. No longer the shadowy absentee authority figures of a previous generation, men are falling in love with their babies and becoming more comfortable with nurturing. It is no longer unusual, for instance, to see a group of fathers at the playground, briefcases parked along the fence, pushing their kids on the swings and chatting among themselves about growth and development—not of corporations, but of toddlers. Certainly some are single fathers, but many have wives at home or at work.

Causing a Stir

This new breed of fathers is causing some of the same upheavals in the business world that the "new woman" caused a decade ago. While not so long ago a man felt that his involvement in his baby's life was properly limited to pacing the floor in the fathers' waiting

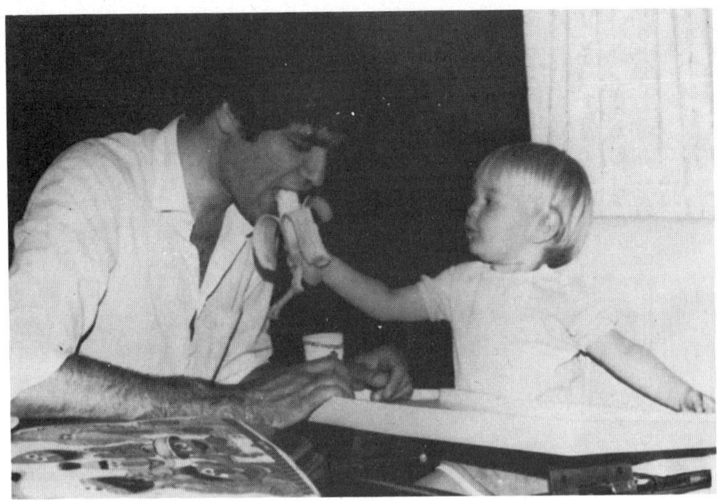

room, today's men are not only at their wife's side during childbirth, but they are asking for the right to stay home and help raise the baby as well.

Though it is still somewhat rare for a man to take an extended leave following the birth of the couple's baby, AT&T, the Reuben H. Donnelley Company, and the U.S. government were cited in Chapter 10 as employers willing to grant protected child care leaves to either parent. The American Broadcasting Company and CBS also provide for protected child care leaves for both men and women, but the National Broadcasting Company doesn't—and has been sued because of it.

Robert Batsche, an NBC engineer in New York, wanted a six-month leave of absence—the same leave available to female employees of NBC—following the birth of the couple's baby. Since his wife is an airline stewardess who flies to Europe and is gone for several days at a time, Batsche wanted to take a leave of absence in order to care for the baby and help ease his wife's return to work. The case is scheduled to be heard by the United States Supreme Court. Such requests for extended paternity leave are sure to multiply as increasing numbers of couples search for ways to handle dual careers and child care responsibilities.

Another trend that is also likely to become more common as the number of two career couples increases is for the father to reduce his work schedule while the mother continues to work full time. This arrangement is sometimes the couple's first choice, or, as in the case of Marilyn Harris, a district manager for AT&T, the only choice.

Marilyn took a year's leave of absence following the birth of her baby, and upon her return to work she broached the possibility of a less than full-time schedule.

"I inquired about working part-time at AT&T," she explains, "but found that management viewed all jobs at my level (supervisory) as full-time jobs. Management here is still rather inflexible on the subject of part-time work, equating it with part-time commitment to job responsibility.

"However, my husband was able to modify his work hours with Bell Labs due to his department's commitment to Affirmative Action. He now works five-hour days, five days a week. There are one or two women in his department who are also working shorter hours.

"My husband's co-workers congratulate him on his commitment to fathering. My husband holds home and family as a high priority, and enjoys his shorter week and extra time with our son.

"But I do wish I could be the one working part-time."

Shared Responsibilities

While as yet few men are asking for extended leaves to help care for their children, men *are* becoming involved in their children's lives in ways that only a few years ago would have been unthinkable for most men. A father who does the dishes and the laundry and drops the children off at preschool in the morning is no longer considered less masculine; he's regarded as a person carrying his rightful share of household responsibilities. The sight of a father doing the grocery shopping with an infant strapped to his chest in a baby carrier is no longer the object of stares and speculation. Men have even been overheard around the office coffee machine discussing the relative merits of disposables versus diaper service.

But the new father's involvement goes much deeper than dishes and diapers. "Fathers appear to have far more capacity to nurture little children than was formerly thought," according to an article titled "The New Fatherhood" which appeared in *Parents Magazine*. "Present research underscores the importance of fathers being involved even in early infancy. For example, in families where the father is emotionally supportive, the mother does a better job of breastfeeding, according to a study by psychologist Frank Pedersen of the National Institute of Child Health and Human Development. Fathers also contribute a special style, a unique rhythm, to infant play; they romp and roughhouse more than mothers. They also tend to stimulate more exploratory behavior and less stereotyped forms of play."

But as fathers get closer to their children, they find themselves faced with the same conflicts that have haunted working women:

Fathers like Dave Holmberg, shown here with Kelsey, add a special dimension to their children's lives.

How to balance the demands of a career with the needs of the children in such a way that both prosper and neither suffers.

"There is evidence that fatherhood is at least as important to men as career success," the *Parents Magazine* article continues. "Contrary to stereotype, according to Joseph Pleck, program director at the Wellesley College Center for Research on Women, men report far greater psychological involvement with their families than their jobs, and family experience contributes more than work experience to their overall well-being."

Achieving a new, comfortable-for-all balance between work and family will undoubtedly be the priority issue for the dual career family of the 80s.

Chapter 13

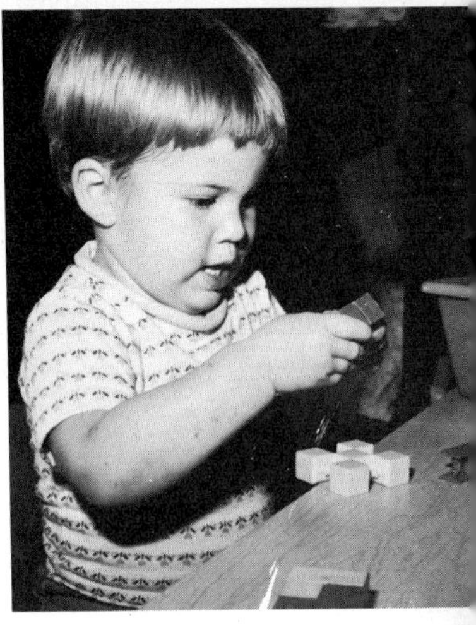

Who Will Care for the Baby?
Choices in child care

There is a whole generation of American women who have grown up enraptured by the adult fairy tale of our times. You know, the you-can-have-it-all fairy tale that promises a fulfilling career, a loving husband, and an adorable baby. It doesn't even require a magic wand. Just wishing for it will make it come true.

But like all other fairy tales, this one leaves many questions unanswered. Such as, who's caring for the baby? How does the mother feel when she starts her workday knowing she's left a sobbing toddler behind? What happens when the baby's earache and an important business commitment collide head-on?

Few of us have any idea of the realities of what lies ahead when we plan on incorporating a baby into an already overfull schedule. Caring for an infant is itself a full-time job, as the uninitiated quickly discover during the first week home from the hospital. How such an adorable seven pounds of humanity can create more laundry than a football team, need less sleep than any insomniac, have more lung power than the Dallas Cowboys' cheerleaders, and require as much packing for an afternoon at grandma's as a world traveler needs for a year abroad are mysteries that have defied the most brilliant minds of our times.

More amazing still is this supposedly helpless creature's ability to make the two previously sane and sensible adults who are wrestling with all of this feel as if they are the luckiest people alive because he belongs to them!

Maternal-Infant Attachment

There seems to be a direct, proportional relationship between the importance women are led to believe they should attach to their careers and the strength of the feelings they are led to believe they will have for their babies. As our society has placed increased emphasis on the fulfillment a woman can expect through gainful employment, it has downplayed the depth of the love she will feel for her newborn baby. No wonder so many career women, far removed from sisters, cousins, or others they can observe at close range with their infants, are so totally surprised by the intense love they feel for their babies.

Many women do, for a variety of reasons, go back to work after their babies are born. But we don't believe any mother, no matter what she was told or what she thought before her baby was born, finds it easy to leave her infant in someone else's care. Mothers and babies need each other. Even though the umbilical cord has been cut, they are still emotionally and physically dependent on one another, just as nature intended them to be. Intense feelings of maternal attachment have been responsible for safeguarding the survival of the human race for 2,000 years. No twentieth century career, no matter how stimulating or fulfilling, can negate such basic biological instincts.

Leaving a baby for a few hours, let alone a whole working day, is one of the hardest things any woman ever does. School teacher Linda Erlebach puts it this way: "I really thought that leaving the baby at the sitter's wouldn't matter, that my career was important in my life. Even after the baby was born, I still believed it—until I left her with the sitter. Don't get me wrong, I probably have the best sitter in the world. I just hate to leave my baby. I miss her all day long."

"Trying to find someone to care for Jonathan so I could return to work was very traumatic," recalls Chris Akin, who resumed her career as a librarian part-time when her baby was six months old because her husband was changing jobs and his income would not be steady.

"It was hard to accept the fact that I would have to leave him. But once I found someone who I knew would love him, it was easier. And now that I have been back at work for over a year, it really has all worked out very well."

Nancy Wolkenhauer has been able to continue her career with Amtrak without sacrificing her close relationship with her son Luke.

Baby's Adjustment

How your baby will react to being separated from you will depend on his age, and to some degree his temperament. Surprisingly, even the tiniest infants seem to sense when they are being packed up to go to the sitter's or when mother is getting ready to leave. Although he does not react specifically to having you walk out the door as an older baby would, he may be fussy and cry while you are getting ready to leave or after you have gone. Even a tiny baby knows his mother by her smell, the feel of her skin, the sound of her voice, the rhythm of her heartbeat, by the way she picks him up and holds him. Though an infant cannot verbalize that he knows you are gone, he is most certainly able to distinguish when someone besides his own mother is caring for him. And mother, for her part, aches for her baby throughout the day.

At six to nine months of age, most babies go through a period of separation anxiety. They want mother in sight *all* of the time, and will sometimes cry mournfully if she leaves long enough to go in the kitchen to get a cup of coffee. This can be the hardest time of all to begin leaving a baby with an unknown sitter since separation anxiety will compound the normal adjustment of getting accustomed to another caretaker. Even a baby who has been left previously may suddenly begin to wail when you leave for work when he turns six months or so of age.

Later on—and for some babies it comes as early as eight or nine months—the baby will begin to be more interested in socializing and new adventures. Once baby hits this period, it is easier to leave

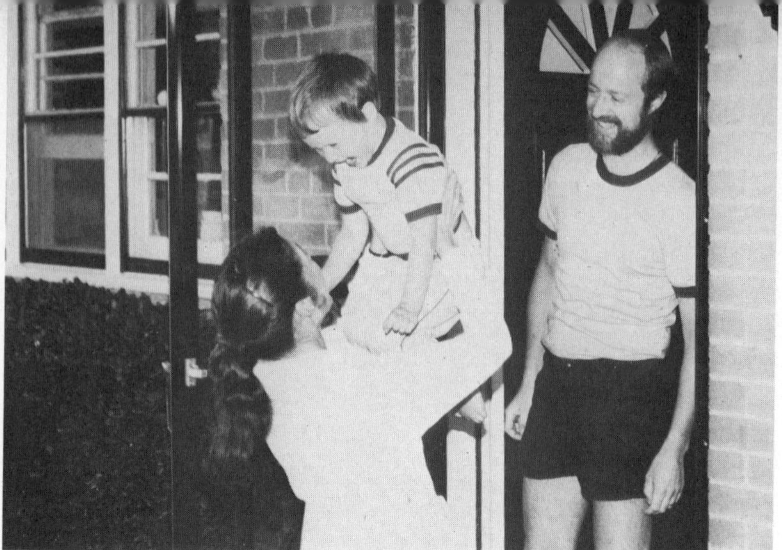

Coming home at the end of a busy day at work brings a warm welcome for Diane Lack from her son Ryan and similarly for Carol Smith from her son Timothy and husband Geoff.

him in someone else's care, especially if you are only gone for a few hours at a time.

In situations where the mother has been consciously working toward being able to leave the baby in someone else's care, and when she is determined to have her plan succeed, most babies will adjust to being left with a sitter. Particularly if the separation is limited to only a few hours a day, a loving caretaker will probably be able to keep most babies happy. Even so, be prepared for some tears the first weeks, and perhaps intermittently after that, as the baby adjusts to the new routine of being left in someone else's care for extended periods.

"No time spent away from your child is good—that is the hardest part," says university teaching assistant Virginia McGowan. "When Meghan was getting used to the sitter, I worried about whether she was being left to cry. It is important to be able to talk honestly and openly with whoever is caring for the child."

Family therapist Karen Combs recalls that, "Colleen began going to a sitter at six months of age. At first, she would cry when I left. By eight months of age, she had stopped crying and acted excited to see the other children."

No mother is ever able to be casual about the sound of her own baby's crying. No matter what your job, leaving a crying baby behind will be the hardest thing you do all day.

Mixed Reactions

You will want to be aware, too, that you may at some point experience very mixed feelings about the baby's caretaker. You want your baby and the caretaker to have a good relationship, but it is sometimes very hard to see your baby grow to love this person; it may seem that he loves the sitter almost as much as he loves you, especially if he begins to call her mama.

Cynthia Hazard admits, "Sometimes I feel jealous because the baby really enjoys the sitter, though at the same time I'm glad."

Cathy Cory, a PhD candidate in clinical and health psychology, recalls, "My son liked his babysitter very much, which hurt my feelings."

Knowing ahead of time that you may encounter these feelings, and realizing that such ambivalence is perfectly normal given the circumstances, can help you to deal with the situation constructively.

Some babies, and mothers, just don't adjust well to the separation. These are the ones you have run across in this book who have said that the emotional price that was being paid for continuing to work just wasn't worth it, so they stopped working and found another creative outlet or another way to make ends meet.

We know that when, for whatever reasons, mother returns to work, everyone involved has to make adjustments. We also know that infants and babies need to be with their mothers, and so we urge you to explore every means of staying with your baby full time until he is old enough to handle the separation, whatever age that might be for your individual baby. We also encourage you to be sensitive to your baby's needs when leaving him with a caretaker, and to modify your arrangements in whatever way is necessary until the situation is one that is comfortable for him.

Our premise, then, is that the best child care is the least child care. The longer you can extend your maternity leave and postpone your return to work, the fewer total hours you can be gone, and the shorter you can make each period of separation, the better for you and the baby.

On the other hand, chances are that continuing your career will mean that at some point you will need to make child care arrangements for your baby/toddler/preschooler. There are many choices for you to consider, and we offer the following information to help you to make the best decision for you and your child.

First Choice—A Loving Father

No one knows and loves a baby like his own parents. In your absence, if the baby's father is available, he would be the first choice to care for the baby. He is more likely to be closely attuned to the baby's needs, he can keep the baby in his own familiar surroundings, treat the baby to his own brand of play and entertainment, and minimize interruptions of the baby's accustomed routines. The

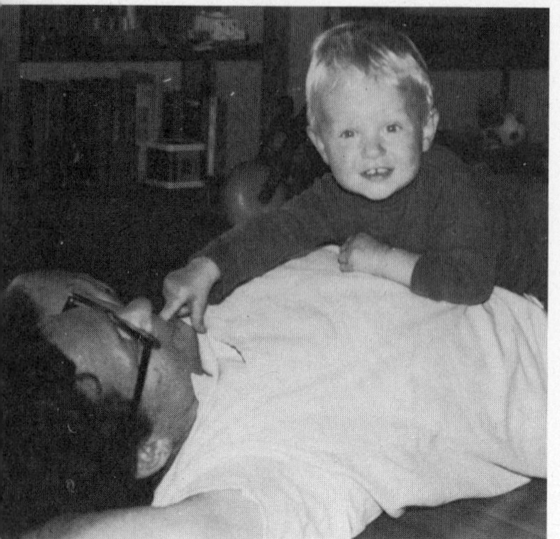

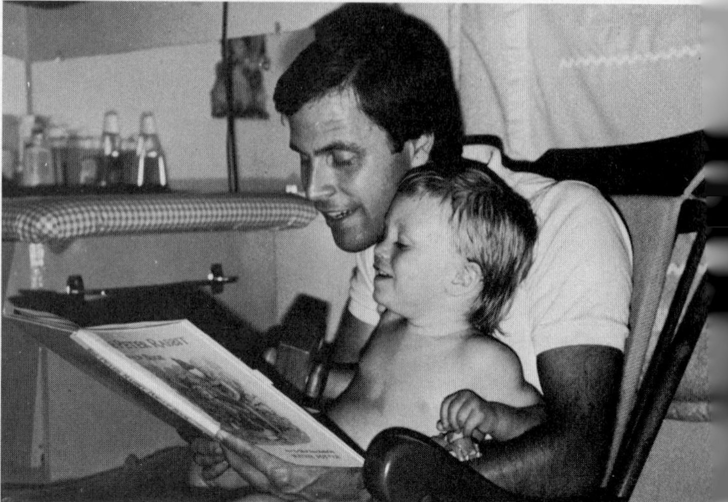

In the absence of mother, dad can offer the kind of loving care every child needs.

transition of being cared for by mother to being cared for by dad is the least jarring and the easiest for the baby to accept.

One mother explains it this way: "The fact that my baby was with her father when she wasn't with me made it easier for me to leave her. I knew she would receive so much love from him, and that he really wanted to be with her. They developed a closeness they could not have had otherwise. She even called him mommy for a while."

Whatever jockeying of schedules is necessary to allow dad to care for the baby in your absence is worth the effort, especially when a child under a year of age is concerned.

Grandmas, Aunts, and Other Loving Relatives

A loving relative who has an emotional investment in the baby is almost always the best choice for a caretaker. While there are many fine sitters who do come to love the baby almost as their own, in the end, all too often, looking after your baby is just a job, a way to earn money, to an outsider.

Family members have the long-term interests of your baby at heart, and are more likely to be patient with him, to soothe and comfort him, to stretch his mind and delight in his smiles than a non-relative would be. Remember, too, that babysitters come and go, and what you want most is for your baby to have one constant, dependable caretaker, not an ever-changing parade of new faces.

Take a close look at the family tree and see if you can't shake out someone who would be willing to lend a hand with your little one.

Is There a Nanny in Your Future?

Don't laugh. This English tradition has just recently found its way across the waters to the United States. Some dual career couples want the best child care for their children—and can afford it. An enterprising Chicagoan responded to the void in quality individualized child care by founding a school called Nanny, Inc., believed to be the only such school in the country. The eight-week course includes child development, childhood diseases, first aid, nutrition, bathing and dressing, language instruction, and contract negotiation.

President and owner of Nanny, Inc., British native Beth Smith was quoted in the *Chicago Tribune* as saying, "We're attempting to get the concept across that the caregiver is an important person in the child's development, and more than a babysitter."

A more common arrangement than hiring a nanny on this side of the Atlantic is to hire someone to look after the house and the children.

Psychologist Patricia Holliday and her husband decided that dependable, full-time child care in their home would be well worth the price tag attached to it.

"It was very important to us to find someone who would continue to work for us for all of the years we needed her, because we wanted Tiffany to form a close relationship with her, to bond with her, to love her, and for the babysitter to love Tiffany. Willie, our babysitter, makes life wonderful for all of us. She manages to cook, clean, and wash our clothes. But, most important, she plays with Tiffany, teaches her how to do things, takes her on walks, and thinks about her even when she is at her own home. She's really like a part of our family. We pay a full salary with paid vacations and such, but it is well worth it for the individual loving care Tiffany receives."

A less expensive option to a full time babysitter/housekeeper is to hire someone to come in for a few hours a week. Anita Untersee, who works out of her home, explains, "I have a woman who comes in twice a week for six hours to clean and help me with the baby. I don't know how it will work out ultimately because it is more expensive than day care, but I feel much more in control this way."

Babysitters—Your House or Mine?

If hiring an outside sitter turns out to be your best option, here are some points to consider.

First, be sure she understands exactly how you want your baby to be cared for. Be very specific that he is not to be left to cry for any reason, that you want him in the mainstream of activities except when he is napping, that you want him to be held and touched and

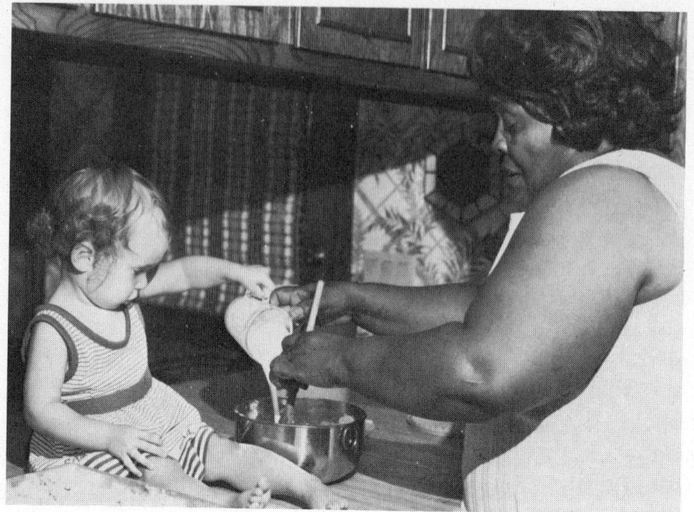

Willie Lee Harper, full-time cook, housekeeper, and baby-sitter for the Hollidays, has formed a close, loving relationship with Tiffany.

talked to. Don't be shy about giving the sitter your baby carrier and asking her to use it. Watch prospective sitters interact with your child. The things we have mentioned should come naturally, or they're not likely to come at all when you are not there to watch.

Social worker Moira Rayner White did a lot of looking for a sitter, but the search paid off. "After a long search we have found a wonderful loving woman who agrees with our philosophy of raising children and supports our breastfeeding. We bring the baby to her home for the morning. We are very pleased with the arrangement."

Linda Ruth Forys also found a very good situation for her baby daughter. "My sitter treats her like gold and the arrangements are working fine."

It usually costs more to have the sitter come to your home (if you can find one willing to do it), but since most children under two feel more secure in their own homes it is an option worth considering.

California doctor Yolanda Leparulo has "a single woman who comes to my home to care for my daughter. She provides her own transportation and does very light housekeeping. I also have a one day a week cleaning lady. My daughter has adjusted quite well. She has established a very positive relationship with her sitter and asks about her when she's gone."

On the other hand, you may have a very sociable toddler who thrives on the change of scene and an assortment of toys other than his own. Let your own child be your guide.

The Sitter's Children

There is no easy answer when it comes to the advisability of hiring a sitter with children of her own. Some mothers have felt that their baby benefited from a family situation, and that the babysitter's children were extra sources of love and entertainment for their child. As Ruth Titschinger points out, "My son enjoys being with the babysitter's children, and the interaction with them has helped him develop social skills."

In other cases, mothers have felt that the sitter didn't have enough time or emotional energy to care for the baby when she had preschoolers of her own to look after.

Whether the sitter brings her child (or children) to your house or your child goes to hers, there can be problems with "territorial rights." If your child goes to her house, her children may be unwilling to share their toys—and be very vocal about it. If her children come to your house and take over your child's possessions, your child will be left feeling threatened and angry. In either case, the real problem may be that her children may resent having to share their mother. You will both want to be aware that this type of conflict could develop.

Make every effort to assure yourself that your sitter is willing to accept a long term commitment. Nothing is more traumatic for a baby and more frustrating for a mother than to be looking for a new sitter every month.

In-Home Day Care Facilities

As more women are looking for a way to earn a living and more women are finding themselves in need of child care, the in-home day care business is booming.

An in-home day care provider is a woman, often with young children of her own, who has equipped her house to care for several (usually from three to eight) children. Many states and municipalities are now requiring such home-based facilities to be licensed, so check to be sure that any home you are considering has a license if one is required. This is your assurance that proper health and safety standards are being met.

Personnel administrator Nancy Johnson found a very good in-home day care situation for her child. "I would often come to get her and find the two of them in the rocking chair with the sitter singing songs to her. My daughter became more friendly and outgoing. Another plus was having other children to play with while she was there. It was great socialization."

In-home day care operators tend to have a serious commitment

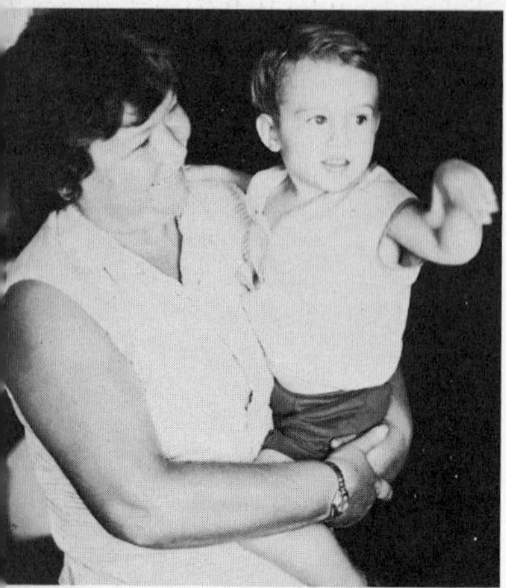

Liz Dursema provides loving care for Tim Hazard while his mother is at work.

to the job since they have usually invested money in play equipment and toys, and perhaps training and licensing. This considerably lessens the possibility that your child care arrangements will vanish with a phone call saying, "I'm sorry, but I won't be able to look after Tommy anymore."

If a home-like setting is important to you and you feel your child would do best with only a few other children instead of the twenty or more that are usually found in a commercial day care center, this may be a good option for you.

On the other hand, if you have a baby or young toddler who still needs large quantities of individual attention, be wary of any situation with more than one or two other children. Your little one's need for concentrated, individual care should not be slighted or minimized. This is an important developmental stage, and it is important to respect and fulfill his basic need for developing an attachment to a caretaker without having to compete with an armload of other children for her attention.

The caretaker's individual style is far more important to your child than the color of her playroom or the equipment she has in her back yard. What will make your child happiest—or unhappiest—is the kind of attention she gives him and the way she relates to him. Make sure the chemistry between the caretaker and your child is good.

Monitor the total situation continuously. Ask questions about your child's behavior and reactions while he is at the sitter's and watch for changes in his behavior while you're together. Things change, and the best of situations can turn into a less than optimum arrangement for your child. Don't hesitate to make a change when one is in order.

The experience of computer systems analyst Cindy Karl illustrates the many wrong turns, dead ends, and frustrations that can be part of finding acceptable child care arrangements.

"Our next door neighbor started keeping our oldest child when she was three months old. I wasn't happy with this because I couldn't tell her about things she was doing that I didn't like. The next lady who kept our daughter was great, but it only lasted for seven months. Kristy went to a playschool next, which she hated, so she was only there for two weeks. Then we got her into a church run nursery school which she loved. But the changes were upsetting to all of us."

Elizabeth River, who teaches toddler-parent education, changed her child-care arrangements as her baby's needs changed. "I got my present job when the baby was fourteen months old and hired a child development student to help me care for the baby so I could bring him with me to class. Sometimes I felt torn between my parent and teacher roles, but for the most part it went well.

"When he was eighteen months old, the class was so popular that I added another section and my three hour day changed to five hours twice a week. So I had the sitter begin taking him to her home for the last two hours to give him a nap. Since he was already comfortable with this person, it worked out well.

"The summer he turned two I found a day-care home and began going there with him, then gradually leaving him for short periods so that by the end of the summer he could comfortably stay for several hours. We are still using this day-care home and find it a wonderful addition to our family. Owen has friends he enjoys from this warm, caring environment."

Whether you are using a private sitter or an in-home day-care facility, if you have a young baby who is still nursing frequently, you are probably wise to find child care close to your place of work. You can then go to the sitter's to nurse the baby at lunchtime, and perhaps during a morning or afternoon break as well. You'll also be more accessible if the baby becomes ill or needs you suddenly for some other reason. And remember that the time you spend traveling from home to work is time you're paying someone to care for the baby, when that time could be yours to spend with him.

Commercial Day-Care Centers

The quality of commercial day-care centers runs the gamut from absolutely excellent to barely tolerable—or worse. If you have a preschooler who thrives in a group setting with lots of activity and stimulation, a day-care center may be your child care choice.

Marilyn Harris felt that her child did well in a day-care situation. "At day care, he is exposed to other children his age and different play situations which I feel are enjoyable and stimulating for him."

Psychiatric nurse Sharyn Stolzenbach started her baby in a day-care center, but moved her when she saw it had turned into a detrimental situation for the baby.

"I first tried a small infant/toddler day-care center, because I couldn't find anyone to come to our home. The first few weeks were fine because there were only a few babies. Then—horrors!—suddenly there were about twenty babies, three staff members, and my family-bed baby was spending her time in infant swings and playpens because she wouldn't sleep in a crib. She also developed sympathetic crying and cried every time anyone else did."

Because the quality of these centers varies so widely, we urge you to investigate carefully before signing on the dotted line. Spending one or two mornings at the center observing is one of the best investments of your time you will ever make. Is the atmosphere friendly and relaxed? Do the children seem to play well together or is there a lot of fighting and crying? Is there a good teacher-child ratio so that there is enough individual attention for each child? Are the structured activities things that your child would enjoy? Is the physical facility bright and cheerful? Are the individual needs and preferences of each child respected?

How many children the center accommodates is another factor to consider. Your child will probably come home with every contagious illness that goes around until he develops stronger immunities. The bigger the group and the younger your child, the more chances there are that he will continually catch something.

Check with other mothers whose opinions you trust and see where they send their children. Experience is usually the best guide, and if other mothers are enthusiastic about a particular center, this is a good recommendation.

One Word of Caution: If you have an infant or young baby, a commercial day-care center does not usually provide the optimal environment. Babies need an abundance of individual attention that simply can't be had in a day-care center. Even if the staff members had enough time, your baby would probably be cared for in a round robin fashion by several caretakers.

A suburban Chicago health department official told of being in a clean, modern day-care center that was licensed for eight infants as well as a number of toddlers. "I watched the woman go down the line diapering each one," she said. "By the time she finished with the last one it was time to start all over again at the beginning. There wasn't a minute for her to hold or talk to any of these babies." This kind of basic custodial care is not what any mother who can avoid it wants for her baby.

On-Site Day Care

With so many women with preschool children now in the labor force, you might wonder why company-sponsored day-care centers continue to be almost non-existent. The answer is simple—they cost money. Or at least most companies still believe they cost more than they are worth. But other companies, propelled by a spirit of innovation and the management savvy to know that what is good for employees is good for the company, have taken the plunge and established successful on-site day-care facilities. And those who have done it feel that the expense—which in some cases may run as much as $2,000 or $3,000 per year per child—is more than offset by the rewards.

A December 1982 article in *Parade Magazine* quoted a representative of Intermedics, Inc. of Freeport, Texas as saying, "Our com-

Patrick Dunal leaves the house in good spirits to spend the morning at the day care center.

pany saw that to get the good people they wanted and to keep them, they would have to realize that these people have children."

One of the chief advantages to parents of on-site day care centers is the ability to have their children nearby and, often, to have some voice in how the center is operated. Because such a day-care center is an employee benefit rather than a privately run business, the company is often willing to contribute in some way to the center's operation, giving it more stability and more "extras" than are currently found in most day-care situations.

Although babies and toddlers up to about eighteen months or so seem to do best in a situation where they receive a great deal of individual attention, an on-site day-care center can offer a number of advantages for preschoolers who are old enough to enjoy a group setting.

The time of separation is lessened by an hour or more with an on-site day-care center. Mother doesn't have to drop the child at the sitter's, travel to work, and then reverse the process in the evening. Mothers are usually free to eat lunch with their children, and perhaps pay a mid-morning or mid-afternoon visit as well. In case of accident or illness, the mother can usually be at the child's side within minutes. From a whole range of perspectives, on-site day care has the potential of greatly reducing the child care burden now weighing so heavily on working parents.

■ **"Employees are more willing to speak up for what they want today than they have been in the past."**

Anita Shreve reports that "At the Zale Corporation, a large, national jewelry company headquartered in Dallas, working mothers (or fathers) may have lunch with their children or visit them at any time in an on-site facility minimally subsidized by the company. 'The senior management at Zale has a long history of sensitivity to family-related issues,' says Michael Romaine, Zale's vice-president for community relations and the founder of the center. 'When they heard about the concept of on-site day care, they felt that our people could use this. About a year and a half into its operation the center was self-supporting in regard to staff, food, maintenance, and utilities. The building represents a five year tax write-off for Zale.

"'I keep telling companies they can do this to make their employees happy—and it doesn't even cost them anything. It's impossible to measure productivity gains, but 40% of all parents who use the center say they came to Zale because of it.'"

Other companies that provide child care centers recite a litany of benefits—improved recruitment of quality employees, less turnover, reduced absenteeism, better morale, increased job productivity, good publicity, and favorable community relations.

The *Parade* article states that during 1979, the first year Intermedic's center was open "employee turnover dropped by 23%. Absenteeism in the manufacturing division alone dropped by 15,000 hours—the equivalent of the time an employee with a perfect attendance record would work during seven and a half years of forty hour weeks. In addition, four months after the center opened, walk-in job applicants became so great that the company did not need to advertise for help."

Among the other corporations offering on-site day care are the Hoffman-LaRoche pharmaceuticals complex in Nutly, NJ; the Wang Labs electronics complex in Lowell, MA; Corning Glass Works in Corning, NY; and the publishing complex of Official Airlines Guides in Oakbrook, IL, according to the *Parade* story. The common denominator is that nearly all of these companies have staffs made up primarily of women who have skills that are in short supply. Day-care centers have proven to be an effective recruiting tool to get these women—and keep them.

Unions have yet to take up day care as an issue because their mostly male members have not expressed a need. Charleen Knight, Assistant Director of the Women's Department of the United Auto Workers said that Region I in the metropolitan Detroit area sent out 80,000 questionnaires a few years ago asking about child care. Less than 10% of the questionnaires were returned.

"There continues to be a smaller number of members who really need child care services than workers who don't need it," Ms. Knight concludes.

Attitudes and Reality

Studies indicate a great disparity between attitudes toward on-site day care and the establishment of such facilities. A survey of 374 major corporations was conducted in 1981 by Catalyst, a New York based nonprofit organization that fosters the full participation of women in corporate and professional life.

The survey found that "54% said they favored corporate support of community-based day care, but only 19% supplied it. Another 20% said they favored on-site centers, while only one percent sponsored them. Nine percent said they favored direct subsidies for child care tuition but, again, only one percent supplied them."

But things are improving, and corporations are slowly beginning to respond to child care needs. Catalyst reports that "Twenty-nine percent are already providing days off for children's illnesses. Other child care options that corporations could explore include: Credit for child care offered through a flexible benefits program; financial contributions to existing child care facilities to expand and upgrade them; purchase of corporate slots in existing community child care; working with employees to establish a near-site, not-for-profit center through financial and in-kind contributions; and on-site corporate-run child development centers."

Columnist Joyce Lain Kennedy reports in the *Chicago Sun Times* that "the National Employer Supported Child Care Project in Pasadena, California, counts 43 corporate, 151 hospital, 14 government, and four union centers."

More and more employees want some kind of child care benefits, and more of them are willing to say so.

An article titled "Business responds to family concerns," in the *Christian Science Monitor* quotes management consultant Norman Crowder III as saying, "Employees are more willing to speak up for what they want today than they have been in the past. Younger workers, especially those with a working spouse and preschool children, are telling management that they're not interested in a pension forty years from now. They want immediate benefits, such as employer sponsored child care."

But there are some problems to consider in providing on-site day care for employees.

"It doesn't work in a place like New York City," says Kristin Anderson of the Center for Public Advocacy Research, "because space costs so much. With space at $55 a square foot, they're not going to use it for a day-care center."

Many women who work in large urban areas don't want a company sponsored day-care center. "Many of these women commute long distances by public transportation," and they don't want to

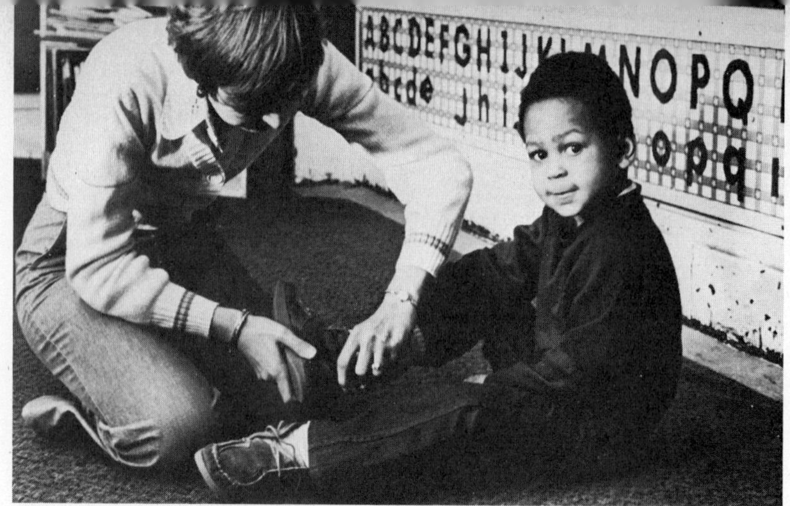

Leon Crutcher gets some help from Kayla Jorgens at the Northside Child Development Center which is partly sponsored by the Control Data Corporation.

bring their children into the city with them. "They would rather make child-care arrangements in their own neighborhoods."

The exception to this is mothers who have babies. "They do want to bring their babies with them," Ms. Anderson points out. "Babies are more portable and mothers want them near their place of work so they can nurse them."

But in situations where on-site day care isn't practical or possible, there are other options to pursue for companies that are interested in giving more than lip service to employees' needs.

"Montefiore Hospital in the Bronx provides training for in-home day care providers," Ms. Anderson says. "The hospital keeps a list of these providers, then the nurses can choose which home atmosphere they want for their children. The providers are given free training and are licensed. They can apply for a revolving loan through the hospital for things like bringing their homes up to safety codes or purchasing new toys."

At Bellevue Hospital in New York City, hospital employees are given a reduced rate at a particular day-care center, and first preference for any openings there.

"Why has it taken so long for even a handful of corporations to respond to such basic family needs? The answer seems to have less to do with questions of cost than with a reluctance to give up comfortable old habits," according to an article titled "Desk set; the new triangle—mothers, fathers, and the office," published in *Vogue* magazine in 1982.

But the handwriting is on the wall, put there not by a toddler with a crayon in his hands but by the combined forces for change that demand recognition of the fact that employees are people with families. The *Vogue* article concludes with a refrain that has been repeated throughout these pages: "The biggest changes—in attitudes and support given—will probably result from the upward movement of women in corporations."

Chapter 14

Breastfeeding
A commitment to the best beginning

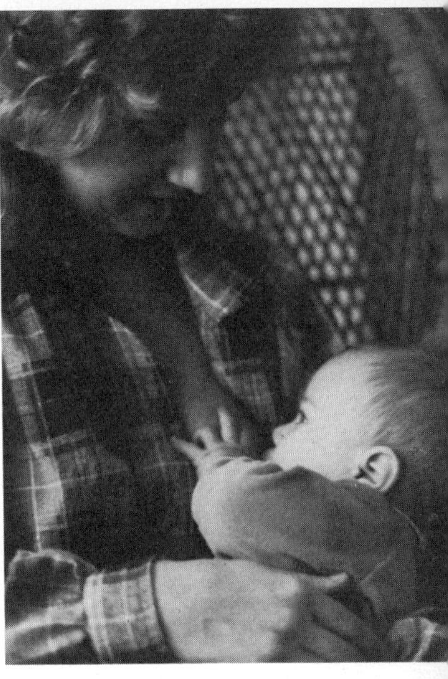

As career women in record numbers are deciding that they will not be cheated out of having a baby, they are also deciding that they will not be cheated out of another important experience—breastfeeding.

While at first glance it might seem that professional women would be the last to want to add breastfeeding to their already lengthy list of responsibilities, statistics prove otherwise. And perhaps this trend is far less contradictory than it seems.

Career women are accustomed to taking the responsibilities in their lives very seriously. They are achievers who are accustomed to giving their best to whatever job they take on; they are willing to accept the personal sacrifices that are usually involved in achieving success. And they also know that the sacrifices are nearly always well worth the effort.

So it's not so surprising that once the decision is made to have a baby, the decision to breastfeed often follows almost as a matter of course.

"I knew that if I were going to rearrange my life enough to accommodate the needs of a baby, I was certainly going to rearrange it a little more to accommodate breastfeeding," a thirty-year-old career woman-mother explains. "Giving birth was only half of the story—I wanted to experience the closeness of breastfeeding, the

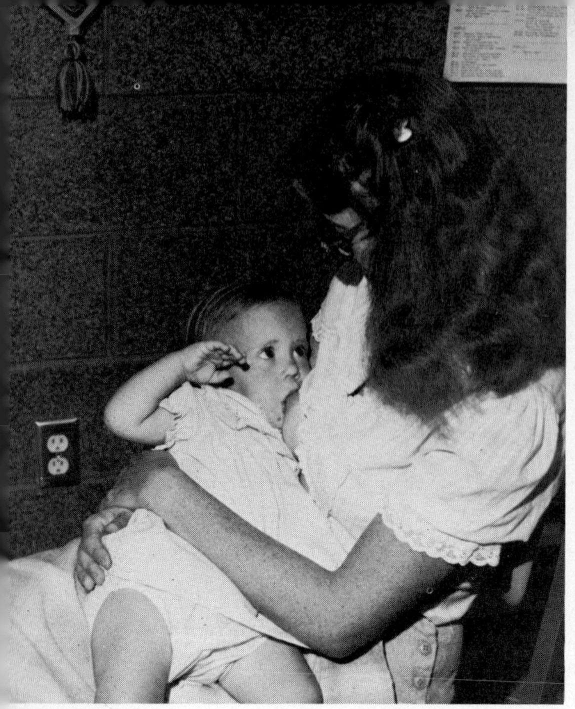

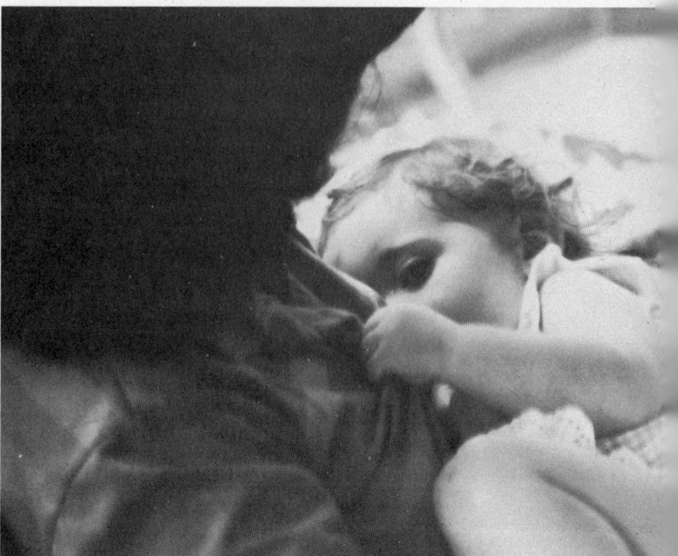

satisfaction of seeing my baby grow and thrive on my milk. Why would I want to bring him into the world if I weren't willing to give him the best possible start in life? Breastfeeding was just too important to miss out on."

The determination of career women-mothers to breastfeed is probably one of the major influences in the rise in the demand for a reduced workweek. Many women cite the desire to breastfeed as one of the primary factors that motivated them to modify their working arrangements.

Dannette Blakeslee, a teacher who reduced her workday to six hours, did so "because of my personal belief that breastfeeding is vital to a baby's health and nurturing."

"With my two older children, breastfeeding did not work out," explains Becky Peckler, a data processor who works twenty hours a week. "I knew I would have to do everything possible to make it work with Jillian. Going back to work at all was a choice I didn't want to make, but our financial situation forced me to.

"When I realized I would have to return to work, I started looking into making arrangements that would allow me to be away from home at the time Jill would most likely be asleep so we would not miss any nursings. I knew how important it was for the baby and I to be together as much as possible, not only to establish a good milk supply but to develop a strong relationship as well."

Margaret Risk-Bryan echoes Becky's feelings. "My first son was, unfortunately, weaned at two months of age. I decided that I wanted to do the best for my next baby, and I knew that working in an office

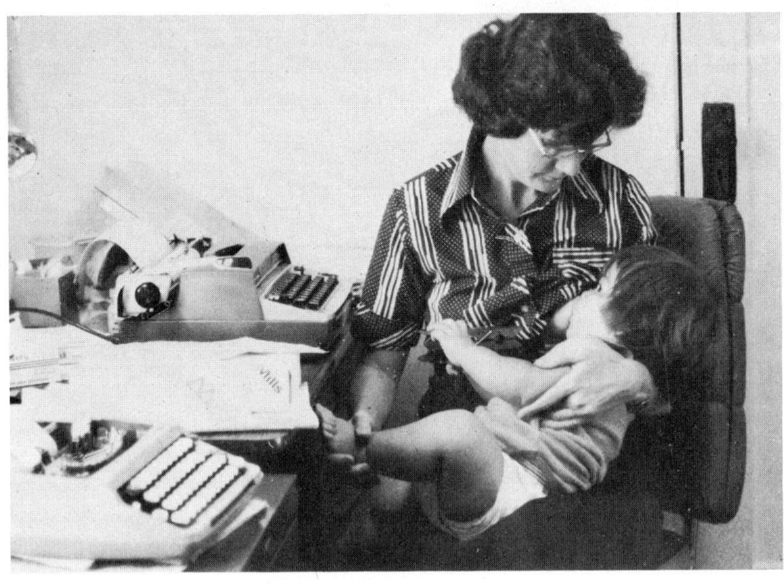

Working mothers do not want to deprive their babies of the benefits of breastfeeding. (l. to r.) Nansi Casper with daughter Nikki; Monica Miele and Heather; Ellen Davies and Stefan.

would not be compatible with breastfeeding. So when I decided to have another child, I took a new part-time job that had the possibility of working on a free-lance basis."

"My child benefited both physically and emotionally from the time we spent as a nursing couple," says nurse Shari Kelly. "It was important to me to make work fit my son's schedule so that I could nurse him for the first year of his life."

Although many women who work full time can and do breastfeed their babies, modified working arrangements—working only part time, working at home, taking the baby to work, or working at night while the baby sleeps—greatly simplify breastfeeding problems. Because, fewer, if any, feedings are missed, overfullness, leaking, and plugged ducts are less likely to occur. There is less need to be bothered with pumping, storing, and transporting your milk, and less likelihood that the baby will wean from the breast as the result of being given too many bottles. For those who are able to postpone returning to work until the baby is six months or older, missed feedings are often little or no problem, especially for mothers who are gone only a few hours a day.

Nurse Mary Doll began working two days a week when her son was four months old, and says she never had difficulty leaving enough breast milk for him, or getting him to accept a bottle. "I used to be afraid I wouldn't have enough stored milk on hand, but I've always been able to keep eight to twelve four-ounce bottles of my milk in the freezer," Mary reports. "I relieve my overfull breasts by pumping some milk at my dinner break."

Susan Thies, also a nurse and the mother of three children, works four days a week. She tells of her situation. "I had breastfed my other two daughters and would not think of giving Rachel formula. I work the 3:00 to 11:00 P.M. shift and usually take my supper break around 6:00 P.M. when my husband is home and can bring Rachel over to nurse. I always try to leave breast milk in the freezer for later, but if it is a quiet evening at work I call my husband and he brings her over again. I work in a very small hospital and RNs are hard to find. The Director of Nursing has not minded my baby coming to work. My co-workers have either been supportive or quiet. Many seem to enjoy watching Rachel grow."

Debbie Armstrong, a physical therapist who works four hours a day, found that her daughter preferred waiting for mother to taking a bottle. "I had completely breastfed my daughter until I started working again when she was five months of age. At that point I started introducing small amounts of solids, just enough so the sitter could give her a little to hold her over if I should run late or have car trouble. I also left expressed breast milk for her. She took it for a few months, but weaned herself from the bottles of expressed milk at seven months of age, and just waited for me to get back."

Denise Peacock, a secretary who works six hours a day, three days a week, had a similar experience. "Reid was seven and a half months old when I returned to work. I pumped milk which I left for him. He would usually take one bottle while I was away, but within six weeks he preferred to wait for mother to return."

Ruth Fleming, a systems engineer from California who works twenty hours a week, went to work when her baby was six months old. "I thought that I would have to at least partially wean the baby. At first I expressed my milk, but soon gave it up because she wasn't interested. It only took her a week or two to move all of her nursings to morning or night. I plan to continue nursing her as long as she likes."

While some babies accept a bottle from a sitter fairly easily, for others the going is a little slower. Dental hygienist Linda Forys explains what happened with her baby. "Before I returned to work, I began pumping my milk and feeding it to her from a bottle so she would get used to it, but the first week at the sitter's she still would not take the bottle from the sitter, even though it was my milk and not formula. But now she willingly accepts it."

Teacher Dannette Blakeslee was able to go to the sitter's house "only two minutes from where I work" to nurse her baby at lunchtime. "If a faculty meeting was planned for after school, I would go to the sitter's again to nurse the baby, then return to school." She used this system for all three of her children, now aged five, three, and six

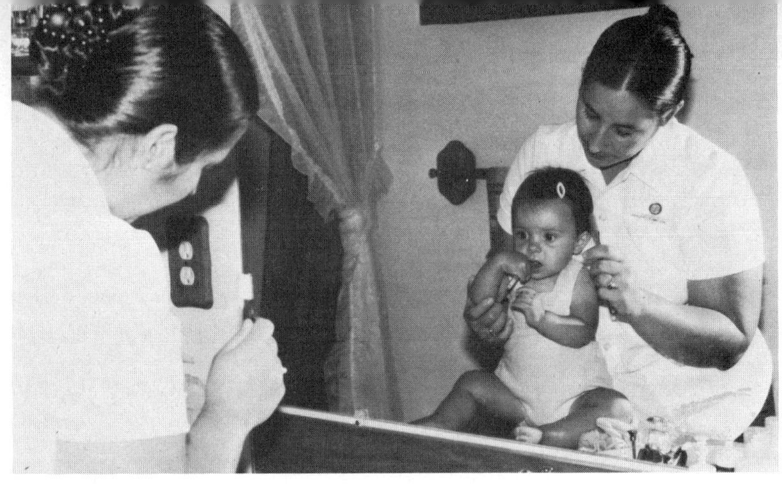

As a dental hygienist, Linda Forys knows the importance of teaching Marianne good dental hygiene.

months, and, because she was finished working at 2:00 P.M., found that "they only needed one bottle at 9:00 A.M.

Norma Innes, an assistant professor of math at Miami-Dade Community College, worked mornings and arranged for her husband to bring the baby to her to be nursed during the summer term when he was teaching afternoon classes at the same school.

"While I worked, my husband took care of the two children (three years and six and a half months old), and then brought them to me so I could nurse the baby. Now that it's fall, I get up early, nurse and pump simultaneously, leave the kids with my mom, then nurse and pump again when I get home. While I'm away the baby gets one meal of cereal with breast milk, and bananas. It works out well."

Occupational therapist Lynda Dunal went back to work twenty-five hours a week when her baby was six months old. "I occasionally had engorged (overfull) breasts the first two or three months back at work when I couldn't get to the baby for a midday feeding. My breasts also leaked—all I had to do was think of him! I would either use the client's washroom and express some milk, or wear pieces of cut up disposable diapers in my bra. I also wore vests a lot!"

Sarah Forbrush Jett, a dental hygienist who works part time, expressed and stored milk at work. "My son would nurse before I left for work. Mid-morning I would slip into the bathroom and express my milk. It took about fifteen minutes. I stored it in a small refrigerator until lunchtime. Then I would drive home for lunch and nurse my son. He drank the morning's expressed milk in the afternoon while I was back at work. I would be home again for his dinnertime nursing. The milk I expressed at work during the afternoon would then be used for his mid-morning feeding the next day."

Nurse Cynthia Abood has breastfed two babies while continuing to work. "With the first child, I went back to work full time at six weeks. He was brought to my office to nurse, so I planned lunch and comprehensive time according to his schedule. He weaned to a cup at nine months.

"I stayed home for three months after Evan's birth, then worked only part-time for a while. He came to the hospital to nurse at suppertime when I worked the 3:00 to 11:00 P.M. shift, and continued to nurse for three and a half years.

"The whole system worked beautifully, and I feel very close to my children because of breastfeeding.

"Since I have had experience with nursing and working, I can share with the new mothers who deliver here and want to do the same. I thoroughly enjoyed my breastfeeding experience and know that my boys were given the best start possible."

Baby Goes Along

Women who take their babies to work with them have different problems, and different solutions.

"I decided to keep my breastfeeding low key to avoid my employer's being concerned over the customers' reactions to my nursing in public," explains Robin Katen who took a job as manager of an animal shelter when baby Kevin was two months old. "I nursed only when there were no customers present, and had to cut some nursings short when people arrived, which sometimes upset Kevin."

Elizabeth Kinsler, who switched from being a high school teacher to working for her husband's fuel injection business so she could keep their baby with her, had a different setup.

"My husband built a kitchen/nursery/office for me at work so we could bring the baby with us. It seems to be working out quite well. We are a nursing couple in a shop with twelve men, so I retreat to my office where we can nurse in privacy. Most of the men are single, and are curious at times about nursing and different stages of child development."

Programmer analyst Carol Petroski took her infant daughter to work with her twenty hours a week and experienced few problems. "Sometimes I had a hard time getting work done due to the attention everyone was giving my baby. I had to take my daughter for walks occasionally when she got restless and needed my individual attention. Of course, I wouldn't charge for those hours, and no one seemed to mind my taking unpredictable breaks. The baby was able to nurse whenever she wanted."

Deborah Coble, a flutist with the Syracuse Symphony Orchestra who went back to work when her baby was four months old, faced somewhat different problems. "I enjoyed some weeks when I was

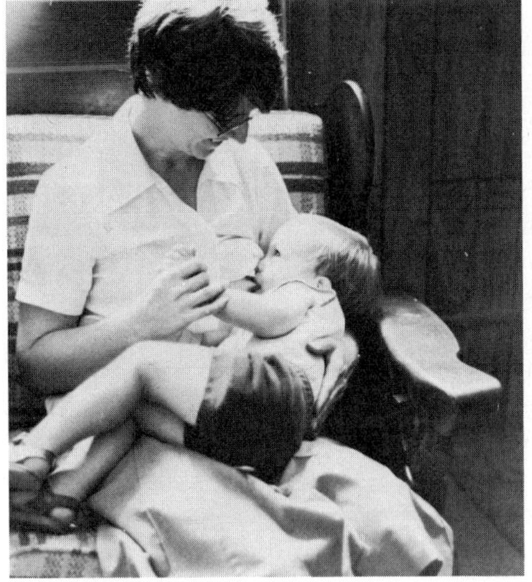

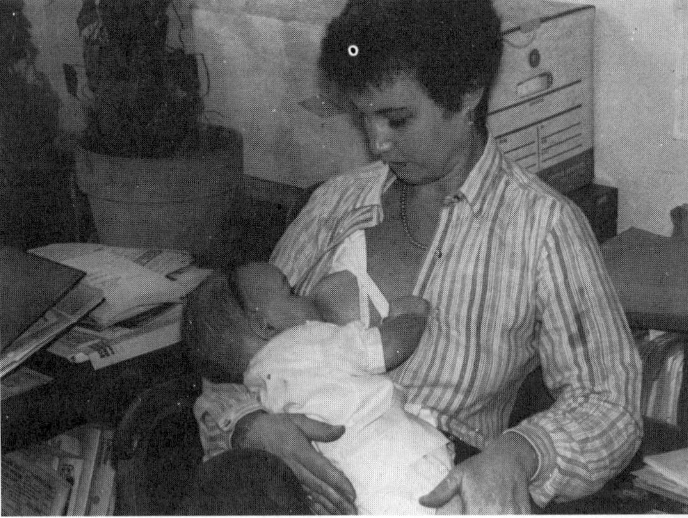

Cynthia Hazard (left) visits the sitter's home on her lunch hour to nurse Tim; Nikki Anne Ravey takes a nursing break with Katherine, who comes to work with her.

home quite a lot, and others when I was quite busy. At least I was able to maintain my milk supply fairly easily.

"Luckily we had no concert tours in the early months. When the baby was about seven months old we went on tour, but it was close enough for me to drive home between the concerts. I took a breast pump along to relieve some of the fullness, but had a rough time using it without her nursing on the other side. I was pretty uncomfortable, but she nursed well when I got home. At least she didn't forget how!"

Phyllis Carlyle, a bridal consultant who works out of her home, feels she has worked out a good system. "I am primarily a full-time mother cherishing and enjoying my baby. Kevin had nothing but breast milk until he was six months old. I expressed three or four bottles a week to cover work sessions, when Kevin would go to a mother's-day-out program. At ten months he is nursing three times a day—morning, afternoon, and bedtime—and eating two or three meals a day. He is a healthy, happy, good-natured baby, and his mama doesn't understand why anyone would not want to nurse!"

Practical Hints

The following information is taken from La Leche League's *Practical Hints for Working and Breastfeeding.* You'll only need these techniques for collecting milk and feeding it to your baby if you'll be leaving your baby in the early months or if you will be separated from your older baby for long periods of time.

Collecting Your Milk

- No other milk or formula is as good for your baby as your own breast milk. Many mothers are able to provide enough milk to satisfy all their baby's needs while they are away. This involves knowing some techniques for storing breast milk properly and giving it to the baby. You'll want to be sure your sitter is aware of the need for certain precautions in handling the milk you leave for your baby.
- Some mothers start pumping and storing their milk ahead of the time they will be returning to work in order to have a reserve supply available. Others pump only while they are away and have enough for the baby's feedings on the following day.
- The number of times you'll need to pump or express your milk while you are away from home will depend on the total length of time you are away from the baby. It's usually best not to go more than three or four hours without removing milk from your breasts.
- There are a number of inexpensive manual breast pumps available today, but many mothers find hand-expressing easiest and most convenient. Here's how to do it: Wash your hands first and have a clean, sterilized container ready (plastic is preferable to glass). Cup the breast in your hand with your thumb above just behind the areola (dark area), and your fingers below, supporting the breast. Squeeze your thumb and fingers together rhythmically while pushing back toward the chest wall. Do not slide your fingers along the skin. Rotate your hand all around the breast in order to empty all of the milk ducts. After working on one breast for three to five minutes, switch to the other breast, then repeat on both breasts.
- Follow the manufacturer's directions in caring for any type of pump. Usually it is necessary to clean the parts carefully after each use and sterilize the pump once a day. Talk to other mothers about the types of pump they find effective. LLL does not recommend the type of pump which requires squeezing a rubber bulb to draw out the milk, as the mother has little control over the amount of suction and these are usually not very effective.
- Your milk will need to be kept cool at all times. If no refrigerator is available where you work, you can use an insulated thermos or small cooler. Put ice into the thermos in the morning to get it cold, then pour out the ice and add your milk. You can keep ice in the cooler and add the con-

tainers of your milk throughout the day. You will also need to use one of these methods to keep your milk cool on your way home.

- The sitter needs to know that you plan to leave your own milk for the baby and what precautions will be necessary in handling it. Also be sure the sitter knows that you do not want the baby given formula or other foods without your permission.

Take Care of Yourself

- Try setting your alarm for at least twenty minutes before you have to get up. Nurse the baby during this time (even if he's still half asleep) so that he's content while you dress and prepare for the day. Then nurse again just before you leave. It'll calm you both and make separation a bit smoother.
- Be prepared for more evening, nighttime, and early morning nursings. Bringing the baby to bed with you is a definite plus. Consider doing this for at least part of the night, if not for the entire night.
- Many working nursing mothers are able to nurse their baby full time on their days off or on weekends with no problem making the adjustment.
- Drink plenty of fluids and eat a nutritious diet of wholesome foods. Get most of your daily liquid in water, juice, or milk. Limit your caffeine (coffee, tea, cola) to two or three drinks daily.
- Find time to attend La Leche League meetings.

Information on ordering a copy of "Practical Hints for Working and Breastfeeding" can be found at the end of this book.

Information and Encouragement

Any woman interested in breastfeeding would do well to get in touch with La Leche League even before her baby is born. La Leche League offers information and encouragement through personal help, monthly discussion group meetings, and a wide range of publications. THE WOMANLY ART OF BREASTFEEDING, a basic how-to book, has provided answers to questions about breastfeeding for two generations of nursing mothers.

Occupational therapist Linda Dunal, who nursed her son Patrick, says, "Thank you, La Leche League, for your book THE WOMANLY ART OF BREASTFEEDING. It helped me over the plugged ducts and discouraging times. I still pick it up; it reinforces my beliefs."

Louise Oppenheimer-Flax, who nursed her daughter Corinne even after she returned to her teaching career, adds, "Our League Leaders' encouragement and the information in THE WOMANLY ART were invaluable."

In spite of how busy you are already, spending a few evenings at La Leche League discussion group meetings can be one of the best investments of your time and energy. Nursing babies attend along with their mothers and there's no substitute for the kind of support and encouragement you'll receive from being in a roomful of breast-feeding mothers. As Jan Costello, editorial assistant, points out, "La Leche League made mothering much easier for me and certainly more fun."

As for the benefits of breastfeeding to a working mother, Janis DePar, an RN who works two evenings a week, says, "Nursing Nicki when I get home is the most relaxing thing I can do. I can't imagine working and not nursing my baby." And Caroline Barnhart adds, "I recommend nursing to any working mother . . . It works beautifully."

Chapter 15

Superwoman
Then and now

Some years after Superwoman first made her appearance in the 1970s, the media began surfacing reports that she was a myth—or that if she had been real, she had surely long since died off from the sheer exhaustion of trying to keep up with her image as the perfect wife, adoring mother, and fast-paced career woman.

We know for a fact, however, that Superwoman is very much alive, and although she is still struggling to reconcile her public image with her personal needs, she is finding life much more to her liking today than she did a decade ago.

The truth is that any woman who takes on the simultaneous roles of wife, mother, and wage earner has absolutely earned the right to the title of Superwoman. Dashing from one role to the next while miraculously holding onto her sanity and keeping her perspective relatively intact is a feat for which no mere human being can ever be really prepared, but one which legions of women, determined to make it all work, are tackling head-on.

What differentiates today's wife-mother-career woman from her counterpart of a decade ago is the fact that she has had the opportunity to learn from her predecessors and knows full well that she cannot reasonably expect to give 100% of herself on all three fronts. She has a far more realistic sense of what is and isn't feasible, and is willing to make a variety of sensible compromises in order to avoid having to sacrifice any one dimension of her life in favor of the other two.

She knows, too, that her time and energy resources are finite, and that she has to establish priorities and make decisions about what is really worth her time and energy and what, given the circumstances, will have to do without her attention.

As Marcie Schorr Hirsch, co-author of *Managing Your Maternity Leave,* says in Anita Shreve's article, "Careers and the Lure of Motherhood," "It's not that I'm not willing to work hard anymore. But I don't want to work hard at everything all the time."

Guilt and Resentment

The career woman-mother of the 1960s and 70s, who had to be a better "man" than every other man in the company, soon realized that her success at work came with a high price tag in terms of home and family. Her husband and children were accustomed to having her available and on call at all times; now she had an employer who expected the same. Somebody had to lose, and the biggest loser of all was usually the woman herself who was awash in guilt, knowing that whatever she did, however hard she worked, one side or the other—or both—was going to scream that they weren't getting their fair share from her.

It was a no-win situation. With unrealistic expectations on every side, there had to be some big disappointments. Whether the woman decided to set aside her briefcase and go back to tending the homefires or chose to continue on with her career regardless of the price she was paying in her personal life, she was filled with resentment and guilt because both sides were expecting more than she could possibly deliver. And neither seemed to care too much what it was doing to her.

While the career woman-mother of the past decade had no guideposts and few role models, today's women have far more realistic expectations of themselves and the compromises they will need to make in order to combine a career with marriage and motherhood. Although some women still try to fill all three roles to perfection, most are quite able to see that it can't be done, and are willing to adjust their expectations accordingly.

Scaling Down Job Demands

The first realization to come, hopefully before the baby arrives, is that continuing to hold down a full-time job will pretty much relegate motherhood to a part-time sideline. Today, more and more women are refusing to be satisfied with giving their babies only what is left over after a full day at work; they are insisting on scaling down their present job or looking for a new one with mother-sized hours.

Cindy Karl, a computer systems analyst who worked full time after her first baby was born, admits, "Working full time definitely affected my ability to mother my daughter. When you work full time you can't give your child 'quality' time. When you get home, you are tired." Today Cindy and her husband both work under flexible arrangements so that their children, four years and six months of age, only require surrogate care for two and a half hours a day.

"It is very hard to find a part-time job, quality child care, and keep the house going," Cindy says. "I couldn't do it without an extremely supportive husband.

"You need to be very careful not to bite off more than you can chew. My mother used to say you can do two out of three when it comes to being a wife, mother, and full-time career woman. She was right. I feel I made a commitment to my husband when we got married and a commitment to the children when they were born. That puts my career in the back seat."

■ More and more women are refusing to be satisfied with giving their babies only what is left over after a full day at work.

Mary Mosquera, who divorced and went back to work full time when her daughter was three, says, "I tried working full time for a while. I even found the kind of job I really wanted, but it wasn't fair to my little girl. Even though the job itself wasn't stressful, the stress of working all day and getting home at 6:00 or 6:30 P.M., never left time for my little girl. She'd ask for my attention, but I didn't have time to give it to her.

"So I quit and got a job from 9:00 A.M. until 3:00 P.M. Those couple of extra hours a day at home made all the difference in the world. Because I was single and working part-time within a certain income, I received a subsidy of free day care at the best day-care center in the city. Without that help, I would not have been able to afford working part-time."

Computer operator Connie Seymour who went back to work from 2:00 to 6:00 P.M. when her daughter was three months old, recalls, "The best part was that we could greet the morning slowly. We could cuddle and nurse without worrying about rushing out the door to a job. As she has gotten older, it is very nice for me to be at home with her for lunch and dinner."

Connie adds that, "While many people believe in quality time over quantity time, I think it is very important to have a happy medium. A child needs a large quantity of everything."

Physical therapist Lynn Nelson, who has a one-year-old and a three-year-old, worked part-time until recently when she returned to a full-time schedule to make ends meet after she and her husband bought a farm.

Working only part-time may mean sacrificing some career goals, but nothing can replace the time spent being a mother to your child.

"When working part-time I appreciated my time with my kids more and made better use of it. Now that I'm working full-time I feel somewhat out of touch with my kids. I just don't believe the statement 'quality time means more than quantity time.' Sometimes after working hard all day I don't have any 'quality time' left. I'm working on improving it, but it's hard. We are planning on my only having to work full time for twelve to eighteen months."

The decision to work only part-time often, perhaps even usually, means putting career advancement on hold for months or years. But it is a small loss when compared to the gains that accrue from giving yourself time to grow as a mother, and giving your baby the optimal environment for growing into a secure and happy person.

Donna Treaster, who has worked part-time as a consulting social worker for several nursing homes for the past seven years, and has taken two babies to work with her, admits, "I worry about it sometimes. When I quit working full time ten years ago, my friends and I were earning $12,000 a year. Now my friends are earning $30,000 a year and have challenging, interesting, high-level jobs. Will I return to the job market at an entry level of $12,000 at a non-challenging job? Or will my part-time consulting work enable me to return to full-time employment with new skills and experience? I don't know. But I suspect it is better for me that I work this little bit than not at all."

"If I had continued to work full time I could have had a big city office with European travel," says writer/editor Karen English who cut back to working half-time for a major publishing company when the first of her two children was born. "But instead, now I have enough work to keep my skills from disappearing, two super kids, homemade cookies in the jar, car pools, a happy husband, and new career goals. I hope I never have to work full time again. I'm not ready to trade my nursing toddler for a designer business suit."

"I've given up promotions and seen others rise above me who used to be below me," says insurance underwriter Barbara Albert. "Just recently I was offered a full-time job at what would have been a substantial increase in money and prestige. I turned it down, but it was great for my ego. I am sure that when my children are older I'll be able to find a place in this company that will be rewarding to me. Meanwhile, I love being a mother—and that's the reason I gave for turning down the job."

Personal Fulfillment

For some mothers, continuing with their careers, at least on a part-time basis, provides them with a feeling of personal fulfillment they cannot find elsewhere. While they enjoy motherhood, they feel better able to cope with its demands when they have the additional satisfaction they find in the workplace.

"Overall, I find that doing work I enjoy, even for only two or three hours a day, helps me to be more patient with my children," explains Martha Katz-Hyman who is employed part time as an archivist for the American Jewish Historical Society. "I am able to continue with my career on a level we feel is best for our children. It does make for a hectic week—I find that things don't get done as quickly or as smoothly as I might like—and I am often tired at the end of the day. There are some days when all I can do after work is take care of the children. There are days when I feel that the children come out on the short end of the stick, but this is not often. In general, this is a good arrangement. For me, working part-time has worked out well."

Archivist Martha Katz-Hyman has continued her career on a part-time basis because she knows her children Moshe and Michael need her.

"Some days I am glad to go to work and have some adult conversation," admits Cindy Boesch, a social worker who job-shares twenty hours a week. "But by 5:00 P.M., I am always ready to go home. It's such a joy to walk in the door and see my daughter grin and wave her arms, and my son come running. Being away four hours a day makes me more appreciative of them, I think, and some days I swear that they grow in just the short time I am gone."

School teacher Barbara Lovley explains: "I have the teaching position I have always wanted, and therefore I am at ease and happy with *me,* so that when I am at home I am more satisfied as a mother and in turn can give more to my family."

"I feel that contact with other adults and with my students makes me a happier mother," says Arlinda McLaughlin, an elementary school teacher who works half days. "I do not have to long for a career away from home, and I do not have to long to be home with our children. I have time for both. I feel that my job stimulates me, and I find I provide more creative and educational opportunities for my children as a result."

"Continuing to work has enabled us to maintain our lifestyle and be relatively free of financial worry, a high priority for us," says school counselor Sharon Karpinski. "Working was never really a matter of choice. It was a decision my husband and I made early in our marriage and had to do with problems we were determined to avoid. It has been the best decision for us and nursing our babies has definitely helped me have the close relationship I wanted with my children."

Emotional Drawbacks

As fulfilling and stimulating as a career may be, there are always trade-offs and drawbacks when a baby is part of the picture.

"I have encountered several major problems," says college instructor Judith Simon, a biostatistician/epidemiologist. "Finding good, reliable babysitters; finding a way to handle my responsibilities at work when sick children take up a large chunk of time (the baby once had three ear infections in a month); and coping with the sad feeling that often creeps into me that I would rather be at home with the kids than at work.

"Continuing to work has been good for my self-image and is enabling me to keep moderately active in my field so that when I 're-enter' at some time in the future I will still have contacts and recent experience. But I do feel sad about the daily separation."

Canadian nurse Marian McLean finally realized that the only solution that was going to make her family happy was to quit work entirely and be at home full time with her children. She explains: "With our first child, I worked a split rotation. Another RN and I were responsible for one position and we could split it any way we liked as long as one of us showed up. It should have been ideal, but even so it was more separation than we could tolerate as a family. Our marriage suffered more than our son since we kept trying for me to work on my husband's days off so we didn't have to leave the baby with someone else.

"When I was working, all of the adjustments a new parent has to make were just that much harder. It was almost as if the baby was one more job to organize and take care of so our lives could continue to run smoothly. Only I was constantly frustrated because that's not how it works with a baby. The baby was fussy and clingy—no wonder. We had some very difficult times and the strain nearly destroyed our marriage."

There are both positives and negatives, pluses and minuses, in combining motherhood and a career. Anita Untersee, who works primarily from home in order to be close to her six-month-old baby, admits, "Often I am distracted and can't give the baby the attention I'd like to. On the other hand, spending every day alone with a small baby doesn't appeal to me. Having my job and contact with the outside world makes me feel that I am still an interesting and vital person. Still, sometimes I miss just being able to take care of the baby and the housework without feeling pressured to do more."

Fatigue—the Ever Present Enemy

Any woman combining a career and family responsibilities can expect that feeling tired will be as integral a part of her as the color of her eyes or the sound of her voice. Even those who used to bound out of bed with the sun to greet the morning in their pre-motherhood days find themselves pulling the covers over their heads and begging silently for just fifteen more minutes of sleep. Those who were less energetic to start with are often almost completely overwhelmed at times with the demands of their dual roles.

There is no joy that compares with having a new baby to hold and love, but plenty of work and a fair sprinkling of sleepless nights are attached like an umbilical cord. All new mothers are subject to fatigue from the demands of a newborn, but for working mothers the road between infancy and school age is paved with bleary eyes and tired bodies.

"I was, and am, exhausted all the time," admits Hannah Fane, a single mother of two children who is a PhD candidate and college instructor. "I think I have managed to mother my children well, but I have paid a price in stress and fatigue. For many years I had no time at all to myself, but it was worth it."

Teacher Dianne Cooper, also a single mother who has a four-month-old daughter, echoes that feeling. "When I come home I am tired. Although I nurse her and hold her, I am too tired to play with her until I get my second wind later in the evening."

"I'm always tired," says nurse Susan Thies, mother of three children. "I find I spend a great deal of time in the morning holding and playing with Rachel, as if trying to make up for being gone in the evenings."

Nurse Pat Lewis, who also has three young children, adds, "When I work too much or too long, I am tired and irritable, plus the kids have a lot of pent up emotions to let out after being with a babysitter all day."

"Sometimes I feel that Corrine makes me too tired to teach, and that teaching makes me too tired to mother," admits Louise Oppenheimer-Flax.

Ryan Lack is getting an early start in learning to help with the housework.

"I don't have one free second and I am usually tired," says physician Therese Church, who has a year-old daughter.

"I sometimes feel like I am forever juggling with time," says Moira White, a social policy analyst who works half-time with the Ottawa-Carletan Immigrant Services. "But the advantages—being able to work in my chosen field and still continue to nurse the baby and spend the majority of the day with her—far outweigh the disadvantages."

"By going back to work only part time, I assumed I would be able to come home, clean house, play with Jonathan, and still have dinner on the table when my husband came home," recalls librarian Chris Akin. "I don't know who I was kidding—I couldn't keep the house clean even when I wasn't working at all! But after realizing that I couldn't do it all, we made some simple changes and modified our expectations."

"Before I remarried, I was divorced for eight years," says Margaret Risk-Bryan who works as a free-lance editor from her home. "I have learned through my experience as a working, studying, single mother that one's physical and emotional energies are finite. Unfortunately in my situation my son suffered from my need to work to support us. What I experienced without choice as a single parent I do not want to repeat by choice with my new baby."

"My biggest problem is my own attitude," says clinical psychologist Christine Sexton who is employed half-time by Boniface General Hospital in Winnipeg. "My training has taught me to be an achiever in my profession, and now I can't do as much. But I cherish the time I am at home, and perhaps feel it to be even more special by contrast with my working hours. I have also learned a lot about efficiency so I can maximize my time with my toddler."

Carla Bombere sums it up well: "You have to be a positive thinker to keep it all going, for there are many moments when it all seems so overwhelming."

A Supportive Husband—the Essential Ingredient

No man is an island, and no woman can or should carry the entire responsibility for home and family all alone. Children, whether the wife is working or not, are a shared commitment. When the wife is employed outside of the home, then errands, housework, meals, and other household responsibilities need to be shared, too.

But the fact is, as study after study confirms, that even when the wife is employed full-time, 80%—or more—of the household responsibilities still fall to her. In addition to putting in eight hours at the office, she usually puts in another four to five hours a day at home doing cooking, laundry, and cleaning. The total number of hours a day such a woman puts in working, both at the office and at home, rival those of the most hard-driven corporate executive.

When the responsibility of mothering a baby or preschooler is added to the list in such an already heavily unbalanced situation, the scales are likely to tip and crush the poor, exhausted woman under a load of responsibilities she can't possibly cope with. Current research indicating that wives demand more of themselves both at work and at home than husbands, and that they worry more that success in their careers will interfere with family life, contains not the slightest element of surprise to the working woman of the 80s.

But today, most women seem to be learning not to expect the impossible of themselves, and a growing number of these women are blessed with husbands who are willing to shed their suitcoats and outdated images of masculinity and accept a greater, though still perhaps not equal, share of household and child-care responsibilities. Without a shared commitment to the lifestyle they have chosen and a team approach to managing the home front, a dual career family is in for a rough time.

Realistic expectations head the list of the items that a two career couple needs to communicate about and agree on.

"Couples may find that their lifestyles are eased if they become more realistic about how much and how well they can do," reports Catalyst's publication, *Corporations and Two-Career Families: Directions for the Future.* "People who place unrealistic demands on their own performance both at work and at home, and who blame themselves when things go wrong, pay a price in increased stress and poorer health. . . . Investing time, energy, and money in achieving a satisfactory combination of career and marriage is well worth

A supportive husband who shares in household responsibilities is the key to success for many working women.

the effort. . . . The *combination* has more of an effect on health than *either* satisfaction with career or satisfaction with marriage."

Studies report, and the experience of many dual career couples confirms, that husbands are more likely—and willing—to share child care than household responsibilities.

"Wives had most and husbands had least responsibility for laundry, cooking, grocery and household shopping, cleaning and housework, and child care, in that order," the Catalyst report continues. "Wives also had more responsibility for handling bills and finances."

Husbands tended to carry the major responsibility for the traditionally male tasks—car and home maintenance and repair, yard work and gardening.

In what nearly every career woman-mother will recognize as a classic understatement of the obvious, Catalyst reports that "Recent research has tended to suggest that working wives are holding down two full-time jobs."

Finding a comfortable division of household responsibilities is one of the most crucial challenges faced by dual career families—and one which has enormous long range implications for their continued survival as a couple. A couple's ability to communicate concerning their needs and expectations can either strengthen or destroy their marriage. And the need to share and communicate during the hectic, stressful years of raising a young family takes on added importance when both parents are employed.

Says Ellen Bright, whose husband cares for their twenty-two-month-old and four-month-old children while she works at night, "My husband is realizing after a few arguments that my job is important to me, but I'm not Supermom and need some help with the meals, housework, and the kids. So he does help. He'll start the dishes, but only does the plates and glasses. He soaks everything else (for days). But the point is he is realizing that there is a lot of work involved with housekeeping."

"My husband and five-year-old son always fix the evening meal," explains Carolyn Barnhart, an associate to the dean at the University of Wisconsin. "When a working mother first comes home, all children, whether nursing or not, want to be close to her. Because my husband prepares the evening meal, I am able to give the children my attention from the minute I walk in the door."

Virginia McGowan, a teaching assistant at the University of Toronto, has a husband that millions of working women would give a lifetime of promotions to be able to clone. "He cares for his daughter, cleans the house, makes breakfasts, lunches, and dinners, and does the laundry when required. He even finds time to pat the dog! All this, and he is also working very hard on research for his degree."

"Lifesavers for me have been a cleaning woman one day a week, a crock pot, and a dear husband who helps me with the children and never complains about the seemingly permanent clutter or the burned disaster we occasionally have for supper," says professional musician Diane Dollak, mother of five children. "My husband doesn't cook but he will always call out for Chinese food or bring home hamburgers in an emergency. In turn, I make a real effort to keep up with the laundry and meals, and to keep in touch with him and not take for granted his patience and willingness to support me."

Madeleine Holmberg, a legal assistant who has taken her year-old baby to work with her since shortly after she was born, has been blessed not only with a supportive husband, but a mother who gladly pitches in and helps, too.

"My husband cooks our dinners and helps a great deal with the housework and child care," she explains. "My mother, a practicing attorney, always seems to have a sixth sense about me and can always tell when I am getting too exhausted and comes to our rescue. But it keeps getting better week by week, month by month, and after a whole year I can't imagine doing it any other way."

Adaptations and Expectations

Perfection is not for this world, although some people are amazingly difficult to convince of that and insist on continuing to try for it. It's easy to spot them. They're the ones who, exhausted or not, can't sleep for thinking about the unfinished work at the office; the ones who have ulcers and heart attacks because they have never understood that relaxing is as vital as eating to continued good health and well-being; the ones who do the work of five people because they insist that every job has to be done exactly right and, of course, they're the only ones who know how to do it "right."

The woman who accepts the dual challenges of motherhood and a career has a stress load that is equal to that of the most high-powered executive. But it doesn't have to mar her enjoyment of these two important facets of her life if she is willing to make adaptations and adjustments as they become necessary, and bring her expectations in line with what she can realistically and sanely hope to achieve.

While each couple's solutions to the particular problems that face them will be uniquely their own, being aware of the most likely areas of trouble can help couples to recognize and work on conflicts before the situation has a chance to get out of hand.

Mentioned most frequently as disadvantages of combining a career and motherhood, respondents in Catalyst's survey named: "Not enough time together; too much pressure; too much to do; not enough leisure; no one has full-time concern with household; no home back-up; children don't have enough parenting."

"Allocation of time" headed the list by a wide margin as the worst problem faced by dual career couples. Financial issues, poor communications, and conflicts over housework were second, third, and fourth.

Combining motherhood and a career is not the impossible dream. But it takes a lot of work, and the ability to put things in perspective.

"It is very possible to nurse a baby and continue a career," observes ballet teacher Deborah Chase-Cargill. "But like everything else worthwhile in life, it is not always easy and certain adaptations are continually being made."

Jennell Woodard, from her own years of experience as a working woman-mother, offers these suggestions for helping to achieve a satisfying balance between home life and the demands of the working world.

1. Consider taking time out for special weekends to go on a hike, picnic, bike ride, or play backyard games. Drop everything else and *play.*
2. If some of your children are older (as young as five years, in my experience), give them special small jobs. It will teach them responsibility and will provide an opportunity for the parents to praise them lavishly. Even if they don't do the job perfectly, they'll feel they are helping out. But keep your expectations reasonable—don't deprive them of their only chance to be children.
3. Look for ways to make your home efficient. Toss all unnecessary items. They take up space and will need to be dusted. Look for easy-to-prepare meals that the children

may be able to help with. Fixing dinner together may provide a great time to talk over the day's events.

4. Realize that we all have off days. None of us has a picture perfect family. Be willing to forgive yourself. Let your children know that you love them and that you are doing the best you can.

Time—the Most Precious Commodity

Someone once said that whatever amount of free time you have, somehow the responsibilities in your life always expand to fill it. In the case of the working mother, the responsibilities expand not only to fill it, but to reach to the Twilight Zone and beyond.

Allocating the finite amount of time that is available to meet the seemingly infinite demands that divide and multiply with ever increasing speed presents itself as a new challenge with the dawn of each new day.

Accepting that there will never be enough time to do everything is the foundation upon which all of the other decisions concerning the expenditure of time need to be based. Once a couple accepts this reality, the process of assigning priorities for using the available time becomes far simpler.

The first priority, as it should be, is spending time with the baby/children.

■ Combining motherhood and a career takes a lot of work and the ability to put things in perspective.

"Working has limited my time with the children," admits teacher Patricia Priore, "but I love mothering and I like working, too. My husband and I have tended to cut back on after-school activities and weekend activities with friends in favor of family things. We like to bike ride, play games, take walks, or go to the zoo."

"Certainly the disadvantage to working is that my day is pretty full, and I find myself turning down many social opportunities unless they involve our children," says job-sharing elementary school teacher Arlinda McLaughlin. "I guard my time at home more carefully than if I were home all day. The advantages of this situation are great, though, because our children go with us more often than in most families. We seek many activities that involve the entire family. Because we have some built-in separation, we make it a point to be together the rest of the day."

"I'm doing something during the day for myself," says Lynda Dunal, "so when I'm with Patrick it's 'our time.' I try to make myself fully available to him from the time I pick him up at day care. I enjoy every moment I am with him. Weekends are always very special family times."

Lynda, like many other working mothers with babies and toddlers, has found that bringing her son into bed at night fills a variety

of needs. "Patrick was a night-waker for several months. I was so glad I was nursing so I could just bring him into bed with us and we could both fall asleep as he nursed. My husband often didn't even know that Patrick had awakened. And what a delight to wake up to that grinning face next to ours! He may not need the milk as much as he needs the closeness and comfort he gets from snuggling up to me. I feel that by nursing I can repay him for some of the time I don't spend with him during the day, and we can be close at night."

"Before my three-day work cycle begins, I get three outfits together so there is no concern about what to wear," explains cosmetics consultant Mary Lou MacGregor. "Meals are planned ahead, ready in the freezer, so there is no worry about 'what's for dinner?' when I get home.

"Usually the day after working we do something special together as a family such as a trip to the zoo, or a river drive, or any of the things Owen and Christina like to do. They go everywhere with me. It's so easy to pack a diaper and go. It seems so natural, so wonderful to be together. The joys of my life happen when I am with my family."

Housework and Harmony

For the working mother-career woman, there is no thought of keeping up with the housework, or if that thought somehow slips in, it is to be banished as quickly as possible. When it comes to housework, the only goal is to keep from drowning in it.

"I have the feeling I'll never catch up on my housework because

Taking time to relax and enjoy family activities together is a vital element in successfully combining a career and motherhood.

my days at home are spent with the kids," admits court deputy Barbara Tickner who job shares her position with another mother. "But I have always let the housework slide rather than take time away from the kids."

Having outside household help is an option that career women-mothers are taking in increasing numbers. Catalyst's study points out, "Although sharing household responsibilities is important, it will not change the number of hours available. Time is finite. To maximize time, couples could pay for some household services. Although help is expensive, it is a long-term investment in both careers and the marriage."

However the housework gets done, whether the meals come from your own kitchen or the deli, the thing that will ultimately count the most is what the parents give of themselves to their children.

"I often feel torn between career goals and family needs," says parent education teacher Elizabeth River. "When my children or I start to show signs of stress, I force myself to slow down. I love my current job, and I don't think I would have ever found this rewarding job of working with parents and toddlers if it hadn't been for my need to work part-time.

"I wanted the rich, total, fulfilling, frustrating, joyous, painful, loving experience of mothering this child of mine."

Who would want it any other way?

■ Part 5

Babies, Careers, and Priorities: Blueprint for tomorrow

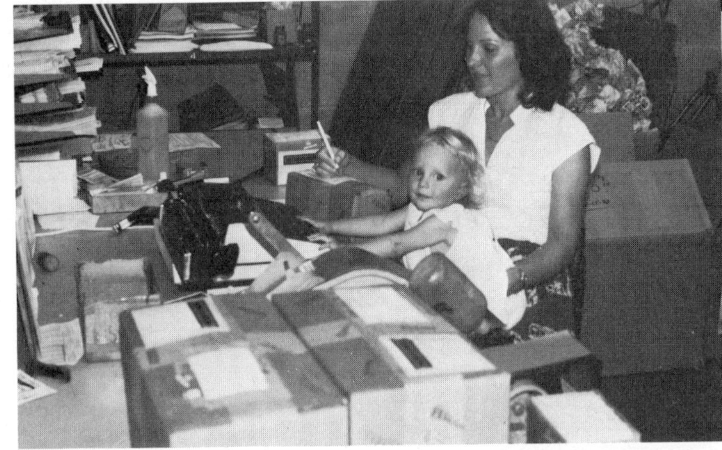

Chapter 16

Profiles of Initiative

Redesigning the American work ethic

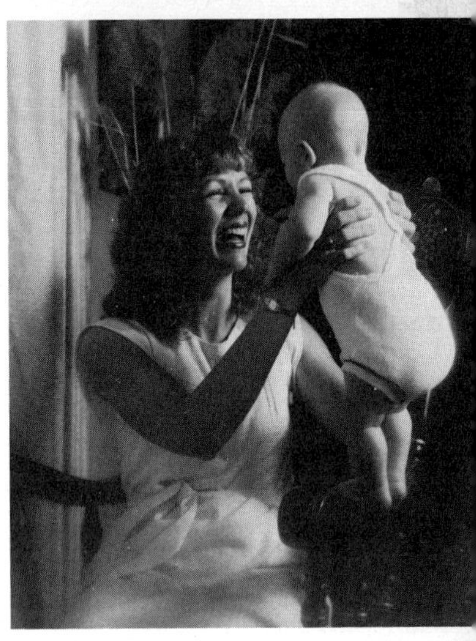

For all the myths and rose-colored nostalgia, perhaps there is something to be said for the good old days. True, there weren't very many options for more than half of the population—the half that had been born as females. But then, there weren't as many hard choices that had to be made, either. Women who might have had some glimmer of a life beyond the dust mop knew that they had no choice but to stay at home, stay married, and make the best of it. Even though women of all manner of persuasions and inclinations were expected to stuff themselves into pretty much the same "happy homemaker" mold, there was undoubtedly a fair measure of security in knowing what was expected of you, and doing it.

Today, women are no longer expected to conform to a uniform, well-defined set of expectations. The limitations—and the security—of the 1950s have given way to the freedom—and the uncertainties—of the 1980s, where women can and do combine, divide, arrange, and rearrange career, marriage, and motherhood.

How and where do women strike the best balance between the need/desire to work and the need/desire to parent? They do it in conventional ways and outlandish ways; they do it through quiet, gentle determination and hard-nosed negotiations; they do it by sheer luck and, not infrequently, by raw guts.

But regardless of *how* women achieve the balance they want, they all find the best balance in precisely the same place. And where is that place? It is the place that feels right to *her,* that works well for the individual woman and her family, where family and career meet comfortably and blend smoothly, where one element doesn't need to be sacrificed for the other.

How and where each woman finds the degree of commitment to the working world that is best for her, and exactly where she strikes the balance between the demands of work and the needs of her family is as unique to her as her own fingerprints. But although situations and solutions vary, the commitment to mothering, and mothering well, is uniformly the same.

In the following pages, we would like to introduce you to five such women who understand the importance of being true to themselves and who searched until they found their own unique solutions to combining motherhood and a career. Although their situations and solutions may be worlds away from your own, there is a lesson for all of us in the commitment and perseverance they have shown as they have struggled to combine the diverse elements of their lives into a satisfying whole.

■ Deborah Fash, Speech Pathologist

Before I became pregnant, I firmly believed that there was nothing at all wrong with putting a baby in a good quality day-care center. But my husband felt differently, and he said that we weren't going to have children at all if they were going to spend their days with a babysitter.

Then during my pregnancy, I began to form an attachment to the baby, and my feelings began to change. I found myself becoming less interested in my career, although I didn't as yet realize how difficult it would actually be to leave the baby. Halfway through the pregnancy we decided that I would quit my job when the baby was born in order to be able to care for him full time. Even though I felt confident that this was the right decision, I felt guilty about leaving my career.

When I quit my full-time job, I thought that I would be unable to work at all. I thought that it was all or nothing. I can see now that I really underestimated my possibilities, as I think many other women do who don't want to work full time but think they have no other options. We were really scared about making it financially when I quit, but knew that we had enough savings to last for a few months.

As it turned out, we didn't have to worry for long. In the weeks after Brian was born I was contacted by five different agencies that were looking for a part-time person. When Brian was four months old, I accepted the most part-time of these positions.

I now work in a Head Start program on a contract basis with semi-flexible hours. I began by working two hours twice a week, then increased to three hours twice a week. This year, as Brian nears two years of age, I will probably move up to four hours twice a week. I am able to do all of my paperwork at home, on paid time, and often take Brian with me for the occasional meetings I have with my supervisors or other staff members.

My supervisors and co-workers have been wonderful. They gladly accommodated me when I was only willing to be away from Brian two hours at a time and they never complained if I had to cancel because Brian was sick. They often asked me to bring him in to see them and suggested that he accompany me to certain staff meetings.

There were several aspects to this particular situation that worked heavily in my favor: The director of the program is a grandmother who really enjoys babies; many other staff members also have children and really understand a mother and baby's need to be together; and the Head Start program itself is child-centered. It also didn't hurt at all that it is somewhat difficult to find a qualified person for this kind of position in a small town.

Once Brian was born, meeting his needs and being his mother became the most important thing in my life. I wouldn't have left him full time unless our lives depended on it. No one else can do what I do for him. I wanted to raise him my way, with my values.

I think that our society makes it very hard on a career woman who wants to raise a family. I did well in graduate school and was told that great things were expected of me. When I quit work so that I could stay at home and raise my baby, those words rang in my ears. Even though I wanted a baby and

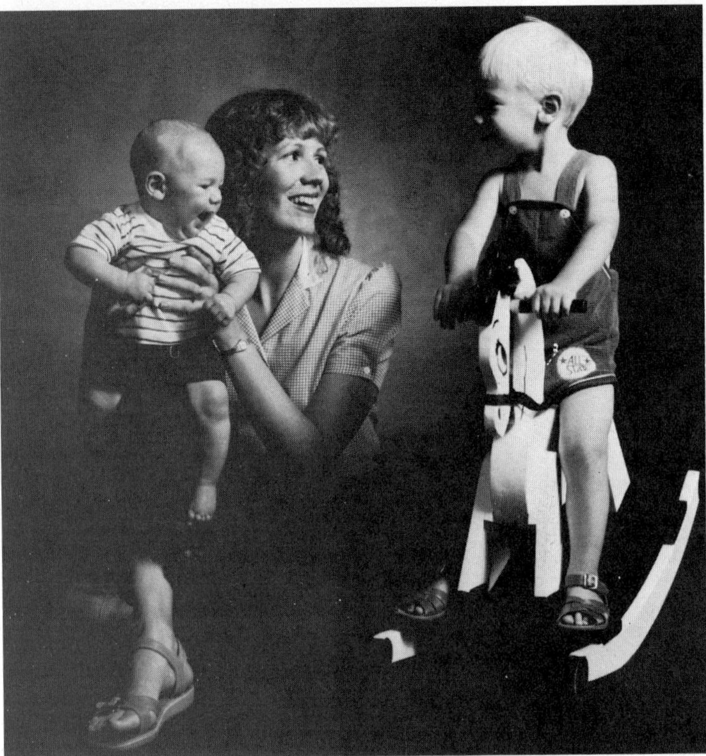

wanted to raise him myself, I felt almost guilty about quitting. But I know I did the right thing, and I feel real sadness for mothers and babies who must be separated for extended periods of time. When I was leaving Brian for only two hours at a time I worried about him, and hurried as fast as I could at work so that I could get home to him as quickly as possible.

My income dropped by $12,000 when I switched from full-time to part-time work, but with the income tax deduction we got for Brian and the drop into a lower tax bracket, we only lost $4,000 in spendable income. The money I earned made the difference between staying afloat and sinking financially. Working part-time does not allow us to make major purchases or to live luxuriously, but the time I am able to spend with Brian is much more valuable than anything money could ever buy.

Certainly I am not advancing in my career by working only a few hours a week as I do now, but it does enable me to "keep my foot in the door." If I were to quit for more than two years or so I would have to go back to school, and the nearest university offering course-work in speech pathology is four hours away. I can't keep my skills as high as I would like because I am not willing to attend training conferences without Brian. But, on the other hand, I am learning a lot about language development from my son! ■

■ Suzanne Otwell, Legal Assistant

I grew up in the 1950s, in an era when women were raised to believe that you went to college, got married, had kids, and let someone else worry about producing an income. Well, times have changed! I wish now that I had given more thought to a career instead of just "jobs"—preferably a career that could have been set aside for some years while the children were small and then resumed with some ease. It never occurred to me that someday I might be supporting the family, as I am doing now.

Five years ago when my husband lost his job, I began working in a law office as a legal assistant for a few hours on Saturday. My husband was able to be at home to care for the children, then four and eight years old. When the youngest reached school age, I began working two days a week from 9:00 A.M. until 3:00 P.M. so that I could be home with the children after school. The system has worked fairly well except when school holidays roll around. That calls for a real juggling act, swapping days with another part-timer with whom I job share. Fortunately for me, the job is flexible. I manage the finances of three elderly clients, which requires me to be in the office only a few hours a week, and I visit them in the nursing home as needed. I have a fair amount of leeway in when I do things. I simply keep track of my hours and I am paid accordingly.

I also work a second part-time job as a legal secretary. After my husband was reorganized out of his job two months ago and again unemployed, I began working more hours to help with the family finances, and now work three days a week in the law office where I am employed as a legal secretary. My husband is working from home as a free-lance writer, so he is almost always there at 3:00 P.M. when the children, now nine and twelve years old, come home from school.

Both of my employers have been sympathetic to my often bizarre arrangements. Neither has pressured me to work full time, though I may soon have to. We are about to lose the hospitalization benefits my husband had through his former job, which is almost a bigger loss than the salary. My coworkers sometimes think I am a little crazy for all of the juggling around that I do. And in fact, now that both children are in school, it may soon be easier to work one full-time job and reap the benefits of health and life insurance and the other fringes that come with full-time employment.

Holding down two part-time jobs has made my schedule kind of crazy—one day here, two or three days someplace else. This can be difficult for all of us, so I make it a point to keep a schedule on the refrigerator and keep the schools well informed.

But I am glad to be able to contribute financially. My husband was able to support us for the years when the children were small; now it is my turn to help him out by contributing to the family income. Right now I am the only one in the family with a regular paycheck.

I feel fortunate to have been able to be at home full time until the youngest child was four years old, and now I certainly have an increased appreciation for the woman who comes home tired at the end of the day but still has to be fresh enough to cope with the demands of a young family. I feel that the early years I spent at home with my children have enabled them to cope well with my temporary absences as they have gotten older. And fortunately my husband has been pretty available to them, too.

During these years when I have settled for non-professional jobs in order to preserve flexibility of time and be more accessible to the children, some of my college friends have told me I was "throwing away my education." Well, this week I worked on Latin and an American history project with my seventh grader, helped my fourth grader with her report on Maryland Indians, and helped her practice the baritone horn. Now, *that's* a liberal arts education! ■

■ Darolyn Butler, Sales Representative

As a traveling Western wear sales representative with a territory that included east Texas and southern Louisiana, I decided before I even became pregnant that I could combine motherhood with my job by switching from a car to a motor home so that I could take the baby with me when I traveled.

When my first baby was born three years ago I hired a sitter to travel with us, packed up my thirty-one foot motor home, and off we went. I was back on the road four weeks after giving birth, watched my diet carefully, and never had a moment's trouble nursing the baby. My milk never failed me. Even after I fell off a horse and fractured my spinal vertabra, I was able to nurse the baby while lying in the ambulance.

I was able to spend wonderful, devoted times with the baby during the drives from one account to another. I often thought that I had more time with her on the road than I did when I was at home with all of the distractions of office and household duties.

Even though I sometimes worked eighty to a hundred hours a week, I was never more than a few moments away from the baby. When I had meetings to attend, my sitter would bring the baby in and I would simply excuse myself for a nursing break. Everyone seemed to understand and even admire my insistence on breastfeeding. During the two years I nursed my firstborn, I never gave one bottle of formula. A permanent sitter always traveled with us, but the baby always knew who the "meal wagon" was, so there was never any confusion about who mother was, either.

My income increased steadily from the time my first baby was born in August of 1979 until January of 1982 when the popularity of Western wear began to decline. The company reduced my territory about the time my second baby was born in June of 1982. Although they never actually said that the birth of my second baby played a part in the decision, I've always felt that it gave them what they thought was a good reason to cut my territory. After all of my plotting and planning to be a good mother while keeping my career going full steam, the career was finally sidetracked by a stereotyped male decision.

I'm now working as a sales representative for a new company with a territory covering south, central, and east Texas. I still travel with the children in our motor home when I need to be on the road. I've also gone into partnership in a new enterprise which is showing some promise of success.

Combining work and motherhood has been a very positive experience for me. Having my work and my babies makes me an extremely happy person. It enables me to afford to have the drudgery work done by someone else, leaving my time free for mothering and working. During my peak sales years in the early 1980s, I had a full-time babysitter/housekeeper/cook and a full-time secretary.

I found that I enjoyed traveling even more in the company of my baby and the comfort of a motor home. The children helped my business by establishing my solidarity and maturity, and people seemed to be impressed with my desire to mother so completely that I would take my children with me over hill and dale.

I like to do anything that I do as well as I possibly can, and combining my traveling career with mothering seemed almost too easy according to some onlookers!

It is perfectly possible to breastfeed and mother while continuing to make headway in a career if one is determined to do it. ■

■ Sheila Young, Craftsperson

Although my youngest child, now almost thirteen years old, hardly qualifies as a baby, I, too, am facing the mothering/career dilemma, although from a somewhat different perspective.

After much thought and consideration, my husband and I have recently separated. My five children are all in their teens, two of them in college, so I was a stay-at-home mother during times when it was easier to make that decision. Even though I graduated from college with a degree in accounting, I never actually put those skills to work in the business world.

During the past two years, knowing in my heart what was down the road in my relationship with my husband, I began looking carefully at the work options that were available to me. I worked part-time for a while during the time my husband and I were still together so I could see how well it would work for me to be employed outside of the home.

I did a lot of soul-searching during this time, since these important decisions would affect me and the children for years to come. I decided that if there were any way to avoid it, I didn't want to burden my kids with two drastic changes at once. Even in the best of family circumstances, it takes its toll when a happy stay-at-home mother goes out to work full time. In the end I decided that to couple the loss that my children would feel because of the separation with the loss of their stay-at-home mother was more than I was willing to ask of them.

I also realized that because I had not ever been employed outside of my home, I would have to start at the bottom of the ladder and work my way up, which would mean that the net return for the hours I would be away from home would be very small. I would have been willing to do it, but felt it would have been too hard on the family financially and emotionally to make it worthwhile.

So I decided, instead of seeking outside employment, to try to turn my craft-making skills into an at-home business. When I took a close look at my hobby and my need to produce an income, I felt there was

a good chance that one could make the other possible. I have now set up my own business, making and selling hand-loomed personalized knit hats. Financially it may be risky and in the long run I will have to contend with retirement options, health plans, and life insurance, as well as the need to make new contacts and fill my social needs as a divorced woman. But for right now my main concern is the emotional well-being of my children, and I feel strongly that I can best fill those emotional needs by being here at home. As much as I believe in being home with young children, it is almost more important to be at home with teenagers, especially if this has been your lifestyle and you are going to be facing major adjustments in your family unit.

I am very grateful that I have an alternative to working outside of the home to explore. I feel fortunate that I love the work I am doing, and believe that this particular career path will pay big dividends—though not necessarily financial ones—in the future. I have been a La Leche League Leader for eighteen years, and I know that La Leche League has been and continues to be a major influence in my life, even now as my youngest child approaches thirteen. It has been La Leche League's philosophy that has given me that courage and conviction to pursue my at-home business in spite of the risks, because I know that what I value most is safeguarding the children's emotional well-being. For me, working from home is the best way to meet that goal. ■

■ Colleen Zubkow, Nursing Coordinator

I was employed part-time as Director of Care for a nursing home until two weeks before my daughter was born. I finally resigned after taking a one-year maternity leave because the nursing home was not willing to negotiate arrangements that would allow me to meet my baby's needs—and my need to meet those needs.

I did not work outside my home at all until I was approached by a local home care program when Shea was eighteen months old. After giving long, hard consideration to their job proposal, I submitted a detailed professional resumé with an additional two pages entitled "How I Am Prepared To Work." I set out my requirements for how I felt the position should be handled, and I also spelled out my personal beliefs on the importance of mother-baby togetherness. I made it very clear that I was not interested in the job unless I could work it my way—with Shea's needs first. I was at an advantage because I was fortunate enough to have the very education, background, and work experience required for the job. This made it more likely that they would accept my conditions, but I wouldn't have wanted the job any other way.

My proposal for part-time work, twelve to fifteen hours a week, with the stipulation that Shea could be with me at all times, was accepted. My manager thought I was a bit radical and extremist, but otherwise he was receptive. After he and his wife had their first child, however, he became noticeably more tolerant and supportive. The majority of the people serving on my board of directors are grandparents, which seemed to work in my favor. Perhaps it is partially because they come from a generation that largely opposes working mothers that they seem to be so impressed with my approach to mothering and working.

Baby Shea could and did come with me to work at all times until she was ready and willing to separate from me, at about two years of age. She went to all board meetings, assessment committee meetings, and staff conferences. I spent about four hours a week at the head office, doing the rest of my work as Nursing Coordinator out of my home. I have an office at home complete with desk, phone, filing cabinets, and answering service, and can fit my working hours around the needs of my family.

My biggest challenge was disciplining myself to work at home—it was so easy to procrastinate, to put it off until tomorrow.

The total situation has been full of bonuses for both Shea and myself. I was free to change, cancel, or restructure many aspects of my work whenever necessary in order to be able to meet Shea's needs. This was the crucial factor which was responsible for making everything work out so very, very well. There was little conflict between Shea's need for me and my work obligations.

I love working part-time. I especially love having only part-time stress. I am much more effective as a nurse now than when I was working full time. I do not burn out as easily, and find I can recharge quickly with so much time away from work.

Why would I choose to work only under circumstances such as these that allow me to put my baby/child first? Because many people can equal or outdo me in my nursing position, but no one could mother and nurture and care for Shea as I can.

I am quite replaceable in the career world. But as Shea's mother, I know I am unique and irreplaceable. ■

Corporations Proving It Can Work

Xerox, IBM, General Motors, AT&T, International Telephone and Telegraph—each is widely recognized as a corporate giant.

But there are many other companies that stand equally tall in the business world. They are giants not by virtue of their size or Dun and Bradstreet ratings but because they have had the vision to see that their employees are people with needs, and the foresight to institute policies that reflect and respond to those needs.

In the following pages we will look beyond the balance sheets and into the corporate hearts of three such organizations with exceptional levels of responsiveness to the needs of their employees.

Though the size, structure, and net worth of these companies vary widely, they all share a common denominator: Each one understands that what is good for the employee is good for the company, and each has boldly modified, accommodated, restructured, and revamped its policies in order to safeguard the well-being of the organization's most valuable asset—its human capital.

Control Data Corporation

Strike up a conversation in nearly any group of corporate executives; mention topics like industry pace setter, multiple work options, innovative management, eyes-on-tomorrow planning; then watch as every head in the room turns toward Minneapolis, international headquarters of one of the most brightly shining jewels in the crown of American business: Control Data Corporation.

Control Data began in 1957 with the goal of developing large scale computers capable of handling massive scientific and engineering problems. The development and manufacture of tape drives, printers, disk drives, and terminals quickly became part of the picture, and soon Control Data also had a billion dollar a year international peripheral products business.

With products and services now being sold in forty-seven countries and annual revenues in excess of $4 billion a year, Control Data employs 58,000 people worldwide, 48,000 in the United States. Nearly ten percent of Control Data's U.S. labor force work under one of five modified work options that the company offers. In addition, fully one-third of all employees in the company's non-manufacturing divisions work under some form of flexible hours.

In the process of becoming the national showcase for the viability of modified working arrangements, Control Data has demonstrated to a rigid, tradition-bound business world not only that a choice of work options is popular with employees, but that they are profitable for the company as well. Far from being too costly and too cumbersome as so many businesses imagine, Control Data has demonstrated that modified work options are a viable, workable alternative. As Control Data's experience so clearly indicates, what is good for employees is good for the company.

"For us, hiring part-time employees started as a business necessity," explains Frank Dawe, Control Data's Vice President of Personnel and Administration. "Various divisions in our corporation would have peak times, so it became appropriate for us to have part-time employees to handle the extra workload during peak times.

"In more recent years, due to the expansion and contraction in high technology industries brought about by fluctuations in the economy, we found that we needed to have flexibility within our work force. We researched the possibilities, and found that the best solution was to hire supplemental employees."

Supplemental employees, as defined by Control Data, are those who work twenty-five hours a week or less. Nearly 5,000 people in Control Data's work force fall into the supplemental category. Some fifteen percent of these are professional level people, including engineers, draftspeople, programmers, and employee relations personnel.

"Some of our supplemental employees want to work less than a full week, and some use this route as a means of gaining entry into the company hoping to become full time later on," Dawe says.

While most part-time employees feel fortunate to have one or two paid holidays, Control Data, as of July 1984, will be offering a full range of benefits to its supplemental employees who worked 900 or more hours during the previous year.

"We feel we have an obligation to these people to provide them with prorated benefits: sick leave, disability benefits, health insurance, vacation, and pension," according to Dawe.

But Control Data's policy goes one giant step further.

"If an employee who doesn't yet qualify for prorated benefits needs immediate health insurance coverage, we have a catastrophic benefits program, fully paid for by the employee, that will provide immediate coverage."

In addition to its supplemental employee program, Control Data has a number of other work options for those whose lives fit better into something other than the traditional nine-to-five office mold.

Flextime: Intrigued by the German system of gliding hours, Control Data introduced flextime into the company in 1973. Although the employees who work under flextime put in a full workweek, they are free to adjust their hours, as their needs or preferences dictate, around the core time of 9:00 A.M. to 3:00 P.M. How widespread is the flextime option at Control Data? "Basically, a manager has to show a reason why an employee could not participate in the flextime program," Dawe explains. "It's available to just about everybody."

Dawe estimates that about half of the employees who take advantage of the flextime option do so for family reasons. "Single parents, both male and female, make use of the flextime arrangement to get the children off to school in the morning. In other cases, couples with only one car use flextime to coordinate their working hours so that they can come and go at the same time.

Work Station, Control Data's response to the national energy crisis, was created in 1976. "We were concerned as a major corporation about doing something to help alleviate the energy problem," Dawe says. "So we had some employees begin to work at home so they wouldn't have to travel into the office, and some work part or all of the time out of one of our other offices closer to their home even though that office was not their primary work site."

Currently, Control Data has about forty employees participating in the Work Station program. "We thought it would be bigger," Dawe admits, "but when we started we didn't select the right people to go into the program. Management did the selecting of the participants early on, but it didn't work out as we expected. Many of the employees we chose missed the social interaction with their fellow workers and so they were anxious to get back to their normal work site. We've found that social interaction is the key factor." Employees who don't need it do well in the program, and those who do need it drop out quickly.

"For those who like the arrangement, we have found that they are more productive than the workers in the major work sites. They're motivated to do their best, and the accommodation fits the pattern of their lives.

"Carefully administered, we think this program has great potential."

Homework, which allows employees with permanent or long term disabilities to work at computer terminals from their homes, was initiated in 1978 by Control Data Deputy Chairman Norbert R. Berg "who felt strongly that we should provide a means for our disabled employees to be productive," Dawe explains.

Dawe estimates that fifteen to twenty people, all of whom were already employed by Control Data when they became disabled, are currently involved in the program.

"We've been pleased to see that other companies are now using the same principle to employ disabled individuals in their own organizations."

Job Sharing, although it exists at Control Data, is low man on the work options totem pole. "We only have a handful of job sharers," Dawe reports. "A few are in the professional ranks, but most of them are clerical."

The Selby Bindery: The real showpiece among Control Data's

employment innovations is its Selby plant, located in the Minneapolis inner city, that employs *only* part-timers, 249 of them in all. Working mothers come in for five hours a day, and then student employees come in for the remaining three hours to complete the shift.

"The program has been very successful from every point of view," Dawe points out. "The Selby plant is a profitable operation for us."

Control Data also operates inner city plants in Rush Heights in Baltimore, Washington D.C., and an Appalachia area in Kentucky. "We've had very good experiences with all of our inner city plants," Dawe says.

Day Care. Recognizing that affordable day care is an acute problem for inner city mothers, Control Data and a group of other local businesses established the North Side Child Care Facility in 1970, light years before the rest of the business world recognized that employees had children, much less that they needed to be cared for.

"We had a lot of mothers who were missing work because of child care problems," Dawe explains, "so we decided it would be in everybody's best interest to establish a day care center to help out. Absenteeism and tardiness both dropped dramatically as a result."

The day care center, with the help of government subsidies and contributions from participating organizations, is self-supporting.

People, Profits, and Progress. "We have established an environment for all of our employees that provides them with a sense of their own self worth," Dawe explains. "We offer a climate of stability, we reward employees for performance, we give our people the right training to do their job. It has always been our feeling that if we do all of these things, we can't help but be successful and have a satisfied work force. This management philosophy works both to the benefit of the company and the individual."

Dawe feels that all indications point to a reduced workweek for all workers in the years to come, and that there will been increasing availability of flexible work options for those who want them.

"The traditional workweek of thirty-five or forty hours is going to come down, as it already has in Europe, in order to reduce unemployment," Dawe points out. "We'll see the workweek reduced in the United States, too.

"Options to the traditional workweek are going to increase. Highly skilled employees are going to be in short supply, and the company with the most work options is going to be the company that attracts and keeps the people they want."

Is it reasonable to think that other companies could follow Control Data's lead in providing a variety of alternatives to traditional work patterns?

"You can never superimpose one culture on another," Dawe concludes. "It has to blend in. But anyone can do what we're doing." ■

■ La Leche League International

Although multi-million dollar corporate giants like Control Data Corporation are often the front runners in innovative employment practices, sometimes it is the very small company, acutely aware of its employees' personal needs, that institutes personnel policies which are light years ahead of the rest of the business world.

Consider, for example, the little one room, three person office tucked away on the second floor of an obscure building on the outskirts of metropolitan Chicago some twenty years ago that was offering modified working conditions that most of the rest of the business world, even today, hasn't yet begun to think about: a workday that regularly ended at 3 P.M. so mothers could be home with their children after school; summers off for mothers with small children; special summer hours for mothers of older children so they could be finished for the day at lunchtime; the option of using paid sick days to stay home to care for a sick child; pro-rated fringe benefits for all employees working twenty or more hours a week.

Back in 1963 the people in this tiny office had never even heard of a Human Resource Director, much less had the benefit of such a specialist's expertise. Nor were these people visionaries who were able to accurately foresee the kind of flexible employment options that would be in demand a generation later when career women-mothers began to flood the labor market.

How then—and why—was this little organization able to see so precisely what kind of modifications working mothers needed in order to successfully integrate work and family life?

The answer, of course, is that the people formulating the policies were themselves mothers, mothers who insisted on making the work fit the mother, not the mother fit the work, so that the needs of the children would not be compromised. The organization was La Leche League.

When the League's one room office opened in the spring of 1963, Betty Wagner, its lone employee and one of the organization's founders, closed up shop every day at 12:00 noon so she could pick up her kindergartner at school and go home for the day. The second person to be hired, LaVerne Spadero, also left every day at noon to go home and fix lunch for her school-age children, but she returned to put in a few more hours in the afternoon after the children had returned to school. The third woman added to the staff in the fall of 1963, La Leche League founding mother Edwina Froehlich, recalls that she had planned to work a full day that year, from 9:00 A.M. till 3:00 P.M., because the youngest of her three sons had started first grade. "But I spent more of the year at home taking care of kids with the chicken pox and measles than I spent in the office."

As the organization's membership mushroomed during the early and mid 1970s, the office staff grew as well. By 1977 the original staff of three had expanded to forty-four.

"Our employees were almost all mothers with school-age children," explains founder Betty Wagner, who now serves as the organization's Executive Director "and each was pretty much free to establish her own hours. We were always willing to accommodate mother hours, and we *expected* a mother to stay home and take care of her children when they were sick. No one ever had to be concerned about losing her job because she took time off to care for a sick child."

Several of La Leche League's mother-employees wanted to be able to be at home with their children during the summer months, so "right from the beginning we established the practice of hiring high school and college girls as summer replacements for those employees who wanted the summer off," Mrs. Wagner says.

Those who chose to continue to work during the summer could work the optional summer hours—7:00 A.M. until 12:30 P.M. "This was a popular option for women whose children were old enough to be left for a few hours every morning," Mrs. Wagner recalls. "Mom could still be home in time to fix lunch and have the whole afternoon free for activities with the kids."

By the late 1960s, paid vacations and holidays became available to all employees who worked twenty or more hours a week. As the office staff grew enough in the early 1970s to make life and health insurance benefits practical, all employees who worked at least twenty hours a week received a pro-rated fringe benefits package.

The original policy of closing the office for the day at 3:00 P.M. so mothers could be home with their children after school has remained unchanged and has continued to be popular with employees.

Although personnel policies that even today are considered quite innovative were standard procedures in the La Leche League office twenty years ago, the League lagged behind in one area: maternity leave.

"For a long time we didn't have any policy at all on maternity leaves," Mrs. Wagner explains, "because up until the late 1970s all of our employees who got pregnant quit working and stayed home full time after the baby was born."

But the tide of social change finally touched the shore at the La Leche League office, too, and in 1980 a policy was established which offered the option of an unpaid leave of up to six months with a comparable job and salary assured upon return.

Not to be left in the dust for more than the blink of an eye, La Leche League's policy also specifies that a mother returning to work can bring her baby with her "until the baby reaches toddler age, and then will be permitted to come to work as long as there is a safe place, free of stairs and other dangers, for him to stay."

To date, three of the League's employees have returned to work with baby in tow. Ivy Bollig Karas worked full time for seven months filling orders in the Shipping Department with her baby in a front carrier or playing on the floor beside her.

Sue Comer, who works in the Order Department, resumed her employment at the League office when her baby was close to a year old, switching from a full-time job to part-time hours. Her husband, who worked nights, usually cared for the baby while she was at work, but Caleb often came to work with mom on days that dad was unavailable.

When Donna Fobes, who also works in the Order Department, returned to work after her six-month leave of absence, little Christen came, too. Donna ar-

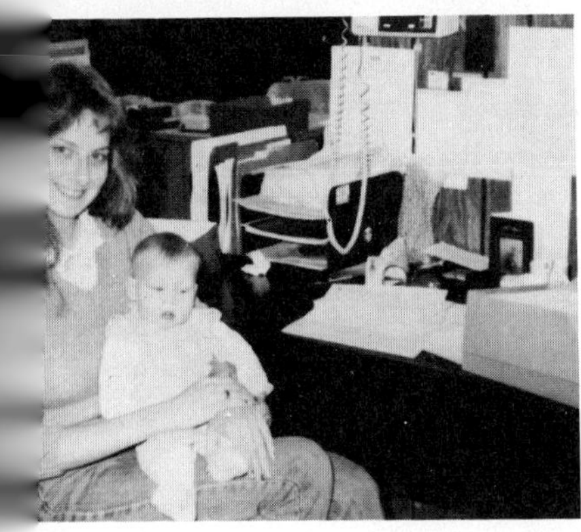

ranged to work only part-time hours at first, and Christen napped and played on the floor right beside her mother's desk.

Much has changed at the La Leche League office over the past twenty years. The staff of three has expanded to include fifty-five employees and the one room, second floor office has been replaced by a two story office building and a 4300 square foot warehouse.

The League's early annual budgets, which sometimes topped $100, are dwarfed by the organization's current gross annual income of two million dollars.

But in this fast paced, ever changing world, one thing at the La Leche League office has remained unchanged through the years: the commitment to putting family first, both at home and at work. ■

■ *Mothering Magazine*

If a book titled "How to Break Every Rule in the Business World and Win" is ever published, chances are good that the authors will be John and Peggy O'Mara McMahon.

The McMahons, parents of four children ranging in age from nine years to fourteen months, felt that they had something to say about alternatives in childbirth and child rearing, and in 1980 decided to take the plunge and say it through their own magazine. They purchased *Mothering*, a three-year-old magazine with a subscription list of 3,000 and single copy sales of about 5,000 per issue.

Peggy, while caring full time for the couple's children, and John, who at first continued his full-time job as an elementary school teacher, transformed the struggling magazine into a first rate publication with 18,000 subscriptions and a total press run of 35,000 issues every quarter. The magazine continues to grow at a steady 15% every quarter.

How did they do it? A great measure of their success can probably be attributed to a strong sense of purpose and the determination to run the magazine—just as they had raised their family—their own way. The McMahons began by laying some ground rules which would give an ulcer to any ordinary magazine publisher, but which, in the long run, have contributed heavily to their success:

- Advertising space would be limited to a maximum of 30% of the magazine's total number of pages. Other magazines carry as much as 70% to 80% advertising, but the McMahons were determined not to let the paid ads overshadow the magazine's message and purpose. And in order to be accepted, products or services advertised would have to be compatible with the magazine's overall philosophy.
- The magazine would not go into debt. "If we didn't have enough money, we just ran fewer copies," John explains. Neither John nor Peggy took a salary from the magazine for the first year and a half.
- All staff members would work part-time out of their own homes. This is still the case today, except for John who is now employed by the magazine full time, even though *Mothering* long ago outgrew its "cottage business" status.

- Staff members, all of whom have preschool or home-schooled children, would be able to bring their children to the weekly editorial and circulation meetings.

  There would be no expensive advertising campaigns, direct mail solicitations, or free copies given away as is customary when launching a new publication. "We relied on word of mouth and networking through our contacts in La Leche League, midwifery groups, and childbirth organizations," John says. "Even today, word of mouth is still our best form of advertising."
- In order to keep overhead to a minimum, there would be no office for the magazine. The McMahons operated everything out of their home—including weekly staff meetings and shipping operations—for the first three years.

Today, even in the wake of the magazine's unqualified success and substantial rate of growth, very little has changed at *Mothering*. Peggy continues to care for the McMahon's children full time, and works on graphics and editorial content primarily in the evenings after the children are in bed for the night.

Staff members, who now number twelve, all continue to work part-time (an average of twelve to fifteen hours a week) from their own homes. All of them continue to bring their children to weekly editorial and circulation meetings, although a woman (who brings her own home-schooled child) has recently been hired to provide creative activities for the older children who choose to participate. As always, babies and toddlers stay with their mothers throughout the meetings.

John was able to put aside his teaching career in the summer of 1981 and go to work full time for *Mothering*, overseeing advertising, circulation, and general management. *Mothering* has moved out of the McMahon's home and is now headquartered in a three bedroom rented house, which provides the ideal setting for the weekly staff meetings.

The McMahons are very aware that a family business often has a way of insidiously subjugating the needs of the family to the needs of the business, and have made it a top priority in their own lives to avoid that trap.

"We're very conscious of the amount of time we put into the magazine, and it is a struggle to prevent it from taking over our family's lives," John explains. "We have made it a practice to take a family vacation during the slow time after one issue is finished and before it is time to start on the next one. We force ourselves to slow down and stay together."

What the McMahons and their staff have demonstrated to a society that prizes productivity over parenthood, balance sheets over babies' needs, is that even in today's regimented, mechanized, synthesized world, it is quite possible to be a productive worker while being a full-time parent.

Mothering magazine's most lasting legacy is likely to come not from its pages, but from its pioneering example of the successful total integration of family life into a business organization. ■

Chapter 17

A Media Chronicle

Innovators in the workplace

COMPANIES START TO MEET EXECUTIVE MOTHERS HALFWAY

Jorgensen brings daughter to Legislature

Raising baby together

An idea that was born in a trunk

New breed of father enjoy sharing child care

Rearing this baby is an office project

Baby joins mom at Capitol

Teachers make job sharing work at Dirksen

■ Children of Working Moms Find Office Schedules to Their Liking

by Jewell Cardwell

Elissa Pinto and Ian Moyer have been keeping regular office hours almost since birth, and they haven't had to pay a nickel in Social Security taxes.

Yet their parents would be the first to admit that they're two of the most socially secure persons in the world.

That's because Elissa and Ian go to the office each day with Mom.

Though it's relatively rare, taking the kids to work is one way working mothers cope with the problem of finding adequate child care. However, this option usually is limited to mothers who are their own bosses.

Akron gynecologist-obstetrician Linda A. Parenti, mother of five-month-old Elissa, said she started thinking about taking her child to work when she first found out she was pregnant.

"At first it was just a joke between me and my husband," Dr. Parenti recalled. Dr. Parenti's husband, Thomas Pinto, is in education administration.

"He would ask me what I was going to do with the baby. And I would tell him, 'I'm going to take it with me to work.' But then the more I began to think about it, I figured 'Why not?' After all, I'm my own boss, and I pay the rent. And I wanted her with me."

Wendy Moyer is the mother of three-year-old Ian. She is the director of a largely volunteer staff at the Kent Community House, a social service agency which coordinates self-help groups.

Now a single parent, Moyer has three other children: Dana, sixteen; Erica, fourteen; and April, nine.

Ms. Moyer said her original motivation in bringing her children to the office was one of practicality: She breastfed her babies. "Also, it was difficult for me to find people who I felt secure with," she said. "I wanted people who would pattern child-rearing after mine. And I have a strong belief in mother for the child."

When Elissa was younger, she slept in a bassinet in her mother's office, part of a suite of offices in an Akron medical complex. Now she stays in a baby carrier which gets moved from her mother's office to the staff lounge, to the reception desk, and back again.

A little pillow hung on an office door attests to her presence. It says: "Shh! Baby Sleeping!"

Dr. Parenti says her office staff seems to enjoy Elissa's company. "And the patients (often expectant mothers) think it's great, too," she said with a smile.

"She's a good baby. She doesn't fuss or holler much . . . except, of course, if she's hungry or wet."

Dr. Parenti said she thinks the greatest advantage of having Elissa with her at work is having the time together.

"Some mothers are able to take maternity leave to be with their babies," she said. "But my practice wouldn't run that way. Yet, I didn't want to give her up.

"This way I could see the things happening to her. I was with her the first time she smiled. I didn't want to have to go home and have the babysitter tell me about it. I shared in it—and she got to have Mommy with her."

As a result of coming to the office with Mom, Elissa has become "extremely social," Dr. Parenti asserts.

"She'll go to anybody," the doctor boasted. "I believe that babies who stay with their mothers are happier babies as a rule. They tend to be less fussy, less colicky."

Ms. Moyer, however, points out there can be some drawbacks to bringing a child to work.

"You're going to have more interruptions," she said. "And you have to deal with people who have difficulty accepting the situation. You have a lot more loading and carrying supplies to do with a child."

Ian sometimes naps on the couch in the back office of his mother's two-room office suite. He's also made that room into his "toy camp," and visitors may find themselves stepping over toy trains and planes, building blocks, and crayons. He brings his lunch to work in a little lunchbox.

"For me, one of the obvious advantages," Ms. Moyer said, "is not having to pay a babysitter—and having the opportunity to spend time with my preschool children."

She sometimes brings her older children to her office, "because I think it's important for children to see their parent's life at work.

"I guess mine is a philosophy that says give your baby as much love as you can. I've seen abused children and heard other horror stories, and I still don't understand it. When I look at my baby, I can't see how anyone could hurt a baby. So, I love her as much as I can."

Ms. Moyer admits that bringing the child to the office wouldn't work for every working mom.

"A lot depends on the job," she said. "And quite a bit depends on the child. I had one who was very active, that I wouldn't have wanted to bring to work. As a matter of fact, as Ian becomes more active, I'm moving up the amount of time he's in nursery school."

Dr. Parenti laughingly admits to greeting some of her patients with a dirty diaper in hand.

"I've never had a patient say that it wasn't great," she continued, bouncing her red-haired daughter on her knee. "So many of my patients who were pregnant during the time I was pregnant wanted to see her anyway." ■

■ Agency Lets New Mother Cradle Work Duties and Son

by Dan Page

Who says babies and business don't mix? Laurel Call doesn't.

Mrs. Call, an attorney examiner for the Ohio Department of Insurance and a new mother, said yesterday she plans to return to work full time July 26. She will be accompanied by her first child, John David, who was born June 18.

George Fabe, director of the department, has given Mrs. Call permission to care for John David at work. Department spokesman Pierce Cunningham described the arrangement as an experiment.

"The whole purpose of the thing really is to expedite her return," Cunningham said. "She's vital to the department's health-care cost-

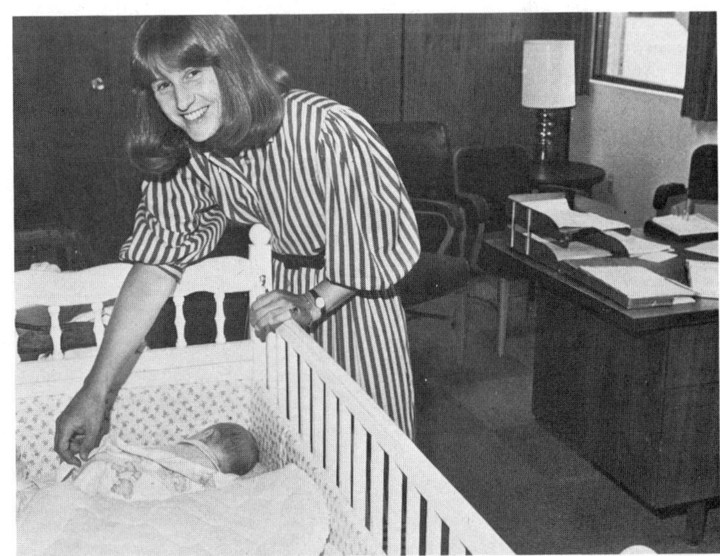

containment effort, which we have put a high priority on.

"A lot of meetings have been scheduled between industry representatives and Laurel Call, and if the child were to become sick, the thinking is that to have the baby there on hand might be better than to have her (Mrs. Call) miss a day of work or an important meeting."

Cunningham said Fabe agreed to allow Mrs. Call to have a crib placed in her office. He said the arrangement is not a new policy or precedent.

"It's not representative of administrative policy," Cunningham said. "It's basically an experiment that we're trying here. If it doesn't work out and proves not to be successful, if it's disruptive to the office routine or we see any number of other problems, it will be discontinued."

Cunningham said Fabe would make that decision. On the other hand, he said, the experiment may work and could be expanded to allow other employees to take part.

"There's no formula or policy at this point," said Cunningham, who added he is unaware of any similar program in Ohio government.

Mrs. Call said John David sleeps most of the day and she believes she will be able to take care of business and the baby.

"There is a conference room at the office, and I will probably conduct meetings in the conference room," she said. "It's right across the hallway, and I would hear him if something went wrong.

"If he continues to be as good as he has been, I don't foresee any problems in the near future," she said. "If he would get fussy, I'm not opposed to changing the arrangements if it doesn't work out. I just naturally hope it does."

Thus far, Cunningham said, the arrival of the crib has caused little stir among department workers.

"There's not been a great hue and cry either for the situation or against it," he said. "I think they have pretty much taken it in stride just to see if it works out." ■

Reprinted from the *Columbus Citizen Journal*, July 15, 1983

■ Rearing This Baby Is An Office Project

by Kathy Waugh

Sarah Valerio sits on the floor of a Chicago office, watching the faces of passers-by.

She catches the eye of office employee Roberta Jacobs, smiles and lets out a squeal of joy. The noise doesn't surprise anyone because Sarah is allowed to do that. She's only six months old.

"I love her," Jacobs says of Sarah, the baby who comes to the office every day with her mother, Pat Valerio.

Valerio wasn't quite sure how

serious her boss was when he offered last October to let her bring the newborn baby to the office.

"I had to work after I had the baby," she said. "We had just purchased a house in Wheeling and were trying to decide how we would manage the cost of the house and the cost of a baby sitter."

But then, out of the blue, came the offer from Valerio's boss, Lou Gold, to bring the baby to work each day at a Chicago home medical supplies company. Although he had never heard of the idea before and has no children of his own, Gold said he thought it was a reasonable way to keep his hard-working employee of seven years.

Sarah is notched in right behind mom's desk and plays on the floor—most of the time—while mom works.

Because boxes and paperwork crowd the small office and offer no room for a playpen and swing, those items are stashed in Gold's office.

He said some salesmen are surprised when they enter the room to offer a price on home medical care supplies and find a baby cooing in a swing, but he said he likes it.

"I figure that, by the time she is three, she will be working here," Gold said. He paused to smile at the baby and get her approval.

"Sometimes it's tough on Pat because I don't let her work slide," he said. "And when I first thought of the idea, I did worry about everyone stopping to play with the baby, but that doesn't really happen."

Lunch hour seems to be the most popular time for playing with the baby, Valerio said. Now that Sarah is older, she doesn't sleep as much and is up and ready to be sociable when lunch time arrives.

Sarah has become a regular part of the routine. She even attended the office Christmas party last year.

Sarah has her bad days, but the fact that she is so good-natured has been the overriding factor in allowing Valerio to keep the baby at work.

But babies don't stay young forever. Now that Sarah is sitting up, it won't be long before she will be crawling, then toddling, through the small office.

"I'm not being pushed to get her out of the office, so it's kind of difficult to let her go," Valerio said.

But Valerio and her husband, Len, are interviewing prospective babysitters who may take over baby-sitting duties this summer.

Would Gold do it again?

"Certainly," he said.

Workers in the office said they don't even notice the baby or hear her, even if she is crying. One might believe that's true until Sarah starts to giggle.

She's caught someone's attention again. ■

Reprinted from the *Sunday Herald*, Hoffman Estates, IL, May 1, 1983.

■ Raising Baby Together

by Dorothy Lipovenko

When they first noticed Dave Maxwell pushing his baby daughter Michaela on the swings weekday mornings, some of the regulars in a neighborhood park in Toronto wondered if he was out of a job. It never occurred to anyone, until Mr. Maxwell explained, that he was looking after Michaela while his wife was at work.

When lawyer Sherrie Barnhorst was too busy to check out a preschool program for two-year-old Eric, her husband Richard made the rounds of play groups near their Beaches home and chose the one he thought best.

Whether by choice or circumstance, the two men are typical of a new generation of fathers who share the responsibility of child care—and like it.

While the new breed of father may be up to his elbows in dirty diapers, he's also enjoying first-hand the special moments of being a father he would otherwise miss if he were just a spectator parent.

Ten years ago, many men would have blanched at the suggestion of getting involved in the daily grind of feedings and baths. It would have offended their male ego, not to mention social convention.

But legions of working women—33,000 mothers of preschoolers and 36,000 mothers of school-age children enter the Canadian labor force annually—have

changed the rigid roles that husbands and fathers are expected to play.

"The younger generation of fathers is doing much more child care," Benjamin Schlesinger, a professor of social work at the University of Toronto who has done extensive studies on the Canadian family, said in an interview. "These men tend to marry women who grew up with the tremendous influence of the women's movement, who are unwilling to take on the formal role of mother and kitchen helper."

And, he said, a commitment of many fathers to greater participation in child-rearing starts in prenatal classes, where they leave "with a feeling of wanting to continue the relationship with the child after it's born."

Heather Maxwell and her husband Dave are among the twenty percent of working couples in Canada who look after a preschooler without outside help.

Mr. Maxwell used to play squash and hockey with the guys in the mornings before going off to his job as director of a recreation centre for Toronto's parks department. For more than a year now, his mornings start with changing twenty-one-month-old Michaela's diaper, followed by fixing a breakfast of hot cereal, fruit, juice, and toast they share after his wife Heather has left for her job as a teacher in a day-care centre.

Michaela's insatiable appetite for books, puzzles, and television's Sesame Street keeps them busy until her mid-morning bath. Weather permitting, the two then head down to the nearby park for fresh air and a romp on the swings, or they run some household errands. When Mrs. Maxwell returns home at noon, the house "may be a disaster but I know they've had a great time together," she said laughing.

"I wanted to go back to work part-time when Michaela was six months old but I was skeptical of leaving her with a sitter," Mrs. Maxwell said, "Dave's hours—1 P.M. to 10 P.M.—weren't leaving him much time with the baby, so I suggested this arrangement. I didn't know if he would really do it, but I wanted him to because I was the one spending most of the day with her."

What began on a trial basis has evolved into a strong commitment.

"I felt I was missing out (on being with Michaela) because of my hours," Mr. Maxwell said. But "when Heather said I'd have to give Michaela a bath in the mornings, I was a shade scared, I'd never done it before.

"It just took a little in-house training." Now, "it's a great arrangement."

With both parents responsible for her development, Michaela benefits from their application of consistent standards to, for example, her diet and discipline.

These parents believe in sharing child-care responsibilities. (l to r) Darlene and David McKee; Sherrie and Richard Barnhorst; Heather and Dave Maxwell.

Similar expectations for work and family life are essential to successful shared parenting, according to Darlene McKee and her husband, David.

For almost seven years, they've balanced an unconventional schedule: Mr. McKee, a musician in a band, looks after daughters Meghan, seven, and Aislinn, three, when his wife alternates two days one week and three days the next as a library assistant. They even split parent duty days at the co-op nursery school that Aislinn attends.

"I've always been a bit of a rebel all my life," Mr. McKee said, turning down the stereo volume. "Sure, I'm tired after coming in at 2 A.M., and the kids get up and they need breakfast or to be taken to school. I don't have time in the afternoons to write songs or do some of the things that I want. But the idea came to me that we owe it to our kids to give them the best possible start. I sort of came to the conclusion that this is the way it should be."

It's second nature to Meghan and Aislinn that their father washes dishes, vacuums, and is readily available weekday afternoons for a jam session in music. But working in a profession with a poor track record for a stable home life has challenged the nurturing role their father has taken on. He's survived pressures from the guys in the band about putting his family first.

Sherrie and Richard Barnhorst agree that their co-operative child-rearing is a natural extension of their egalitarian relationship.

"When you're studying for bar admissions exams together (as they did), you don't expect the other person to do the housekeeping exclusively. And when you have a child, one parent is not solely responsible for child-rearing," Mr. Barnhorst, a lawyer with the Ontario government, said.

"Some men don't develop the confidence (to look after a child) because their wives don't give them a chance," Mrs. Barnhorst said. "I think women are reluctant to give up their authority (in the household). I really had to trust Dick's decision on choosing a play group for Eric—some women might have trouble with that."

Although his work hours aren't flexible enough to accommodate more time on his part for child care, Mr. Barnhorst manages to shop for Eric's clothes on his lunch hours and to accompany his wife on visits to the pediatrician.

"I bring a different kind of energy to dealing with Eric than Sherrie does. Take bedtime for example. We've got Eric settled into a routine but sometimes he wants extra stories read to him or whatever. It's a question of how many hoops will you go through to get a kid to sleep. I'm willing to go through more. . . ." ■

Reprinted from *The Globe and Mail,* Toronto, January 6, 1983.

■ She Has a Computer in Nursery

Reesa Abrams didn't have to sacrifice her career to her desire to be a full-time mother when her daughter was born four-and-a-half months ago.

Abrams, now a management consultant who produces quality software for computer hardware manufacturers, works as a consultant to Digital Equipment Corp. of Nashua, NH.

Digital installed a computer in Abram's home. "It's in the baby's room so I can put the baby in the jump seat or in the crib and work the computer," she explains.

Two days a month, the nursing mother and her daughter go to work together.

"She goes with me to Nashua, into the building, and one of the secretaries babysits with her while I have meetings," Reesa explains.

The home computer allows her to converse with Digital daily. She delivers weekly or monthly research reports to the corporation—either by computer or in person—and believes Digital officials are pleased with the arrangement and her performance.

"It's basically an experiment to see if it works and it's working," Reesa observes. "I'm very happy. It allows me to stay active in the field and to stay at home and raise a child."

The arrangement offers a double bonus because Reesa's husband, Steve, works as a counselor from their home so that both can devote time to parenting.

Reesa said she is hopeful that other businesses will consider similar arrangements for working parents. ■

Reprinted from *The Times Record,* Brunswick, Maine, June 1, 1982

■ Baby Joins Mom at Capitol

Lullabyes and legislation are mingling happily at the Capitol this year where a state representative works side by side with her newborn daughter.

Rep. Donna Zajonc, R-Salem, has set up a corner of her office on the third floor of the House wing for her month-old daughter, McKenzie.

There is a dressing table, diapers, toys, a cradle, and a swing.

Zajonc says she is working to find a balance between motherhood and her job. She said she believes what she is doing is indicative of the future.

The assistant minority leader, who is breastfeeding her daughter, pays out of her pocket for a secretary who doubles as a babysitter.

McKenzie is the first child of Rep. Zajonc and her husband, Ed. ■

Reprinted from the *Corvallis Gazette Times,* Corvallis, OR, January 1981. © Associated Press

An Idea That Was Born in a Trunk

by Ron Wertheimer

Lots of women hope for interesting part-time work when they suspend careers for motherhood. But where should they look?

Well, Susan McTigue was acting director of the art museum at the State University of New York at Purchase when her secretary gave her an unusual gift. It was a copy of a Winslow Homer engraving, clipped from a well-preserved antique issue of *Harper's Weekly*.

Mrs. McTigue, the former curator of decorative arts at the Museum of the City of New York, appreciated more than just the kindness. She knew that the print, while not astonishingly rare, was surely valuable, especially in such good condition.

The obvious question was, "Where did you get this?"

The surprising answer was, "From that trunk in my attic."

Mrs. McTigue soon visited the attic with her secretary. "She opened this trunk and they came spilling out," she recalls.

What came spilling out were copies of *Harper's*, every issue from the magazine's founding in 1857 through 1875.

During those years, *Harper's* covered the big news of the day, including the Civil War and Reconstruction and the downfall of William M. Tweed's political machine in New York City. And in those days, before technology allowed for mass printing of photographs, publications like *Harper's* were full of richly detailed line engravings.

The trunk also had some copies of *Scientific American* from the same era, each one full of carefully rendered drawings of the latest inventions. Mrs. McTigue's secretary knew only that the trunk had belonged to her father. She couldn't explain his collection, in which the magazines not only were uncirculated but many were still in the uncut folios, just as they had come off the press.

Mrs. McTigue knew that there wouldn't be much of a market for the complete magazines. Universities and libraries, she knew, had such items in their collections. But she decided that individual illustrations, mounted and framed, would make valuable and historic decorations.

Here was the answer to the question about her free time, too.

"I've never not worked," says Mrs. McTigue, whose husband, Thomas, is a lawyer. "I knew if there was any way to do something at home, I'd have to find it."

Having found it, she dubbed her business The Fine Print. And when her son, Brian, was born last year, Mrs. McTigue settled in with her secretary's collection, selecting and framing some of the contents. The two women agreed to share in any profits the venture might have.

"Coming from a museum background, pulling pages from magazines is sacrilegious," she says. But pull she does, with great care.

While Brian naps, his mother immerses herself in history. On the table in her cramped basement workroom, she lovingly examines the illustrations.

There isn't much profit, she says. "It's not an income you can live on."

Since she launched her business last year, Mrs. McTigue has sold thirty-five items. She's hoping for more sales during the Christmas shopping season. Some of her collection will be on display during December at the Closter Library. ■

Reprinted from *The Daily Record*, Morristown, NJ, December 9, 1980

■ Eaton Defies No-Nursing Rule

by Curt Seifert and Jim Mullendore

Three-and-half-month-old Ian Eaton came to visit his firefighting mother at the Iowa City Fire Department shortly before noon today.

Ian's mother, Linda, has become the center of a local—fast becoming national—controversy because she has vowed to disobey Fire Chief Robert Keating's ruling that she can't breastfeed Ian while she's on duty.

Ian, his aunt, and grandmother stayed at the fire station about twenty-five minutes—alone and unobserved in a downstairs room—and left, apparently without incident.

According to Eaton's attorney, Jane Eikleberry, Linda breastfed Ian during the visit.

When the twenty-six-year-old mother reported for work as scheduled at 7 A.M. today, she was greeted by a horde of local—and a few national—representatives of the news media.

Within an hour after arriving, Eaton, Fire Chief Robert Keating, Assistant City Manager Dale Helling, and City Human Relations Director Sophie Zukrowski met in the chief's office, Keating said.

Keating said that Eaton was told that her request to nurse the child on duty had been given "careful consideration," but was still being denied.

Keating, as in the past, declined to comment on the situation, except to say that Eaton was on the job as scheduled.

Helling explained this morning that the city was basing its decision in the "no-nursing" rule on three factors.

First, Helling said officials were worried about setting a precedent with other city employees by allowing Eaton to nurse her child on duty.

"If we make this accommodation for one city employee," Helling said, "we'd have to do it for all the others. We have to set a policy that will be consistent for all city employees. This could have city-wide implications."

Second, Helling said officials feel Eaton's nursing could have an effect on her job performance.

"It could delay her reaction time," Helling said.

Helling admitted that male firefighters are incapacitated by normal bodily functions during different parts of the day, as are females, but noted that Eaton "elected" to nurse Ian, calling the act not "totally necessary."

Third, Helling said there could be "legal" implications to allowing Eaton's request.

If firefighters' families are allowed to frequent the station, the city's liability for injuries to family members would be increased, Helling contended.

He said the practice could result in a "calamity" if an emergency situation arose.

In a related action, the Johnson County-Iowa City Chapter of the National Organization for Women announced it was establishing a legal fund for Eaton.

At a press conference commemorating the sixth anniversary of the U.S. Supreme Court's landmark ruling on abortion, Susan Hester said, "We don't feel there is any moral issue involved in the Eaton matter.

"Eaton plans to nurse her child only during her personal time; other firefighters spend this time exercising, showering, studying, or resting; family members often visit during these breaks.

"The question is Eaton's right to employment," Hester said, "She's not asking for any special privilege." ■

Reprinted from the *Press-Citizen*, Iowa City, IA, January 22, 1979

■ Breastfeeding Firefighter Quits; "It Will Be Better"

Firefighter Linda Eaton, who waged a sixteen-month legal fight to breastfeed her son in the firehouse, quit her job Wednesday, saying, "I'd rather be broke and be with Ian."

But Eaton, twenty-seven, the city's only female firefighter, said she would pursue her legal fight and her attorney said more suits could be filed.

Eaton said her reason for leaving resulted "directly and indirectly" from her sex discrimination suit, filed with the Iowa Civil Rights Commission in January 1979.

"I don't believe I can carry out my job to the best of my ability," she said. "I did so (resign) with my son's best interest in mind. This doesn't affect my legal action. I plan to follow through on that to the end.

"I don't feel that I lost or that I quit or ran away from this problem," she said. "I'd rather be broke and be with Ian. It will get better for us."

Eaton, a single mother, held up a copy of a letter from city officials asking her to reconsider her resignation.

"If your decision is based upon recent problems which you have brought to our attention, we have taken steps to prevent further incidents and to discipline those involved in past incidents and we will continue to do so," the letter said.

The city is appealing a March ruling by the Civil Rights Commission that found Eaton was the victim of sex discrimination and awarded her about $25,000 in legal fees and damages. ■

■ Executives Nurse Interest In Breastfeeding

by Holly Hanson

When a top-notch executive for a major oil company gave birth to her first child, she gave little thought to returning to work soon. She wanted to breastfeed her baby, and surely there was no way to combine that with a demanding full-time job.

Her supervisors, however, were not anxious to lose the services of a valuable employee, not even to allow her to take a long leave of absence. Instead, they moved her into a secluded, private office and urged her to bring the baby to work with her. She did, with few disruptions in her schedule or the company's.

An airline employee who was breastfeeding her son faced the end of her six-month maternity leave. When her request for an extension of the leave was refused, she and her husband arranged a complicated schedule that allowed her to continue breastfeeding. Her husband, who worked at night, drove her to and from work so she could nurse their son in the car. He also brought the infant to her every day at noon so she could nurse him again.

Sympathetic to her plight, the woman's union representatives pressured local management to extend her leave by five months. They did, and the woman returned to her job right on schedule.

You can credit this new-found flexibility in American business to an unusual mix of trends that, on paper, seems contradictory at every turn.

On one hand, more women are entering the work force, devoting themselves to their careers with a fervor traditionally reserved for men. They are having fewer children and having them later in life.

On the other hand, women are breast-feeding their newborns in record numbers. In the past ten years, the number of women choosing to nurse their babies has increased from twenty-five percent in 1971 to nearly sixty percent this year, a twenty-five year high, the American Academy of Pediatrics said.

These women are rejecting the efficiency of infant formulas in favor of the periodic inconvenience of breastfeeding to give their babies a healthier start in life. And quite a few of them are juggling high-powered careers at the same time.

What's going on here?

Marian Tompson, co-founder and past president of La Leche League International, a Franklin Park-based information service and support group for those interested in breastfeeding, has this theory.

"First, it's contagious. As one woman hears another say. 'It's an experience I'd never have wanted to miss,' she wants to try it, too," Tompson said. "Second, there's a natural inclination to breastfeed. It's built in for survival.

"Third, there's a back-to-nature movement, so women are interested in doing things as nature intended.

"Last, mothers want to give the best to their babies," she said. "There are a lot of studies that show breastfeeding offers advantages that bottle-feeding has not been able to offer. Breast milk is a live food that protects the baby."

Despite the occasional inconvenience of nursing, there's no better way for an infant to be fed, as Tompson sees it.

Human milk is easily digested and supplies all of the nutrients a child needs in the first six months of life. It also contains important enzymes, hormones, and other substances that provide immunity against some illnesses and allergies, she said.

"There is a great deal of antibody protection in breast milk," said Dr. Marvin Goldman, an Arlington Heights pediatrician. "Naturally produced milk is the best available food for an infant."

But that's not all. A close dependent relationship naturally develops between the nursing mother and her child. This bonding is so important, La Leche League members believe, that mothers should do everything they can to foster and strengthen it.

"When a nursing baby looks up at you and smiles like you're the light of the world, it's an experience you think about when you're old and gray," Tompson said, adding, "The baby needs his mother as much as he needs the milk. Breastfeeding is a relationship as well as food."

For that reason, Tompson said, a nursing mother should try hard not to disrupt the bonding relationship once she begins breastfeeding. This directive sounds simple, but it can pose some problems for both the mother and the father.

For the mother, it means being solely responsible for every middle-of-the-night feeding. For the father, it means no opportunity to feed little Christopher an occasional bottle.

"Some fathers may want to feed the baby, but it really is unnatural," Tompson said. "It's a shame to introduce formula just so the father can try it out."

Instead, La Leche counsels mothers that they should make a commitment to breastfeeding, that most fathers take great pride in watching the growth and development of their breastfed infants, and that all those 2 A.M. feedings handled alone are a small inconvenience for the emotional and physical benefits of steady nursing.

Most pediatricians won't argue about the value of breastfeeding. But they emphasize parents needn't feel guilty about giving the child an occasional bottle or even substituting infant formula for mother's milk once in a while.

Mixing in an occasional bottle is a system adopted by many working women who can't dash home at noon for the mid-day feeding, pediatrician Goldman said. "We have many working mothers who are able to combine breast and bottle feedings without any problems," he said.

Some of those mothers use infant formulas part of the time. Others, however, attempt to avoid the problem of the noon feeding by finding a secluded place at the office to express their breast milk, storing it in a refrigerator for the next day's noon feeding.

It's a system that seems to work equally well for mothers and employers. Dr. Joseph King, director of employee health services at Continental Illinois National Bank and Trust Co. of Chicago, put it this way:

"Every business has a private space a nursing mother can go to pump her milk, and most businesses have some way to store it. We have a refrigerator here, and we'd have no objection to women coming here, pumping their milk and storing it until they go home," he said. "We haven't ever advertised it, but we'd have no objection. I'd be very glad to see it."

Although King is a big fan of breastfeeding—"I think it's great. I'm with La Leche on that."—he draws the line at allowing working mothers to care for and breastfeed their infants at the office.

"I don't mean to be chauvinist," he said, "but I can't see having a place here at the bank for breastfeeding women. I think that would be kind of difficult."

La Leche League members do not agree, of course, and neither do women like State Rep. Susan Catania, R-Chicago, who breastfed her children at work, and actress Lynn Redgrave, who is suing CBS for the same right.

This burgeoning commitment to breastfeeding is persuading a few businesses to juggle work schedules, extend maternity leaves, and set aside secluded office areas to accommodate nursing mothers.

For example, when Kaye Lowman learned she was pregnant with her fourth child, she decided to quit her job as director of public information for the Village of Hoffman Estates, thinking she'd never be able to combine work with nursing.

"There was no doubt I was going to breastfeed and that I intended to quit, so I kept waiting for them to say they were advertising for someone to fill my job," Lowman said. "But they're very flexible and open at Hoffman Estates. They said, 'Why would we replace her? Who said she had to leave?' "

As a result, Lowman brought her infant daughter to the office for more than a year.

"It worked out very well," she said. "All my bosses cared about was that the work was done and on time, which it was. In my case, my office is set apart, and, as an infant, my daughter was either sleeping or playing on the floor. Everyone was extremely accepting.

"It's no problem to breastfeed if you have the right job and the right physical setting," she said. "You can't be in the typing pool, and you can't be tied to a machine eight hours a day. But (breastfeeding is practical for) artists, journalists, public relations people like me, lawyers, doctors—anyone with just enough flexibility and space for the baby so that, when you need to take a break to do something for the baby, you can."

Both Lowman and Tompson believe breastfeeding at the office will win greater acceptance as employers begin to realize they cannot afford to force their valuable women employees to choose between motherhood and a career.

"Working women who are having babies today have sat down and decided they really want them," Lowman said. "They're going into it with their eyes open. They're carefully examining their options, and they're more assertive than they've ever been. They want the best of both worlds. They don't want to choose between a job and a baby." ■

Reprinted from *The Daily Herald*, Hoffman Estates, IL, September 3, 1981.

■ Jorgensen Brings Daughter to Legislature

by David Enger

Kay Jorgensen says she's luckier than most working mothers. Instead of leaving her eight-month-old daughter behind when she goes to work, Ms. Jorgensen can take her along—to the South Dakota Legislature.

Ms. Jorgensen, a Republican member of the state House of Representatives from Spearfish, says her daughter, Meredith Pangburn, spends two or three hours in the Legislature every afternoon.

Ms. Jorgensen's mother, Twyla Jorgensen, wheels Meredith through crowded Capitol hallways in a baby carriage, and sits with the baby in the House gallery or in a hallway next to the House chamber.

"I try to be with her over the noon hour or at least a part of the time in the afternoon," Ms. Jorgensen, thirty-one, says of her daughter. "I just try to spend a little time reading and playing, but that will necessarily diminish as the session progresses" and the workload increases.

"There's more to this than I really expected," Ms. Jorgensen says of her role as a first-time mother. "The incredible amount of time that a child needs and that you want to give is just amazing to me.

"Everyone is patient with me when I'm chronically late to things," Ms. Jorgensen says. "Other legislators are all very considerate."

Ms. Jorgensen's husband, Mike Pangburn, remains in Spearfish during the forty-day legislative session. He is a teacher at Belle Fourche High School.

None of the other thirteen women legislators are living here with young children through the session, Ms. Jorgensen says. None of the ninety-one male lawmakers are keeping children here without their wives.

Twyla Jorgensen, who left her home in Witten to stay with her daughter and granddaughter during the legislative session, says she enjoys helping care for Meredith.

"The attention she (Meredith) gets is always really something, but she's so responsive, she smiles all the time, she doesn't cry," Mrs. Jorgensen says. "I consider it a real privilege to be here, I'm so happy to do this."

Becoming a mother has changed her schedule, Ms. Jorgensen says.

"I don't go to quite as many things at night," Ms. Jorgensen says, referring to the steady round of social activities that organizations hold for lawmakers. "I may go there to say hello, but I don't stay as long as I used to."

Keeping up with the pace of the legislative activities was harder last year, Ms. Jorgensen says.

"By the end of the last session I was exhausted," she says. "The physical drain when you're pregnant is beyond belief; this year's much, much easier."

When the Legislature isn't in session, Ms. Jorgensen works as director of the High Plains Heritage Council, an organization planning a museum in Spearfish.

"I have always worked, and a child is a rather delightful addition to my day, so you figure out how to do the best you can do for your child and still meet your job obligations," Ms. Jorgensen says.

Being in the Capitol is good for Meredith, because she is exposed to many people and activities, her mother says.

"She observes and absorbs very much," Ms. Jorgensen says. "I think it's a very positive experience."

"I never intended to have a child, but it was really kind of sudden that my feelings just changed. I wanted one more dimension to add to my life," Ms. Jorgensen says of her decision to become a mother.

"I'm rather amazed at my whole response to her. I didn't know a child could just totally captivate how you feel and think," Ms. Jorgensen says. "I think it's made me a better legislator. You really do look at the future with a different eye when the concern is not only other people's children, but your own." ■

Reprinted from the *Rapid City Journal,* Rapid City, SD, January 20, 1983. © Associated Press

■ If It's Domestic, Is It Dull?

Edited by Gerri Hirsey

"Domesticity doesn't have to be dull," says Coralee Kern, "or demeaning. It depends on how much dignity you bring to it, and how much you value yourself."

Seven years ago, seriously ill and with a medical debt of $111,000, Coralee Kern began her cleaning service, "Maid-to-Order," from a hospital bed with the help of her fifteen-year-old son. Since then, Maid-to-Order has grown to a $300,000-a-year business, and Coralee's son has grown into a management position in his mother's firm. Recently, Coralee spoke to us from her home/office and explained how a stray idea turned her life around.

"I was in a state of severe depression, terribly ill with a rare lung ailment, divorced, with the prospect of raising two children alone. I didn't know what would become of us. Then an idea came to me. From my hospital bed, I wrote to maid services all over the country, asking prices, services offered—all the particulars. I was astounded at the lack of professionalism in the replies. Nobody was running a top-notch, blue-chip operation. Why couldn't I fill that void?

"Next, I had to check out the market. I pored over the voter registration lists and made up my 'fat cat' list of 2,000 potential customers from the more expensive end of town. We did one mailing, offering top quality maid service, satisfaction guaranteed.

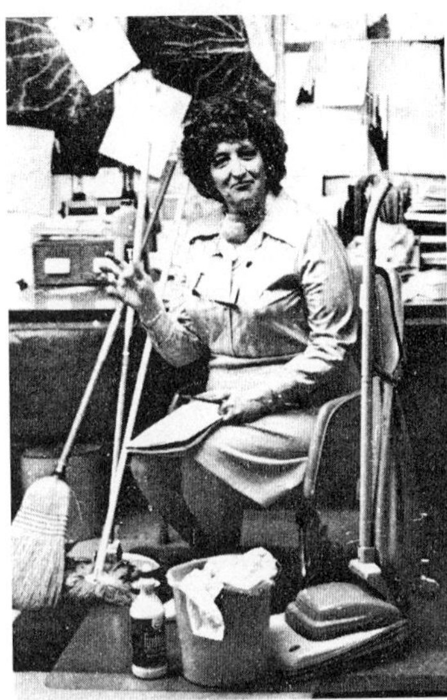

"By then I was home, but still very sick. I didn't want anyone to know, so I rented a small office in downtown Chicago where my son interviewed potential maids. Then he brought the applications home and we discussed them. I got an answering service, too, making a total cash outlay of $4,800. We got such a great response to the mailing, we were in business right away.

"I learned most of the cleaning techniques from the maids, and once I was on my feet, I went out with a bucket and a mop myself. We got a contract to clean model apartments, so we learned by doing a whole building. We tested cleaning products and techniques to develop some kind of standardization—so much for becoming familiar with the practical end of the business.

"We started with thirty maids, and now we have about 300 employees, including maids, bartenders, waiters, and maintenance men. Fourteen business concerns from as far away as Albuquerque want me to franchise Maid-to-Order. And we've added a companion service for the elderly, a vacation apartment and plant-care service, and a party service. Now we're looking into the concept of team cleaning in the suburbs where a team of specialized workers would travel between homes in a van.

"Why do I think it's been so successful? I've persevered. I called every morning to see that maids showed up; I followed up every complaint, answered every phone call. Most of all, I listened. When a client called to complain about the maid I sent to help at a party, she spent forty-five minutes explaining the things the maid should have done and didn't. I wrote it all down, thanked her, didn't charge her for that day, and started our party service based on what she had told me.

"At the bottom of it all, though, the real reason we've done well is that I've always looked after the well-being and dignity of the maids. I am pro-union. I am on the Illinois Committee on the Status of Women and the Governor's Advocacy Committee for Displaced Homemakers. I participate in studies on domestic workers. I envision a time, not far off, when domestic workers will be seen as semi-professionals, like the plumbers and electricians. Listen, I've had fun with Maid-to-Order, and the money's been very important to me—I never had to go on welfare or disability. But, I also feel we may have some influence in changing the status of domestic workers, and that means very much to me. After all, we're learning to value the homemaker as a skilled person—why not the domestic worker?

"I still work from home. And I work very hard. But I'm a very happy woman. Maid-to-Order was exactly that for me. It changed my whole life." ■

Reprinted with permission from *Family Circle Magazine*, February, 1979.

■ Joan Lunden Is Blazing a Trail

by Marian Christy

There's a crib in Joan Lunden's New York office.

There's a prim, uniformed nurse, Lolita, with a rattle in her hand in Joan Lunden's office.

There's a cute, cooing baby in Joan Lunden's office and when she's hungry she hollers, and her demanding wail sounds stronger than Joan Lunden's phone.

Usually the baby stops crying faster than the phone stops ringing, which says something about Joan Lunden's priorities. When it comes to juggling motherhood and career, Joan Lunden is mastering the art. And she is clearly successful at both kinds of work.

This, in fact, is the scene here in the executive suite of "Good Morning America" (ABC-TV), where Joan Lunden, one of the co-hosts on the show, is pioneering a new twist on the $250,000-a-year television career—namely in-office child care for her ten-week-old daughter, Jamie.

According to Lunden, her new contract stipulates that she must have a nurse if she travels on assignment because where she goes, the baby goes. When the chauffeured limousine picks her up at her Westchester home at 5 A.M. Monday to Friday she brings the baby along, nursing Jamie in the back of the car speeding into Manhattan. "I'm also able to study the scripts while I'm nursing," she says nonchalantly.

Could this be a portent of maternal things to come in offices around the country? Joan Lunden hopes so.

"It is a great relief to discover that you can do two things at one time," says Lunden, who appeared daily on television until two weeks before her baby was born last July 4. Soon after Jamie's birth, she had some "real anxiety." It was not a postpartum attack. Joan Lunden was trying to figure how to do what she has done.

"When I started thinking of the possible complications, I said to myself: 'You must be crazy out of your mind!' Then I said: 'Hold on, Joan. Only thing you gotta be is organized.' Once that sunk into my head, I realized that I had to be totally organized."

It sounds relatively easy, thanks to the supportiveness of the network, but actually the painstaking details were worked out by Lunden's lawyers and a battery of network lawyers. Lunden says that her employer had to be "talked into cooperating." She says that her present contract was worked out by her lawyers who told her to "leave the contract to them and to concentrate on being a mommy."

Lunden has the easygoing, unruffled disposition to handle her workload and her baby simultaneously without a trace of visible tension.

"I really like my job," she says. "I don't know of any job I would want more than this one. It was just a matter of facilitating being a mother and being on the show simultaneously. In the end, the network lawyers said 'yes' to everything. I never got involved. I don't know how wonderful the legal meetings were, but it all worked out.

"I'm aggressive but not obsessively so," she explains. "I have made my choice; I have had a baby. I am a home person at heart." Joan Lunden, who had a "most enjoyable pregnancy," says that it is not out of the question that she will get pregnant again and appear in her job as an expectant mother for the second time. "I won't wait a long time," she says smiling.

As if on cue, the baby cries a bit and Lunden says, laughing, that this is a "new sound" around the office. The baby's father is Michael Krauss, a former Today producer who is making pilots for a new syndicated daytime talk show, "Hittin' Home." Part of Joan Lunden's security is the fact that Krauss wanted her to star in his show, and she was considering that option if ABC-TV had not agreed to her demands about their baby. "It's better this way," she says. "We don't bring home the same problems every night. He has his career; I have my career. And we have our baby."

She says that Krauss is "perfect." She says he is "understanding" of the demands of her career. "He does not get up with me. It's too early. So I tiptoe around. Actually he's my biggest fan. He has made me so much better at what I do." Lunden says Krauss has been and is her friend, her mentor, her advisor, and critic.

Lunden and David Hartman have talked often about the fact that she is, perhaps, blazing a trail of child care options for other mothers.

"I am serving as an example," she says. "Men who head corporations are the men who make the rules for women. And I have shown them that I stayed on the job during a pregnancy, a visible job. I showed that pregnancy was not an illness. That it was not something to hide. I stayed on the air and I looked nice. I showed them that I could be a businesswoman." ■

■ Companies Start to Meet Executive Mothers Halfway

Dougla Pyrke, thirty-four, resigned as director of sales administration for the Bloomfield (Conn.) division of CIGNA Corp. after the birth of her second child last year. Then she gave her boss a job description for a part-time replacement and recommended herself. Pyrke now works three days a week at the insurance company, performing many of her previous functions.

Most executives who become mothers return to their old work routines soon after childbirth, but there are others who—like Pyrke—have always wanted to modify their schedules. Now employers have begun to work out special arrangements for them.

At First National Bank of Atlanta, for instance, Susie F. Siskin, thirty-three, and Joan S. Suttin, thirty-six, both mothers of young children, split an attorney's job between them. Each works three days a week, sharing Thursday, when they coordinate their activities. In Northbrook, IL, Randi Starr Savitzky, thirty-one, mother of two and production manager of McDougal Littell & Co., textbook publishers, spends two of her five weekly workdays in an office in her home, cheerfully wiping jam stains off her computer printouts. "I've been able to meet my children's needs and also meet my professional ones," she says.

Special Accommodations Made. While companies still avoid promulgating official policies—a *Business Week* survey of a dozen U.S. cities did not turn up a single personnel policy on special arrangements for mothers—attitudes have changed sharply from the days when each arrangement was treated as a rare exception to the rule of full-time, on-site work or no work at all. Today, many major corporations approve part-time employment or other special accommodations for large numbers of corporate mothers. At one company—AmeriTrust Corp. in Cleveland—twenty-five mothers have switched to part-time work within the past two years.

New demographics have produced the corporate change. Women increasingly are postponing childbearing until they have achieved enough job status to make their bosses willing to accommodate them. The U.S. Health & Human Services Dept. reports that the number of first births to women thirty to thirty-four rose eighty-three percent between 1972 and 1980, from seven births per 1,000 women to 12.8 births. The increase for women thirty-five to thirty-nine was forty-four percent and for women twenty-five to twenty-nine, thirty-one percent. The number of first births to younger women declined.

Companies frankly acknowledge that they agree to the new arrangements in order to hold valued employees. The *Los Angeles Times* moved energy reporter Doris Byron Fuller, thirty-three, to a *Times* office near her home after her son's birth, because "for top-notch reporters, I feel some accommodation is justified," says John Lawrence, assistant managing editor for economic affairs. Control Data Corp. in Minneapolis set up a home office for technical writer Marilyn M. Bigalke, thirty, to give her more time with her son because "I didn't want to lose her," says her boss, Stanley E. Berglund, who is the manager of Control Data's government systems resource center.

Shorter hours and proportionately lower pay do not necessarily lead to comparable decreases in workload. Basically, they mean working smarter, says Jane Dahlstrom-Quinn, thirty-five, vice-president in charge of legal compliance at United Bank of Denver, who works three days a week to fit in with the therapy schedule of a son born with Down's syndrome. She has dropped activities that were "nice but not essential," such as a committee chairmanship in the American Bankers Assn.

"No Schmoozing." My lunch hour is twenty minutes," says Joan Winstein, thirty-four, mother of a two-year-old son and a part-time vice-president of the First National Bank of Chicago. "I don't schmooze around the coffee machine or read the newspapers." CIGNA's Pyrke schedules meetings back-to-back when she goes to the office and then takes work home.

Careers almost inevitably suffer when mothers curtail work schedules. "It is definitely a setback," says Rebecca M. Rohde, thirty-one, personnel supervisor with Perry Drug Stores, Inc. in Pontiac, MI, who cut her fifty-hour workweek in half following the birth of a daughter in 1981. Part-time work limits the type of assignments Rohde can handle, explains her boss, Samuel N. Ray, assistant vice-president for human resources. "I'm at a plateau career-wise right now," observes Jacqueline W. Goler, thirty-one, a part-time marketing analyst at AmeriTrust Corp., an expectant mother who already has a three-year-old son. And one corporate mother who works part-time at a New York City bank says that an able manager usually makes vice-president in five or six years, but that she waited ten years for the title.

Re-entry Trouble. Still, say the women, working a modified schedule is much better than quitting. "I was acutely aware that women who took several years off had trouble getting back into the work force," declares Marilyn Milam, thirty-six, a vice-president with First Interstate Bank of California, who opted for part-time employment when the first of her two sons was born seven years ago. Employers generally understand the motivation. "My reaction is that women who work part-time are showing a lot of ambition," asserts W. Michael Balsley, senior vice-president of First National Bank of Atlanta.

Banks and financial companies apparently find it easier to accommodate part-time executives than do many other organizations. Some employers will not or cannot provide flexible work schedules. When Marjorie B. Schaafsma, thirty-four, a Grand Rapids lawyer, found a full schedule exhausting after the birth of her daughter last December, she persuaded her boss, attorney William G. Reamon, to approve a temporary four-day week. But Reamon declined to make it permanent, so Schaafsma plans to leave. "I could not care for the baby and be a trial attorney," she says.

Women who do manage to combine unconventional work arrangements with motherhood tend to be enthusiastic about the mix. "I have the best of both worlds, coming to a job I love and still having time to devote to my family," says Denver's Dahlstrom-Quinn.

Fortunately for them, their employers seem equally content. "You don't voluntarily lose key people," says Eugene U. Ricci, president of CIGNA Service Co., explaining why he reduced work hours for Marsha Chappell, thirty-seven, who directs CIGNA's Eagle Lodge business conference center outside Philadelphia, when her son was born last year. "Brains are hard to come by." ■

Reprinted from *Business Week*, October 17, 1983 by special permission. © 1983 McGraw-Hill, Inc.

■ If Home Is Where the Worker Is

The growing tendency of companies to have employees work at home instead of in an office is starting to have significant impact on labor relations planning. With experts predicting that as many as 15 million workers could be earning their primary income from so-called homework by the mid-1990s, major companies are training middle managers for supervising workers from a distance and developing new types of compensation systems. Adjusting to these changes can be traumatic, and this may encourage unions to make homeworkers an important target in their drive to organize white-collar occupations.

Homework was common among blue-collar workers early in this

century, and thousands of garment workers, many of them illegal aliens, are still compelled to do it—usually in violation of federal laws. But the number of legal homework programs for white-collar employees has risen from a handful a year ago to about thirty-five, involving perhaps 600 workers. Aetna Life & Casualty Co. and Investors Diversified Services, Inc., plan to turn pilot projects for at-home data processors and clerical workers, respectively, into permanent programs this year. Chase Manhattan Bank is expected to start a homework experiment with nine data processors in May. And Blue Cross/Blue Shield of South Carolina will expand its program for three clerical workers to perhaps as many as twelve by the end of the year.

Telecommuting, as homework is called when computers are used, will help solve an estimated annual shortage of 10,000 programmers and data analysts during the 1980s. It will expand the labor force because it enables more people to work who have small children or who are handicapped. At its best, it means greater trust between workers and their supervisors. But it also tends to weaken ties between employees and their companies. And the piecework nature of such work increases the risk of employee exploitation.

Estimates vary on how quickly homework will spread, but economist, Elisabeth Allison of Data Resources Inc. says there are now 15 million information-manipulation jobs—such as computer programming, financial analysis, and writing—that could be done at home. Researcher John M. Niles of the University of Southern California, who coined the term telecommuting, has weighed the costs of office space, commuting, and home equipment and predicted that within a decade 5 million people could be working mainly at home. The shift, says Allison, will require "a new pattern of employee relations."

Supervision will be a major problem. "It ultimately comes down to an honor system," says Jay Christensen-Szalanski, an administrator at Seattle Public Health Hospital who works eighty percent at home and supervises two other telecommuters. Many managers find it hard to adjust "because they think they might lose control of their people," Says Nelson B. Phelps, manager for Mountain States Telephone and Telegraph Co. The phone company holds seminars to eliminate this fear. Blue Cross assigns homework only to people who have worked in-house—and thus have earned its trust. Companies keep tabs on workers with frequent phone calls. And Chase Manhattan may have homeworkers visit the bank each week.

Another approach is to monitor workers through their own equipment. "You are visible the moment you log on," says Victor Hart, account manager at Los Angeles-based Freight Data Systems, where twelve programmers work at home. But such measuring and frequent phoning also bring the risk of oversupervision. Moreover, it is a short step from evaluating workers by output to paying them by output, and this, says Dennis Chamot, assistant director of the Professional Employees Dept. of the AFL-CIO, holds "a potential for exploitation." In reaction to violations of child-labor, overtime, and minimum-wage laws, the Labor Dept. in the early 1940s outlawed homework in seven garment industries. The Labor Dept. last year lifted the ban for one industry, knitted outerwear, causing the AFL-CIO to predict "the return of the sweatshop to the home."

No one thinks such abuses will occur in white-collar homework. Still, Aetna plans to pay telecommuters by the project and to use them only for "peak work," leaving them without a regular salary. They will also be eligible for health and pension benefits. Blue Cross's homeworkers are excluded from $2,000 to $3,000 a year worth of benefits, and they pay $2,400 in annual rent for their computer terminals. However, the company says they earn up to $3,000 a year more than salaried office workers.

How much this will help unions organize homeworkers is debatable. Glenn E. Watts, president of the Communications Workers of America, notes that telecommuters "tend to be individualistic people who like to negotiate on their own with the employer." Moreover, the isolation of such workers makes organizing expensive and difficult. But Chamot says that wide differences in compensation could give unions an edge, and Data Resources' Allison predicts that homeworkers at least will form professional groups to provide the social interaction they miss at the office.

Indeed, isolation may limit the homeworker movement. One worker quit Mountain Bell's experiment in order to keep his contacts in the office. And Insurance Co. of North America is moving slowly toward telecommuting. Says Senior Executive Vice-President Allan Z. Loren: "We think, 'Wouldn't it be great if women who can't come to work because of small children could work at home?' But one reason women get into the job market is to have the company of adults." Still, some experts see homework providing social contact by phone. Telecommuters, says Watts, could even hook up to union meetings. ■

Reprinted from *Business Week*, May 3, 1982 by special permission of McGraw-Hill, Inc.

■ Lansing Teachers Offered Job Sharing Plan to Avoid Layoffs

by Yolanda Alvarado

The Lansing School District is attempting to reduce the number of teachers it may have to lay off in June by offering the teaching staff a "job sharing" plan—with half paychecks, half the work, and full health insurance benefits.

Lansing schools Personnel Director David B. Smith said teachers were also offered the option this week of taking full time voluntary leaves for the 1981–82 school year.

"Because of declining enrollments and reduced finances, we are in a period of impending layoffs," said Smith. "We know we are going to have to have fewer staff members than we have this year, but we would really like to stay away from layoffs where we can."

Tom Ferris, president of the Lansing Schools Education Association (LSEA), said job sharing "is an excellent way to explore different careers, to explore different ways of teaching in the school district, and also to prevent lay-offs to an extent."

Teachers who wish to share jobs will have to apply, and each pair must submit a plan which specifies how the sharing arrangement will work.

"We want to know how in-service will be handled and who's going to do what," said Smith. "We want consistency, discipline, and control in the classroom, as well as good communication with students and parents. We want to be sure we are running just as good a program when we are 'sharing' as we were before."

Two elementary teachers teach a fifth and sixth grade class at Reo. Kathleen Baldwin and Sandy Paulos, both mothers of young children, agreed ahead of time how responsibilities would be shared.

Mrs. Baldwin works mornings. She teaches math, social studies, art, and spelling. Mrs. Paulos works afternoons. She teaches the same students reading, science, English, penmanship, music, and physical education.

Mrs. Baldwin and Mrs. Paulos also agreed on a discipline code so students wouldn't be confused by different expectations. Mrs. Baldwin said they meet once a week to discuss the progress and problems of their students. They plan class parties together and occasionally substitute for each other.

"We manage to head off any problems by talking about everything to the last detail," said Mrs. Baldwin. "Besides spending more time with my two-year-old son, I've been able to help with parties at my daughter's school. If I were working full time, I wouldn't be able to do that!

"I go home at the end of the day in a pretty happy state of mind because I don't have the drudgery of a full day," Mrs. Baldwin said. "The kids get two teachers who feel pretty refreshed and who feel good about themselves.

"I would certainly want to do this until my son goes to school. I might want to stick with it forever," said Mrs. Baldwin. ■

Reprinted from the *Lansing State Journal*, Lansing, MI, February 13, 1981

■ Teachers Make Job Sharing Work at Dirksen

by Kathy Schaeffer

The first clue that Room 205 in Dirksen School in Schaumburg is special is the placard above the door with two teachers' names printed on it.

But the fifth-grade students who call that classroom home will tell you there are more important differences between their homeroom and every other one in the school.

Twice each day, those students are greeted by a teacher who is fresh and rested. More often than not, they will get their graded tests and papers back earlier than other students. And, it's doubtful that those students will ever have a stranger as a substitute teacher.

That is because the students have two homeroom teachers, Ann Westby and Linda Rosholt. Westby and Rosholt are the first regular classroom teachers in Illinois to share teaching responsibilities for one class in a pilot job sharing program in Schaumburg Township District 54.

"They're never grouchy," said student Lisa Smith. Classmate Sean Armstrong added, "If they get in a bad mood, you won't have to see them all day."

Westby teaches math, social studies, and science in the morning, and Rosholt teaches reading and language arts in the afternoon. If one of the teachers is absent, the other fills in and teaches all day.

Beyond debate about grouchy teachers and speedy test results, the students said they also see other more substantial differences in their two teachers.

"It's kind of interesting to see

how they both teach," Sean said. "Mrs. Rosholt jokes more." But he added, Westby has been known to bring in watermelons from her garden for "watermelon math" lessons.

Learning to get along with more than one homeroom teacher is one student side benefit of the job-sharing proposal, school officials said.

However, the main reason for the pair's proposal was their desire to spend more time with their families and personal business without giving up their careers as teachers. They spent months researching job sharing and writing a detailed proposal that last spring was approved as a trial program by the District 54 school board.

And, say all who are concerned, it's working.

"It just leaves me with a better feeling at the end of the day," Rosholt said. "I don't fall asleep on the couch at home anymore." And she was able to take up piano lessons with her five-year-old daughter.

"It's wonderful," Westby said. Working only half of the day gives her time to work at her church, where she spends about two hours every afternoon. "I am developing a volunteer ministries program at our church. It's such a totally different thing than working full time. Neither feels like work when you're only doing it half time."

During a recent lunch period when both teachers' schedules overlapped for thirty minutes, Westby and Rosholt quickly briefed one another on the day's activities.

"I have three children who didn't bring in their homework for math," Westby said as she shuffled through her desk, getting ready to leave. "If they don't have it in by the end of the day, they each get a detention. I really hate to ask you to give out those detentions," she told Rosholt.

Then the conversations moved to a youngster who had missed several days of class because she was sick. Rosholt asked Westby whether she thought the girl was feeling well enough to participate fully in class.

"Oh, she's feeling pretty normal. I watched her throw a football," Westby said with a smile.

Often during those lunch meetings the two will discuss other school business or conversations they have had with parents. One key to the success of the job-sharing arrangement is that the two teachers have constant communication with one another.

"We told parents that they don't have to wait until there's a certain person here. If you tell one of us, you've told both of us," Rosholt said.

The two teachers explained the job-sharing program to parents at an orientation open house at the beginning of the school year. There were few questions, and there have been no complaints.

"But I did get one note from a parent that said, 'Please be sure that Mrs. Rosholt reads this, too,' " Westby said. "The parents still aren't real sure about little things like that."

Dirksen Principal Bernard Lucier said much of the success of the program is because of the individuals who are involved.

"The main reason it's working is because we have one unit operating up there, instead of two half-time teachers. Although they're working half time, they're really putting in more time than half," Lucier said. "They're just the type of teachers who are willing to extend themselves."

Because personalities are a major part of a job-sharing arrangement and because those who participate receive only half of the pay and half of the benefits, job sharing is not for everyone. District 54 officials are not expecting teachers to line up by the hundreds to participate.

In the spring, evaluations by students, other teachers, parents, and supervisors will be presented to the school board to help determine whether job sharing will become commonplace. Officials have said there probably would be a limit on the number of pairs who would be allowed to share jobs.

Linda Stolt, Schaumburg Education Association president, said a provision for job sharing probably should be included in the teacher contract that will be negotiated at the end of the school year.

Questions such as whether a job-sharing teacher should earn a full year of credit on the salary schedule or be eligible for tenure have not been answered. With declining enrollment, there also is the question of who would be laid off first, a teacher with all full-time teaching or a teacher with a combination of full-time and job-sharing experience.

"At bargaining time, I'm certain we'll look into it," Stolt said.

Her comments echoed District 54 administrators and board members who are taking a wait-and-see attitude on the concept. ■

■ The Thurmans: Full Time Parenting, Part of the Time

Bringing up baby in the 1980s has its challenges—especially for dual career couples like Audrey and Gerry Thurman of Columbus.

"Before the baby was born, we discussed our child-care options," Audrey said. "We didn't want to leave her with a sitter, so that meant that somebody would have to stay home with her, at least for the first year."

"But we're both very involved in technical work," Gerry added. "It wouldn't have been fair for one of us to have to 'retire.' "

With the help of their supervisors in the Switching Operations Systems Laboratory, Gerry and Audrey created their own unique solution to the problem.

January 1, 1982—about six weeks after their daughter Bree was born—they started working at their regular jobs, part-time. Each puts in a five-hour day at the office while the other is home with Bree. At noontime, according to Audrey, they "exchange a hug and car keys" and switch roles.

Audrey works Monday, Wednesday, and Friday mornings, Tuesday and Thursday afternoons. Gerry's regimen is just the reverse.

"This gives us a consistent schedule," Audrey said. "Our colleagues know when we're in and when we're available for meetings. And they can always call us at home if they need to."

While they're at the office, the Thurmans try to make every minute count. "When you know you'll only be there for five hours, you don't do much socializing around the coffee machine," Gerry said.

And with a baby who "goes off like an alarm clock around 6 A.M." the one who's working the morning shift finds it easy to get to the office early.

"I get a lot of good work done in the morning when there are no distractions," Audrey said.

Audrey and Gerry have a terminal at home, too—his department bought it, hers pays the monthly charges. "But I wait until Bree's napping before I log on," Audrey said.

For Audrey, the arrangement fit in nicely with the life she had envisioned for herself. "I always aspired to a career," she said, "and I always wanted to be a mother. The question was how to do both."

For Gerry, being a full-time parent part of the time wasn't easy at first. "My first part-time day at home was a little scary," he admitted. "I'd never been alone with a baby before. I learned what to do by trial and error. Bree demonstrated a lot of patience with me."

Today Gerry's an old hand at baby care. He feeds her, plays with her, changes her. When Gerry's working in the yard or hitting golf balls at the driving range, Bree's right there in her stroller, taking it all in.

"Bree and I had nine months to fall in love with each other before she was born," Audrey said. "Now she and Gerry have developed a special relationship, too."

"For half a day, every day, she's totally dependent on me," Gerry added. "No wonder there's such a bond between us."

After seven months, the Thurmans seem pleased with their new lifestyle. "We get to stay involved in our profession," Audrey said, "and we're not at home long enough to feel isolated or hungry for adult conversation."

But they admit that their arrangement wouldn't suit everyone. They also admit that they owe a lot to luck.

Gerry Thurman and Audrey Ralston joined Bell Labs within months of each other in 1979, Gerry at Columbus and Audrey at Piscataway. As part of the company's One Year On Campus program, they started work on their masters degrees in computer science at Purdue that fall.

"They assigned graduate student offices alphabetically," Audrey recalled. "Since Thurman comes after Ralston, we ended up being office-mates."

They found that they had a lot more than an office in common. "Mathematics, computer science . . . we're practically twins," Audrey said.

They married in July 1980 and graduated in August. At the time Gerry's lab was expanding and Audrey was able to transfer in.

Working for the same organization, they feel, made it easier to arrange for their new schedules when the baby was born.

"We were very fortunate," Gerry concluded. "And so is Bree. She's getting to know both parents from the start. That's a pretty nice way to be introduced into the world." ■

Courtesy of AT&T, Bell Laboratories. Reprinted with the permission of *Bell Lab News*.

Job-Sharing Alternative Draws Nurses Back to the Hospital

by Carol A. Bardi, RN

With a severe nursing shortage affecting patient care in hospitals across the country, progressive hospital administrators need to try some alternatives to help attract and retain nurses. The American Hospital Association estimates that there is a nationwide shortage of 100,000 nurses, and every year, more and more nurses are leaving the health care profession to go into other fields. According to the *Wall Street Journal*, more than one out of three hospital nurses quit every year, and out of 1.4 million licensed nurses, 414,000 have stopped working because of childrearing duties, advanced age, and transfers to other facilities.

Why are nurses leaving their chosen profession? They are leaving because of heavy work loads, "burnouts," and inflexible scheduling involving most weekends and holidays and night and evening duty. Nurses resign to take other positions because "they feel they don't have adequate control over the content or pacing of their work," according to a study of nurse turnover in Baltimore conducted by Carol Weisman, an assistant professor of behavioral sciences at Johns Hopkins University.

Job Sharing. What can be done to counteract this large exodus of nurses each year? One method that has been tried and proven in other fields is job sharing. Teachers and social workers began job sharing in the mid-1960s, and since that time, job sharing has been elected by bank tellers, researchers, receptionists, and laboratory technicians. In hospitals, staff nurse positions could be filled by job sharers, which would help to alleviate the nursing shortage and the need for on-call and temporary registered nurses.

Job sharing is a voluntary arrangement in which two persons share one full-time position. As applied to the hospital setting, and more specifically to staff registered nurses, job sharing would be a full-time position, eight hours a day, five days per week, staffed by two registered nurses. Because it might not be efficient to split an eight-hour day, each RN could select the number of eight-hour days she or he prefers to work according to the individual's preference. For example, it may be desirable for one RN to work sixteen hours, or two days per week, and the other twenty-four hours, or three days per week. Job sharing differs from permanent part-time employment in that the job sharers would split weekend and holiday duty, each working one weekend out of four and two holidays instead of four. Fringe benefits, such as health insurance, sick time, vacation time, and personal time, would be pro-rated according to the hours each person works.

RNs who are interested in permanent part-time work in a hospital setting would be the likeliest applicants for job-sharing positions. Nurses who are not presently employed because of home responsibility and child-rearing duties and older nurses who are ready for semi-retirement would be logical applicants as well. Many on-call nurses also would prefer job sharing because it would cut in half the number of weekends and holidays required. Most on-call nurses who desire permanent part-time work are unwilling to work every other week-end and most holidays.

Benefits. There are many advantages for hospitals in the job-sharing concept. First, it brings back to the hospital nurses who enjoy bedside nursing but who are tired of weekend and holiday duty. Second, better patient care can be provided through a reduction in the use of temporary and on-call nurses. Presently, many hospitals are using on-call and temporary personnel who are not familiar with the hospital to fill needed positions. By filling these positions with job sharers, the amount of time regular employees spend away from their duties to orient the temporary RNs to hospital procedures, the floor routine, and the physical layout of the unit will be reduced. Third, sick calls would decrease and productivity would increase, as documented in a study done by Catalyst, a job-counseling and placement service for women. The study found that fifty half-time social workers in Boston carried a greater case load than twenty-five full-time personnel. The half-time welfare case workers averaged eighty-nine percent of the client contacts of the full-time case workers. Also, job sharers have more flexibility in their schedules, so they can cover for each other if one partner needs an extra day off for an appointment or illness, thereby reducing the number of sick calls.

Finally, job sharing reduces employee turnover for several reasons. First, turnover is reduced because of the voluntary nature of the sharing, according to Barney Olmsted, co-director of New Ways to Work in Palo Alto, CA. Furthermore, because job sharing enables the RN to spend more time on interests outside of the hospital, "burnout," a common cause of job turnover, becomes less of a problem. Third, job frustrations are alleviated by the support that job sharers lend to one another. The support emanates from their mutual interest in the shared responsibility of patient care.

Like any innovative concept, job sharing is not without some drawbacks. Some might argue that job sharing would be an increased cost to the hospital. However, after a careful comparison of costs, the actual dollar increase is minimal, and the potential for increased productivity, lower turnover, less overtime, and less time spent recruiting and orienting on-call personnel should outweigh the small cost. Increased costs would occur in the areas of fringe benefits, statutory benefits, and employee orientation, however. Because fringe benefit packages and costs differ from organization to organization, these costs must be considered on an individual hospital basis. One approach would be to treat the job sharers as permanent part-time employees and pro-rate the fringe benefits according to time worked.

One way to eliminate the cost of orientation for two persons would be to institute a pilot project that offers job sharing to on-call personnel who are already employed by the hospital. This type of pilot project may qualify for federal funding, which would offset the cost.

Some critics claim that job sharing will be so attractive to full-time employees that everyone will want to try job sharing if it is offered as an option. However, most full-time RNs need the salary and benefits that a full-time position provides. Job sharing is most attractive to those RNs who do not desire full-time work and who are not currently working in a hospital setting.

In summary, job sharing could help alleviate the nursing shortage in hospitals by attracting qualified nurses who desire flexibility in their work schedules. Job sharing does not eliminate weekend and holiday duty, but it does reduce it by half. The advantages of job sharing more than outweigh the disadvantages. As the nursing shortage increases, job sharing will become a workable staffing alternative. ■

Reprinted with permission from *Hospitals*, published by the American Hospital Publishing, Inc., copyright June 16, 1981, Vol. 55, No. 12.

■ Her Town Newsletters Truly In-House Productions

by Elida Witthoeft

Few area residents would suspect that those official-looking municipal newsletters that arrive in the mail every few months are produced in an office equipped with a wooden slide and a doll house.

But to Kaye Lowman, who has carved a small empire for herself as a newsletter publisher, the childrens' toys may be her most important tools. By starting her own business, Lowman has created a job that allows her to stay home with her children and still pursue a career.

Four years ago, Lowman took a part-time job as Hoffman Estate's public relations director. Her duties included producing the village newsletter, work she had never done despite a degree in journalism. Then Lowman found herself pregnant with her fourth child and began dividing her time between

village hall and her Barrington home.

"I did the Hoffman Estates page layouts when I was in labor," said Lowman. "When Carrie was three weeks old I took her and the newsletter to the village."

Meanwhile, Lowman's reputation had spread, and she was approached by Streamwood officials to do their village newsletter. "The Streamwood manager talked to the Hoffman Estates manager, and he (the Hoffman manager) said what I did in my own time was my business," said Lowman. "Hanover Park was the next town to ask. One neighbor sees another's newsletter and asks, 'How did you get that?' "

Lowman's unique service snowballed, and now she is producing at least nineteen newsletters a year, including Elk Grove Village, Palatine, Schaumburg, and Wheeling Township as clients. "It's turned into a full-time job," says Lowman, who also continues her part-time job in Hoffman Estates.

Producing a newsletter takes five working days to complete. It begins when Lowman sits down with municipal officials to discuss the publication's content. "They'll give me ideas," she said. "They might want an update on Lake Michigan water, or the law dealing with township collectors." Lowman then researches the issues, conducts interviews, and even takes pictures.

With the interviewing complete, she then writes all the copy, designs the newsletter, lays out the pages, and gets it all to the printer. She even makes arrangements with local postal offices to have the finished newsletters delivered within a day of when they arrive at the post office.

"People get so much unsolicited mail that you have to attract people to look at it," said Lowman. "Cheap, unattractive newsletters—no one reads them. I always try for an eye-catching picture on front. I want it to look newsy."

"I try to write from the perspective of the citizen. In towns where they (publish) their own (newsletter), the government officials write for other officials, and the politicians write to other politicians," she said.

Lowman's fees begin at $1,300 for a four-page newsletter, and she says she "makes a better living than most women who sit behind desks," and is still at home.

She said each newsletter takes on a personality of its own, although she used to "lie awake at night worrying the stories would get mixed up." But government officials look at each step of her work and help catch errors.

"I've grown to like local government. It's the place where people can make their voices heard. I like the part of telling them what they need to know and what to do to be heard."

Lowman also likes the time she spends with her children. "I'm committed to babies. It doesn't have to be 'either/or.' Many women would be wise to reassess their jobs and do the best for their babies and still be satisfied themselves," she said.

"Lots of work can be done at home with an umbilical cord to the office." ■

Chapter 18

Work and Womanhood
New perspectives

Many things in today's world are in short supply. But the woman of the 1980s and beyond has been blessed with two things in abundance: options and choices.

With little fear of social stigma or unfavorable repercussions, a woman today is able to choose to be single or married, to pursue a career or to stay at home, to raise a family or to remain childless, to combine motherhood with a career or to make raising her children a full-time commitment.

But make no mistake; the availability of so many options is a mixed blessing. Choices can be seductive, promising a greener pasture but delivering a patch of thorny weeds or, worse yet, dry, barren earth.

The freedom to choose from among so many lifestyles carries with it the responsibility to scrutinize the costs that may be incurred as well as the bonuses that may accrue. When the choices made will affect children, even children who are yet to be born, the responsibility to measure anticipated gains against potential losses takes on an awesome dimension. Implicit in the freedom to choose is the obligation to choose wisely.

Women and Work

Prior to the last decade, if you asked a woman who she was, you could pretty well count on having her describe herself as a wife and mother, or as a homemaker. Her identity was completely tied to her family and home life.

Ask a man the same question and he will almost always describe himself in terms of his work—his profession, his position, the company he works for. His personal identity is most closely tied to his work life.

Today, as women enter the labor market with years of training for their chosen profession and a long-term commitment to their work, they, too, have begun to define themselves in terms of the work they do. While her job may represent a second income for the family, it is often equally important as a means of providing a source of identity, a sense of accomplishment, a measure of personal worth. For such a woman, to turn her back on her job upon the birth of a baby is to give up her identity and self-esteem. Giving up her work would mean giving up an important part of herself.

Judson Stone

"We've understood for a long time how much of a man's sense of personal identity—who he is in the world—comes from the work he does," says Judson Stone, a pioneer in the field of industrial mental health who acts as a consultant for both labor unions and the federal government in the formation of work-related public policy.

"Traditionally, women have found their sense of identity through their roles as wives and mothers, and their primary emotional support through coffee with the next door neighbor, walks around the block with the kids, and conversations over the backyard clothesline.

"But because of the options available to women today, the neighborhood support groups have pretty well vanished," Stone explains. "The next door neighbor is off at work, there's no one to stop and talk to on a walk around the block, and the clothes dryer put an end to those important conversations over the backyard clothesline."

With the neighbors at work and the clothesline in a heap on the basement floor, the woman of the 80s is finding that a career offers important emotional as well as economic benefits.

"Many women are finding that their sense of themselves now comes through participation in the workplace, and their emotional support from the network of friendships formed there," Stone adds. As one of the country's foremost experts on the relationship between work and personal identity, Stone has seen firsthand what can happen when a man or woman becomes unemployed or gives up a career.

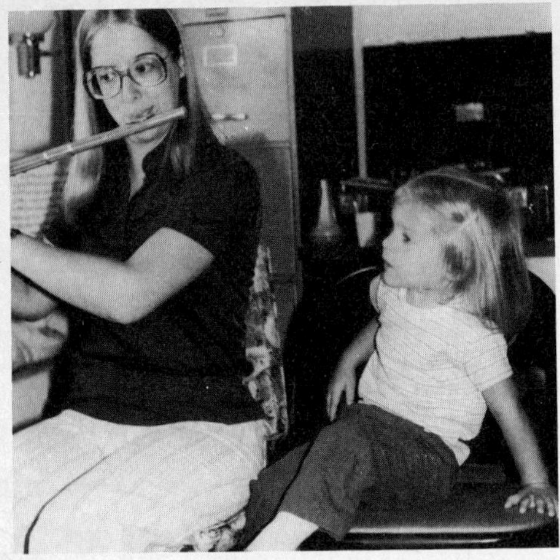

Flutist Deborah Coble has continued her career in music while being a mother to Lianne.

"People who aren't working feel as though they have lost a part of themselves. They suffer anger, grief, depression—all the classic symptoms of mourning. A woman who gives up her career because she thinks she has to for the sake of the baby may have trouble with bonding, difficulty accepting the baby, and a strained marriage relationship.

"If we are not to lose a real part of ourselves, a career is not to be given up lightly," Stone cautions. "Our work tells us who we are and what we are about."

As Deborah Coble, a flutist with the Syracuse Symphony Orchestra puts it, "Being a musician is not just a job. It is a way of life. It is who I am."

A Clash of Needs

But for an increasing number of career women, especially those who can no longer avoid staring the end of their child-bearing years square in the eye, forgoing a family for the sake of a career is not an acceptable option. And so, almost unnoticed, these women have begun reshaping the workplace in order to make it more responsive to their need to work and their desire to have a family. Whether a woman's need to work is financial, social, or emotional, the desire to Be a parent may be equally strong.

"I married at twenty-eight, had my first baby at twenty-nine," explains biostatistician/epidemiologist Judith Simon. "By that time I was too far into a career that was fulfilling and satisfying to let it go. But having children has always been my most important and strongest desire."

"I enjoy doing what I do and want to do it as long as I can," says flutist Deborah Coble. "But my husband and I also feel we have a lot to give as loving, caring parents. Our daughter has added a wonderful dimension to our lives."

And as these women begin to bring about the modified working arrangements that will enable them to blend motherhood with a career, they are discovering an unexpected bonus—that the personal satisfaction they find through their work enhances their feelings about their children, and the joy they find in parenting makes them better, more fulfilled people at work, and everywhere else.

Many of the women who are opting to combine a career and a family say that they feel they are "better" mothers because the fulfillment they achieve in their careers gives them a high degree of personal satisfaction that spills over into their relationship with their husband and children. This kind of statement is sometimes a red flag to mothers who feel it is important to be at home full time with their babies and young children, even though staying home may entail personal or economic sacrifices for them. This is an issue that could be argued endlessly, for the bottom line is that every mother is a unique individual and there is no cast-in-stone set of rules and regulations that enables us to compare one mother with another and declare her "good," "better," or "best." What works well in one woman's life may not work at all in another woman's life. And motherhood is, after all, not a contest but a commitment of love to the children we bring into the world. Our respect for the uniqueness of each individual woman includes recognizing that it is each woman's right to determine what is best for herself and her family.

■ What works well in one woman's life may not work at all in another woman's life.

As Gayle Feld puts it, "Good mothering can't be defined by a narrow set of rules. We all have to do what we feel works best for ourselves and our families. If we are reasonably satisfied with what we are doing, we can pass that good feeling along to our families, who will be happier as well."

"Working has made me happier," admits nurse Patricia Wendt, who took her baby to work with her for six months while she was employed by the WIC (Women, Infants, and Children) program. "When I was home all day every day I was going a little stir crazy. I feel that I have a talent in my profession, and it feels good to put that talent to use. Because I'm happier as a person, I'm more energetic as a mother."

Hospital dietitician Lisa Holden comments, "I tend to get restless and frustrated without an outside commitment that challenges my mind. I really admire women who stay home with their children and have infinite patience with them. For me, working three days a week enables me to come home eager to see the children, refreshed and renewed. It's a nice balance: time away, time together. I think we better appreciate the time we have together."

Anthropologist Margaret Saunders, who is self-employed as a

Anthropologist Margaret Saunders attended a naming ceremony in the Niger Republic of West Africa several years before her own two sons were born.

consultant in African development, explains it this way: "Being employed is very important to my own self-esteem. The children receive better mothering when I am happier with myself. Over the past six years of being parents, we have found that life is more pleasant when I am not gone eight or nine hours a day, but that my being at home all the time is not the best solution for us either."

Occupational therapist Barbara Addis comments, "Since I am away four mornings a week, I am ready to tune into Carrie and play with her when I return home. I appreciate my time with her more. Even though I am sometimes tired, I feel refreshed and good about myself after work because I enjoy what I do."

"Working has been a real benefit," says Susan Edwards who is self-employed as a designer. "I never have to feel tied down by having to stay home with a baby, nor do I have to feel left out of the working world."

"I wanted to continue doing what I enjoy doing as an archivist," says Martha Katz-Hyman. "I felt that it was important for me to have something I did for myself so that I would not resent the demands of children as I might otherwise."

"My career satisfies certain needs in me that weren't being met when I was home full time with Patrick for the first six months," comments occupational therapist Lynda Dunal.

"I worked hard to earn my nursing degree," explains Cheryl Kruwel. "I wanted to work, but I also wanted to raise a family. Doing the work that I enjoy makes me more contented and happy as a person, which spills over into my relationship with my son."

Secretary Nansi Casper, who takes her toddler with her to work, says, "My job is a very important part of the family income, but I also enjoy my work very much. I enjoy having a career that provides me with challenge and mental stimulation. I enjoy being a mother, but I enjoy my career as well."

"I feel I need to get out in the world to have a complete life," admits computer supervisor Jannette Johnson. "I feel better about myself when I am doing something to expand my mind."

"I wanted to keep doing pediatric nursing," says Mary Doll, "but not at my son's expense. By working part time I feel that I can make an important contribution while I am at work, and be the best mother I am able to be while I am at home."

"I appreciate the change in routine," says Helen Stewart, a self-employed attorney. "It makes me glad for the time at work and glad for the time at home. I love both home and office. I would have no problem at all if only there were forty-eight hours in a day."

Economic Need

In these uncertain economic times, a woman may find herself propelled into the work force not through her own desire, but through sheer economic necessity. When it is the need for additional income that takes a woman out of the home and into the labor market, her options may be narrower and her need for emotional support is certainly greater.

"I went to work when my second child was three months old," says teacher Patricia Priore. "My husband was unemployed when his position at the university ended. I would have preferred to stay home while my children were preschoolers.

"But when, for financial or other reasons, both parents are working, then it's great when there are support systems to help the family. For example, breastfeeding my children, with the help of La Leche League, gave us a tremendous rapport and a special sense of identity. My husband's taking on the meal preparations and the shopping added a valuable time dimension and role model for the kids. Our babysitters provided more than emotional security. They gave our children, love, just like a family.

"Although having a foot in two different worlds isn't for everybody, it works for some. Having options and loving support are blessings for which I am grateful."

A Commitment to a Career

Women who have spent years earning their degree or advancing within the company are understandably reluctant to turn their backs on what they have worked so hard to achieve.

"I waited for a long time to have this second baby—there are eleven and a half years between my children," said attorney Susan Miele. "I was impatient for the first one to grow up, but with this one I feel time is flying and she is growing too fast. I don't want to miss the special toddler years. However, a great deal of time and expense went into getting my law degree and I can't throw that away. I feel I have to keep working to keep my career alive."

"I could take a short leave of absence," says Syracuse Symphony Orchestra flutist Deborah Coble. "But if I quit completely I probably would never get my job back."

Or, as nurse Cynthia Abood succinctly puts it: "I did not enter my career never to work at it."

A Precious Time

But the career woman of the 80s understands her baby's need for her and the importance of being a meaningful part of her baby's life. And she realizes how much she herself will lose if she misses out on the opportunity to mother her own children. Far better to just gently stir the career for a few years to keep it moving, even if ever so slightly, than to try to relegate the baby's infancy and toddlerhood to the back burner. Careers can be put on hold; babies grow up and are gone. It was a wise and thoughtful Mother Nature who brought babies into the world needing to be breastfed and cared for, reminding us that mother and baby are very much a unit for many months after birth and that they need to be together. To try to ignore or circumvent this physical and psychological need is to tamper with one of the most fundamental and basic elements of human nature.

■ Careers can be put on hold; babies grow up and are gone.

"Children grow so fast," observes teacher Barbara Lovley. "They need me and I need them. So I can compromise my career and salary and work part-time."

"I can always work," says job-sharing social worker Cyndy Boesch. "I still have thirty plus years that I can work. But there are biological limits put on motherhood. Children are little for such a short time. If you miss it, it's gone."

Nurse Cynthia Lee who works on call explains, "I wanted to *see* my son grow and learn and experience, not just be told about what he did."

"At this time in my life, I feel that being a mother is more important than my career," comments Ann Louhela who works under a flextime arrangement with the federal government. "My child will be a baby only once, and I'll probably be working the rest of my life, so there's a lot of time for a career."

"I believe it's important to enjoy life. I want more than mere

Motherhood is a special time in a woman's life, meant to be savored and enjoyed.

survival," admits job-sharing court deputy Barbara Tickner. "I believe that by spending more time with my children than I could if I worked full time that I am giving them a taste of the alternatives in life, and still providing the kind of home life that I remember from my own childhood."

"I realize how important the first three years are to a baby," says Susan Courville, Administrator of the Ottawa-Hull Childbirth Education Association who takes her baby to work with her twenty hours a week. "I didn't want to miss out on all the special things my baby would do, all the firsts in his life. I know that my children *need* me, especially in the early years. I don't want to regret anything. I want to be able to live with myself later on. If I were working full time, naturally I would be earning more, but I would have to pay for child care, too. Money isn't everything. At least I am at peace, since my baby is with me and I know she is well and happy."

"Parenting is a humbling experience," says college professor Sonia Werner, "yet I wouldn't want to miss the experiences for anything."

"My work must come second to my family," explains Virginia McGowan of the University of Toronto. "How could this world be a fit place to live in if our priorities do not place child and family first? We owe this much to future generations."

"How I love my number-one job—being Owen and Christiana's mother," adds cosmetics consultant Mary Lou McGregor. "The satisfaction, the pleasure, the love I get from motherhood is beyond anything else I have ever experienced. Watching Owen and Christina grow is a great pleasure to me. I am so fortunate to have been blessed with two children who have taught me new dimensions to the word love."

"I am a new explorer in the old world of motherhood," admits college professor Merike Tamm who carries a part-time teaching load. "As a thirty-three-year-old woman who had never held a baby before her own, and who had grown up on the literature of women's liberation, I had braced myself for the tedium of baby care. Every day of pleasure has been a pure surprise.

"If I had not had Aleksander, I would have felt that my life was full and complete—that acquiring a PhD, teaching, writing, discussing politics, traveling, having friends and a loving husband, provided sufficient joy and excitement for any woman's life.

"But no thrill in the world compares with holding your own newborn baby in your arms, and no pleasure is sweeter than feeling your breasts swell with milk and then having them emptied by a tiny, toothless mouth that occasionally pauses to smile at you.

"I came across a quotation the other day which sums up my feelings: 'It is not an ordinary time. In the life of a mother these early years are the focal point, unique and fleeting, a time of tranquility and exquisite beauty.' "

Providing the opportunity for every woman to find a workable blend of parenthood and professional goals is the challenge of today—and the blueprint for tomorrow.

Chapter 19

Of Cradles and Careers
Today and tomorrow

The workplace, as we have known it for the last 100 years, is undergoing, day by day, some subtle but radical changes which are altering and redefining it in a variety of ways. To some, impatient for options they feel are long overdue, these changes are occurring with infuriating slowness. But changing it is, in ways that will provide a far broader range of choice for the woman who wants to add motherhood to her job description.

The concept of inflexible, hard-driven, work-centered lives that is so well ingrained in our society, is beginning to soften around the edges.

"Except for prisons and armies, where else are adults told daily when to come and when to go and where to be and what to do?" asks Stanley D. Nollen assistant professor at Georgetown University's School of Business Administration, in an article titled "The Changing Workplace."

Nollen, also quoted in a *Wall Street Journal* article, points out, "There is a real movement for expanding life choices for women and men, so people won't have to be slaves to the workplace."

The movement for change that is already underway will receive a sizable dose of adrenalin from the coming generation of career

Achieving a satisfying balance between their careers and families provides these women with a sense of personal fulfillment they could not find in choosing one or the other.

women who aren't wondering whether they can combine a career and motherhood—they simply take it for granted that they will.

"Does today's young college woman think she can have both a successful career and a thriving family life?" begins a newspaper story out of Cambridge, Massachusetts.

"If 8,000 undergraduates at seven New England women's schools are any indication of national expectations, then the answer is a qualified 'yes.' " The article goes on to point out that "In terms of career and family, women undergraduates have very similar goals to men undergraduates."

"If more women were working in an even wider range of jobs and companies, they would be able to begin lobbying for the same humanization that already exists in the so-called women's fields," says JoAnne Alter in her book, *A Part-Time Career for a Full-Time You.*

"Unquestionably, flexible workdays and alternative work schedules would be among the demands of new workers as they became more entrenched in their jobs and more valuable to their employers. Part-time would begin to open up at even higher levels and in more job categories as part-timers became eligible for promotions."

"There is movement which will gradually build during the 80s," explains Association of Part Time Professionals' President Dr. Diane Rothberg. "As we change to a more service based economy, there will be more possibilities for part-time work."

"A lot of the change in attitude can be attributed to women who want families," adds Barney Olmsted of New Ways to Work.

Until now, career women of childbearing age have been the

real momentum behind the movement for change in the workplace, but progressive corporations and foundations studying the effect of work on the family are beginning to add their muscle, too.

"Recommendations for practical action by employers, unions, and government to increase part-time opportunities and other innovative work practices are offered by a Work in America Policy Study on New Work Schedules for a Changing Society," reports the Association of Part Time Professionals' national newsletter. "The study recognizes that the 'single most important obstacle to new work schedules' is our country's 'autocratic tradition of supervision, founded on the belief, deeply imbedded by custom and practice, that rigid schedules are essential to efficiency.' It calls for a new 'time management' philosophy that responds to the work needs of the 1980s."

The Association of Part-Time Professionals' newsletter also reported that "Flexible work schedules were selected by the United Way as one of fifteen potential major issues for the 80s. Flexibility is 'compatible with both contemporary lifestyles and the increasing demand for expanding job opportunities.' It also capitalizes on the idea that though proportionately less time may be spent on work, the quality output may be substantially higher when service workers are committed to their assignments."

"Change is in the air," Dr. Rothberg says. "Given the demographics of the country, it has to come."

There are a lot of people who at some time in their lives don't want to work forty hours a week," says New Ways to Work's Barney Olmsted. "There are a lot of different things in our lives that we have to balance and spread through our lifespan. The more people who decide to take charge of their time and restructure their work life, the better off part-timers will be.

"We will get to the point where part-time is one of several accepted options," Olmsted explains. "It could certainly be in the next ten years. If a lot of people are willing to accept the status quo, then it will take longer. But it could happen pretty quickly if enough people decided to take it on as an issue."

Options for the future will continue to become more varied as our understanding of the worker and the ways in which he can most efficiently function in the workplace continue to expand, and as increasing non-traditional working arrangements become available, "couples who might remain childless for fear of jeopardizing their careers will have families," reports *Corporations and Two-Career Families*. "The children, in turn, will benefit from having two parents . . . and stronger role models."

Basic Human Needs

A letter which was published in Ann Landers' syndicated column, titled "Working Mother Yearns for her Baby," described the plight of one working mother.

> DEAR ANN: I am a single working mother and I'm sure there are millions more like me. I spend fifty hours a week away from my baby, and it's getting harder and harder to say goodbye to her in the morning.
>
> I waste a lot of time thinking about my child and resent the fact that I cannot be at home with her. My work performance is suffering because I can't keep my mind on what I am supposed to be doing.
>
> There is no one I can depend on to help me financially. The longing I feel to be with my child is creating physical and emotional stress. Can you come up with a solution?

The ache in the hearts of mothers across the country for this woman and others like her was probably felt from coast to coast the week this letter appeared. No mother who wants to raise her own baby should be deprived of the opportunity to do so simply because an inflexible, unfeeling system of work has yet to realize on a broad enough scale that accommodating its workers' basic needs, including the need of a woman to mother her baby, is an investment in the future of generations to come, and, ultimately, in the welfare of our world.

Few working women are prepared for—and even fewer employers understand—the depth and the intensity of the feelings a

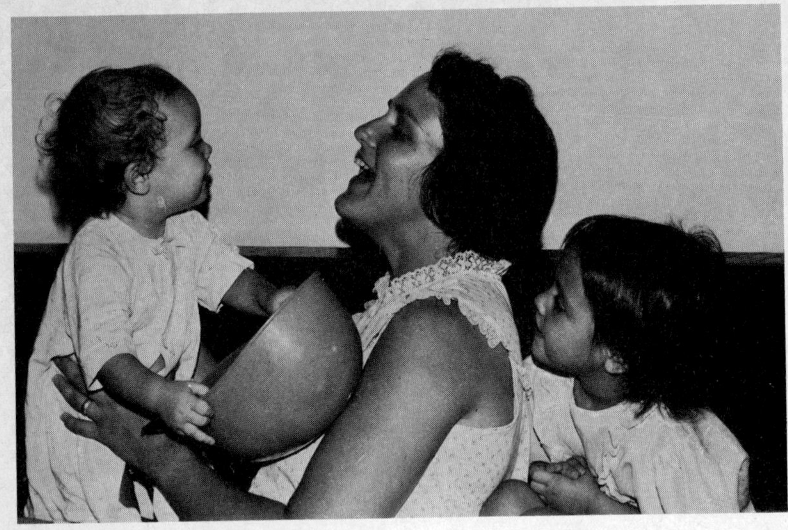

No woman should have to choose between having a career and raising a family if she wants to do both.

mother has for her newborn infant. New motherhood is a season of life that is meant to be savored and enjoyed, not swallowed up by the unrelenting demands of a forty hour workweek.

The need to be with the baby, the desire to love and nurture him, are as much a part of the childbirth process as the baby himself. To deny the mother's need to be with her baby, and the baby's need to be unabashedly adored and enjoyed by his own loving mother, is to deny both of them one of the most basic and vital of human experiences. The implications for society if it continues to ignore the mother's and baby's need for each other are enormous.

Psychiatric registered nurse Sharyn Stolzenbach puts it this way: "I had no comprehension of how intense my desire to be with my baby would be until after she was born. I knew that it would be difficult to leave her, but I thought that financially it was a necessity for me to work full time and so I planned accordingly during my pregnancy. I had an excellent job for an RN—good pay and benefits, enjoyable work, flexible hours, all weekends and holidays off—and I felt that somehow it would all work out.

"But after Kendra was born we had so much fun during my seven weeks off that I just didn't want to leave her. I never thought about all of the costs of working full time with a baby, and did not even consider working part-time as an option. But after returning to my full-time job, I found myself feeling absolutely overwhelmed. The physical demands were incredible. I kept trying to be 'more organized,' but nothing seemed to really help.

"Emotionally, I was a walking disaster. I felt inadequate as a mother, a wife, a homemaker, and a nurse. I can see now that my frustration resulted from setting my standards too high. How could anyone possibly do all of the things I was expecting of myself? I suffered terrible guilt—guilt for not being at home with my baby and guilt for not being in control of these emotions. 'It will get better; I'll get used to it,' I kept telling myself.

"I found myself facing each day in pieces. I was constantly coming undone by things like driving down the road and seeing a mother pushing her baby in a stroller; I would burst into tears. I so longed to be with my baby.

"Breastfeeding was the only thing that kept me going during this period. Those moments of nursing her were my only source of joy and relaxation.

"Working part-time has been the answer for me. Now I have time to be with the baby, bake bread, and be the kind of wife and mother I want to be."

Tomorrow's Promise

The solution that the mother in Ann Landers column asked for is within our grasp. Every woman who seeks and wins a modified working arrangement, thereby initiating one more change in the workplace, brings the day that much closer when the woman who works, for whatever reason, will not have to relinquish the right to be a mother to her baby.

Tomorrow holds out the promise of a new way to work, a better way to live. Tomorrow, no woman will ever again need to choose between having her career suffer because of the baby, or the baby suffer because of her career. Tomorrow, the world of work will recognize that babies have needs, and that their career women-mothers want to be there to fill them.

Tomorrow has been a long time in coming. But these elusive dreams are closer than we know to becoming everyday realities.

It is within our power to make tomorrow arrive today.

Appendix

■ The following books, newsletters, and organizations have been of help to us in preparing this book and may offer additional information that will help you in reshaping your career to include a baby in your life.

HOW TO SPLIT OR SHARE YOUR JOB by New Ways to Work. 1982. 56 pp.

Four stars for this excellent publication which is must reading for anyone seriously considering job sharing. A thorough nuts and bolts how-to manual including how to assess the likelihood that your job can be restructured, things to know before approaching your employer, how to choose a partner, and sample cover letters, resumés, and proposals.

WORKSTEADS: Living and working in the same place by Jeremy Joan Hewes. Garden City, NY: Doubleday/Dolphin, 1981. 165 pp. $9.95.

A pure pleasure to read even if working from home is the furthest thing from your mind. There's plenty of solid information about nitty-gritty details such as zoning regulations, business licenses, taxes, and finances. But the real joy of this book is the author's warm in-depth interviews with people across the country who have beautifully woven together the primary pieces of their lives by not just living and working in the same place, but by totally integrating home and work life. This is must reading if you are considering working from home; great reading even if you aren't.

MANAGING YOUR MATERNITY LEAVE by Meg Wheatley and Marcie Schorr Hirsch. Boston: Houghton Mifflin Company, 1983. 213 pp. $7.95.

Geared to the professional woman who wants time off to be with her baby, but wants to ensure that her job will be waiting for her when she returns. The primary focus of the book is on how to choose the right kind of person (one who won't decide she wants to keep your job for herself) to fill in while you're away, how to stay visible even when you're not in the office, and how to re-establish yourself in the workplace when you're ready to return.

A PART-TIME CAREER FOR A FULL-TIME YOU by JoAnne Alter. Boston: Houghton Mifflin Company, 1982. 394 pp. $8.95.

A good overview of a variety of less-than-full-time job options, including a very readable look at both the history and future of part time work. The book includes many extensive lists, such as the projected growth and decline through 1990 of every imaginable field of work; specific companies and the kinds of part-time jobs they are offering; and a lengthy chapter describing fields of work and types of jobs that offer the best opportunities for part-timers, including educational requirements, salary, and advancement opportunities for each.

JOB SHARING: A new pattern for quality of work and life by Gretl S. Meier. Kalamazoo, MI: The Upjohn Institute for employment research, 1978. 187 pp. $4.50. Available from New Ways to Work.

A largely academic look at job sharing which focuses primarily on analyzing the findings of numerous studies conducted on job sharing in the public sector. Heavy on research; a good resource for those who are looking for hard facts and statistics.

WORKING FOR YOURSELF: How to be successfully self-employed by Geof Hewitt. Emmaus, PA: Rodale Press, 1977. Softcover, 304 pp. $7.95.

A very readable how-to handbook on self-employment covering everything from paid advertising to obtaining grants to what your friends will think when you begin working for yourself. Chapters on farmsteads, crafts, services, and free lancers look at both the trials and triumphs of individuals who are their own bosses.

THE JOB SHARING HANDBOOK by Barney Olmsted and Suzanne Smith. Penguin, $8.45. Available from New Ways to Work.

A great resource offering a wealth of insight and information into the still largely uncharted territory of splitting a job. The book includes just about everything a potential job sharer might need to know—guidelines for everything from assessing the employer's needs, finding a partner, targeting the job, preparing for the interview, and solving common on-the-job problems—making this book indispensable reading for those who would like to go the job sharing route. Profiles of individual job sharers provide insight into how employees in a whole range of fields and job classifications have successfully initiated job sharing into their workplaces.

CORPORATIONS AND TWO CAREER FAMILIES. Available from Catalyst, 14 E. 60th St., New York, NY 10022. $5.00 prepaid.

Solid statistical data based on Catalyst's survey of 374 corporations regarding attitudes toward a wide range of issues pertinent to two career families. Graphs, tables, and charts, plus interpretations of the survey's findings as well as some conclusions about probable directions for the future.

MIND YOUR OWN BUSINESS AT HOME (Newsletter). 1206 W. Webster, Chicago, IL 60614. Advice and information for home-based business persons on improving products and services, marketing and advertising, and counsel from attorneys, insurance brokers, accountants, financial consultants, and government agencies are included in this bimonthly newsletter. Published by Coralee Kern, the guru of the work-at-home movement who built her six figure Maid-to-Order business from a hospital bed twelve years ago. Send a stamped, self-addressed envelope for current subscription information.

NEW WAYS TO WORK NEWSLETTER. 149 Ninth Street, San Francisco, CA 84103. Subscriptions to this quarterly newsletter are $15.00 for non-members, free with $25.00 tax-deductible membership fee.

ASSOCIATION OF PART TIME PROFESSIONALS NATIONAL NEWSLETTER. P. O. Box 3419, Alexandria, VA 23302. Send a stamped, self-addressed envelope for current subscription information. A local Washington, DC, area newsletter is also published.

WORDS AT A STROKE. P. O. Box 647, Clayton, CA 94517. A newsletter for free-lance typists, and secretarial and word processing services. Send a stamped, self-addressed envelope for current subscription information.

Breastfeeding and Parenting Information

LA LECHE LEAGUE INTERNATIONAL
9616 Minneapolis Avenue
Post Office Box 1209
Franklin Park, IL 60131-8209
312-455-7730
Send a self-addressed, stamped business-size envelope for a free *Catalogue* which lists over 125 books and information sheets on breastfeeding, childbirth, child care, and parenting which can be ordered by mail or purchased from local LLL Groups.

Practical Hints for Working and Breastfeeding is an 8-page booklet including the basics of pumping and freezing your milk if you must be separated from your baby. Single copy, 50¢.

THE WOMANLY ART OF BREASTFEEDING is La Leche League's basic handbook on breastfeeding and parenting. Based on the experience of helping hundreds of thousands of women breastfeed their babies, the revised 1981 edition includes a wide range of first-person stories and photographs. THE WOMANLY ART OF BREASTFEEDING has provided needed answers to two generations of nursing mothers on every aspect of breastfeeding. Available in softcover, $7.95, hardcover, $12.95, from La Leche League International, local LLL Groups, and local bookstores.

Alternative Work Options Information Organizations

NEW WAYS TO WORK
149 Ninth Street
San Francisco, CA 84103
415-552-1000

Send a stamped, self-addressed business size envelope along with a request for New Ways to Work's extensive publications list. Specific information on a variety of non-traditional work options is available, as well as more general information on trends and issues. Co-directors Barney Olmsted and Suzanne Smith are widely considered to be the foremost experts in the country on both the theoretical and practical aspects of splitting or sharing a job.

Need help fast? Ms. Olmsted and Ms. Smith are available for telephone consultation, but would appreciate a donation to New Ways to Work in exchange for their time and expertise. Job placement in the San Francisco area is also available. Membership, which costs $25.00 a year, includes a subscription to New Ways to Work's quarterly newsletter and a discount on all publications.

ASSOCIATION OF PART TIME PROFESSIONALS
P. O. Box 3419
Alexandria, VA 22302

Send a self-addressed stamped, business size envelope for APTP's packet which includes a newsletter, publications list, and information about the organization. *A Part-timer's Guide to Federal Part-time Employment* is available for $4.95 postpaid; *Part-Time Work: a bibliography,* also $4.95 postpaid; and *The Job Sharing Handbook,* $8.45 postpaid. APTP also has an insurance program for those who work part-time and do not receive benefits. *Association of Part Time Professionals* President Dr. Diane Rothberg's expertise lies in the areas of research, statistics, and trends rather than individual consultations. APTP also takes an active interest in legislation affecting the opportunity to work less than full time, and is currently working to expand its network of local chapters. A job referral service is available for the Washington, DC area.

FOCUS ON ALTERNATIVE WORK PATTERNS
509 Tenth Avenue East
Seattle, WA 98102
206-329-7918

Send a stamped, self-addressed envelope for a publication list and membership information. FOCUS President Nancy Inui will gladly provide written or telephone advice on specific situations. A donation to FOCUS for individual consultation will be appreciated. In addition to advice and counseling for job seekers, FOCUS acts as a clearing house for part-time and shared jobs in the Seattle area, conducts workshops, provides corporate and individual assistance with restructuring work hours, maintains a reference library on alternative work patterns, and publishes monthly and quarterly publications.

Photo Credits

PART 1 Clockwise from the top: Diane Lack, Donna Rito, and Norman Kloosterman—Photo by Catherine Yaegar, taken at Oakwood Hospital, Dearborn, Michigan; Diane Lack with Ryan—Photo by Jim Mears; Susan Novara with Lindsay; Ina Hopkins—Photo by Kaye Lowman; Linda Erlebach with Theresa.

CHAPTER 1 Page 3. Robin L. Peyson-Nazimiez with Jason—Photo © Betsy Brill. Page 7. Photo by Med Dement. Page 8. Photo by Bob Stelzner.

CHAPTER 2 Page 9. Diane Lack—Photo by Catherine Yaeger, taken at Oakwood Hospital, Dearborn, Michigan. Pages 12 and 13. Photos by Staff Davis.

CHAPTER 3 Page 15. Patricia Holliday and Tiffany. Photo by Med Dement. Page 19. Photo by Eva Green.

CHAPTER 4 Page 23. Carla Bombere with David and Andrew. Photo by Bob Stelzner. Page 25. Photo by Staff Davis.

PART 2 Clockwise from the top: Monica Miele with Heather; Robin Peyson-Nazimiez with Jason. Photo © Betsy Brill; Karen Combs and Colleen—Photo by John Jennewein; Monica Miele.

CHAPTER 5 Page 31. Lynda Dunal and Patrick. Page 37. Photo (l.) by Catherine Yaegar; photo (r.) by Jim Mears. Page 38. Robin Peyson-Nazimiez with husband, Michael, son, Jason, and client, Thomas Abraham. Photos © Betsy Brill.

CHAPTER 6 Page 49. Monica Miele. Page 65. Photo by Kaye Lowman. Page 67. Photo by D. Woodman.

CHAPTER 7 Page 71. Linda Werner and Jessica. Page 72. Photo by Mark W. Oberst. Page 75. Carla Bombere with her sons David and Andrew, and client Ed Springer—Photos by David Nees and Bob Stelzner. Page 78. Isabelle DuBois-McCaughey with daughters Theresa and Vanessa. Page 83. Photos by John Murphy. Page 91. Miriam Hawkins with her husband Phil and children Nathan and Rachelle—Photos by Mark W. Oberst. Page 94. Patricia Holliday and Tiffany—Photo by Med Dement. Page 95. Patricia Holliday with husband Britt and daughter Tiffany—Photos by Med Dement.

CHAPTER 8 Page 99. Madeleine Holmberg and Kelsey. Page 102. Photo courtesy of Joan Lunden. Page 103. Photos by Staff Davis. Page 109. Photos by Frank and Katie Johnson. Page 119. Katie Costanzo with daughter Natalie. Pages 120 and 121 —Photos by Jim Thompson. Page 122. Photo by Bob Bateman.

PART 3 Clockwise from the top: Carla Bombere with Andrew—Photo by Bob Stelzner; Rosanna Ringer with Erin and Colleen—Photo by Craig Ringer; Linda Erlebach with Theresa; Sally Strosahl with Kyle; Sally Strosahl with Andrew and Kyle—Photos by Staff Davis.

CHAPTER 9 Page 127. Ina Hopkins, Executive Director of the Northwest Suburban Association of Commerce and Industry—Photo by Kaye Lowman.

CHAPTER 10 Page 135. Ina Hopkins—Photo by Kaye Lowman.

CHAPTER 11 Pages 141 and 143. Lynda Dunal with Patrick.

PART 4 Clockwise from top: Sharyn Stolzenbach with Kendra; Linda Ruth Forys with Michael and Marianne; Cheryl Pledger with John and Holly—Photo by Frank and Katie Johnson, Phyllis Carlyle with Kevin.

CHAPTER 12 Page 149. Britt L. Holliday with Tiffany—Photo by Med Dement. Page 150. John Pledger with John Gainer Pledger—Photo by Frank and Katie Johnson.

CHAPTER 13 Page 157. Jacob Jansen. Page 160. Photo on left by Jim Mears. Page 162. (l.) Walter Doll with Evan (r.) D'Arcy Dunal with Patrick. Page 164. Photos by Med Dement. Page 172. Photo courtesy of Control Data Corporation.

CHAPTER 14 Page 173. Mary Lang, dental assistant, with Patrick—Photo by Peter Patrick. Page 174. Photo on the left by Narice La Plant Plumb. Page 177. Photo by Cindy Wells.

CHAPTER 15 Page 183. Cheryl Pledger with John and Holly—Photo by Frank and Katie Johnson. Page 186. Nancy Wolkenhauer with Luke. Page 190. Ryan Lack with Diane—Photo by Jim Mears. Page 192. Thomas Johnson, husband of Sally Strosahl, with Andrew—Photos by Staff Davis. Pages 196 and 197. (l. to r.) Darlene McKee and family; Lynda Dunal and family; Cheryl Pledger and family—Photo by Frank and Katie Johnson.

PART 5 Clockwise from the top: Elizabeth Kinsler with Audrey; Sonia Werner with Heidi and Emily; Cheryl Pledger with John and Holly—Photo by Frank and Katie Johnson; Darolyn Butler and children.

CHAPTER 16 Page 201. Deborah Fash and Mike—Photo by Jay Wiseman. Page 203. Deborah Fash with Brian and Mike—Photo by Jay Wiseman. Page 205. Darolyn Butler with Rima and Cecelia. Page 207. Sheila Young. Page 210. Control Data World Headquarters. Page 210. Frank A. Dawe. Page 212. William C. Norris, Chairman and Chief Executive Officer of Control Data, with Mary Black and Diane Wingo who work part-time in the Selby bindery. Page 213. Betty Wagner—Photo by Kaye Lowman. Page 214. Ivy Bollig Karas with Doreen. Page 215. Donna Fobes with Christen. Page 216. The staff of Mothering Magazine.

CHAPTER 17 Page 219. Photo by Hank Reichard. Page 220. Photo by the Daily and Sunday Herald. Page 222 and 223. Photos © The Globe and Mail, Toronto. Page 224. Photo by Don Hinckley, The Times Record, Brunswick, Maine. Page 225. Photo of Susan McTigue. Page 227. Photo by Iowa City Press Citizen. Page 231. Photo by Carl Hugare. Page 232. Photo © Los Angeles Times Syndicate. Page 238. Photo by the Daily and Sunday Herald. Page 240. Photo courtesy of Bell Labs. Page 243. Photo by the Daily and Sunday Herald.

CHAPTER 18 Page 245. Nansi Casper with Nikki—Photo by Narice La Plant Plumb. Page 247. Photos by Ernest Rose. Page 249. Photo by Steward Saunders. Page 252. (l.) Cheryl Pledger with Holly—Photo by Frank and Katie Johnson; (r.) Patricia Holliday with Tiffany—Photo by Med Dement.

CHAPTER 19 Page 255. Carla Bombere with Andrew—Photo by David Nees. Page 256. Sally Strosahl with her husband Thomas Johnson and sons Andrew and Kyle—Photo by Staff Davis. Page 257. (l.) Diane Lack with her husband George and son Ryan—Photo by Tom Risner; (r.) Patricia Holliday with her husband Britt and daughter Tiffany—Photo by Med Dement. Page 259. Rosanna Ringer with Erin and Colleen—Photo by Craig Ringer.